# Just Jack

*Just Jack is a dedication to my late husband Jack who gave so much of himself to this world. Thank you Jack Woolridge*

# Just Jack

The Life and Career of
Dr Jack Woolridge (Dr Wooly)

*Suzanne Woolridge*

Suzanne Woolridge
PO Box 587
Cronulla 2230
NSW
Australia
jwoolridge@bigpond.com

Copyright © Suzanne Woolridge 2025.
All rights reserved.

No part of this publication may be copied, reproduced in any format, by any means, electronic or otherwise, without prior consent from the copyright owner and publisher of this book.

Editor: Karina Machado
BMA Publishing Expertise: Benny Agius
Cover design, text design and typesetting: Shaun Jury

ISBN: 978-0-646-72511-6

# Contents

| | |
|---|---:|
| **Prologue** | xi |
| Chapter One | |
| **In the Beginning 1925–1935** | 1 |
| Chapter Two | |
| **Tom Sawyer Days 1935–1939** | 9 |
| Chapter Three | |
| **Turbulent Times 1939–1946** | 21 |
| Chapter Four | |
| **Jack and Jill 1946–1954** | 33 |
| Chapter Five | |
| **Sutherland to Scotland 1955–1961** | 39 |
| Chapter Six | |
| **Sue's Story** | 53 |
| Chapter Seven | |
| **Meeting Dr Wooly 1961** | 85 |

Chapter Eight
**Invitation to the Ball 1963–1969**     93

Chapter Nine
**A New Beginning 1969–1970**     113

Chapter Ten
**An Around-the-World Adventure! 1970**     139

Chapter Eleven
**Double Trouble 1970–1974**     163

Chapter Twelve
**The Dawn of Echocardiography 1975**     185

Chapter Thirteen
**The Amazing 'Lazy Pat' 1976**     191

Chapter Fourteen
**The Brothel 1977–1978**     201

Chapter Fifteen
**Annus Horribilis × Two 1979–1984**     207

Chapter Sixteen
**Flood Waters 1985–1986**     239

Chapter Seventeen
**The Evolution of 'Inverness' 1986–1993**     255

Chapter Eighteen
**Sweet Dreams, Then a Nightmare 1993–1994**     265

Chapter Nineteen
**A Win, Then Mutiny 1995–1996**     277

Chapter Twenty
**Resuscitation 1996–2000**     283

Chapter Twenty-one
**Two Tragedies 2000–2008**   303

Chapter Twenty-two
**Heartache 2008–2014**   319

Chapter Twenty-three
**Going Home 2015–2018**   325

**Epilogue**   335

**Acknowledgements**   341

**Further reading:**

   **Curriculum Vitae, J.D. Woolridge**   343

      **Publications**   345

   **Curriculum Vitae and Clinical Training,**
      **Suzanne Ellen Woolridge, D.M.U.**   347

   **Record of Travel 1976 to 2018**   355

   **Inverness Stud – List of Horses**   375

Hi Sue

Well, what a wonderful read about a life lived so full.

Your account of medical and cardiological issues is precise, as I would have expected. While that may have been my role to assess those issues I came away feeling very much more and a deeper understanding of both you and Jack.

You have captured him precisely and your interweaving of his early life, horse racing, the stud development, cardiology and later cattle is very well done and an important historical document.

I thought I knew him pretty well but your story adds much more and I had no idea of the relationship issues you faced. Your response to that issue was laudable and a credit to your character and I presume your religious background.

You come across as a very strong, caring, loving and forgiving person and your role in *Just Jack* is so important because without you there would not have been the Jack we knew: The great cardiologist, caring physician, racing identity, husband, father and friend to so many.

Thank you for giving me the opportunity to read the book, I really enjoyed spending time with him again.

Roger
A/Prof Roger M Allan
Cardiologist

# Prologue

How could a boy who played truant from school for almost a year become one of Sydney's leading cardiologists and concurrently develop a prominent and successful Murray Grey Stud and thoroughbred-horse stud with a successful stable of racehorses?

And how could a shy, naïve 15-year-old country girl with little education be part of the pioneering era of echocardiography and vascular ultrasound, and at the same time raise three beautiful daughters, manage Jack's cardiology practice and manage his thoroughbred horse stud and racehorse interests?

While this book may not answer all of these questions, it is my hope that it at least sheds light on my complex and brilliant husband, the soul bond we shared and the fascinating years we lived through on the cutting edge of a new era in medicine.

Our lives eventually intertwined, filling our world with adventures, misadventures, catastrophes, family love and hard work.

This is Jack's story.

It is for his children, grandchildren and great-grandchildren.

His story reveals how success came with conscientious hard work driven by his passion for life, cardiology and his horses. He was charismatic, and everyone wanted to be his best friend.

Jack was ambitious, always wanting to be better than the rest. This competitive attitude drove him to study hard and become a distinguished cardiologist. Interwoven with this, he was a great raconteur with a wonderful sense of humour, often self-deprecating when deflecting awkward situations.

Fierce ambition aside, Jack was always considerate and compassionate towards others, demonstrating unselfish generosity.

He was intensely curious about the world. His great passion for horseracing metamorphosed into a thriving horse-racing and horse-breeding enterprise which was inextricably intertwined with his other great passion, cardiology.

Yet, if you had known him as a 10-year-old boy who revelled in a 'Tom Sawyer' lifestyle in the forests, playing in the river and prawning with the local Indigenous children – you would have wondered what would become of him. And then, if you had known him as a teenager dreaming of a career in sport, you may have questioned where his future lay.

Keep in mind these were difficult years, during and following the Depression, years scarred by World War II, which unleashed its wrath and destroyed the hopes and dreams of young Australians.

Yet somehow, Jack's dream endured.

Occasionally, I suggested he should write his story, but he thought his life was 'ordinary' and 'nothing special,' and, he was too busy with life. If he ever did consider writing his story, he thought it could wait until he retired. Well, it was a long wait. He retired as a cardiologist three months after he turned 90.

Jack passed away in his 92nd year and, a few months later, I felt he was nudging me to write his story.

I will do my best to remember the stories as he told them to me. Of course, after 1961, I was also part of the story. In my retelling, there are some situations where I have used poetic licence to keep the flow of the story, and some names have been changed for various reasons. Also, I have included some historical facts to set the stage for comprehension of the events.

Jack had an extraordinary life, and I was very privileged to be part of it, and so, my family, THIS IS OUR STORY.

I hope you enjoy reading about our adventures.

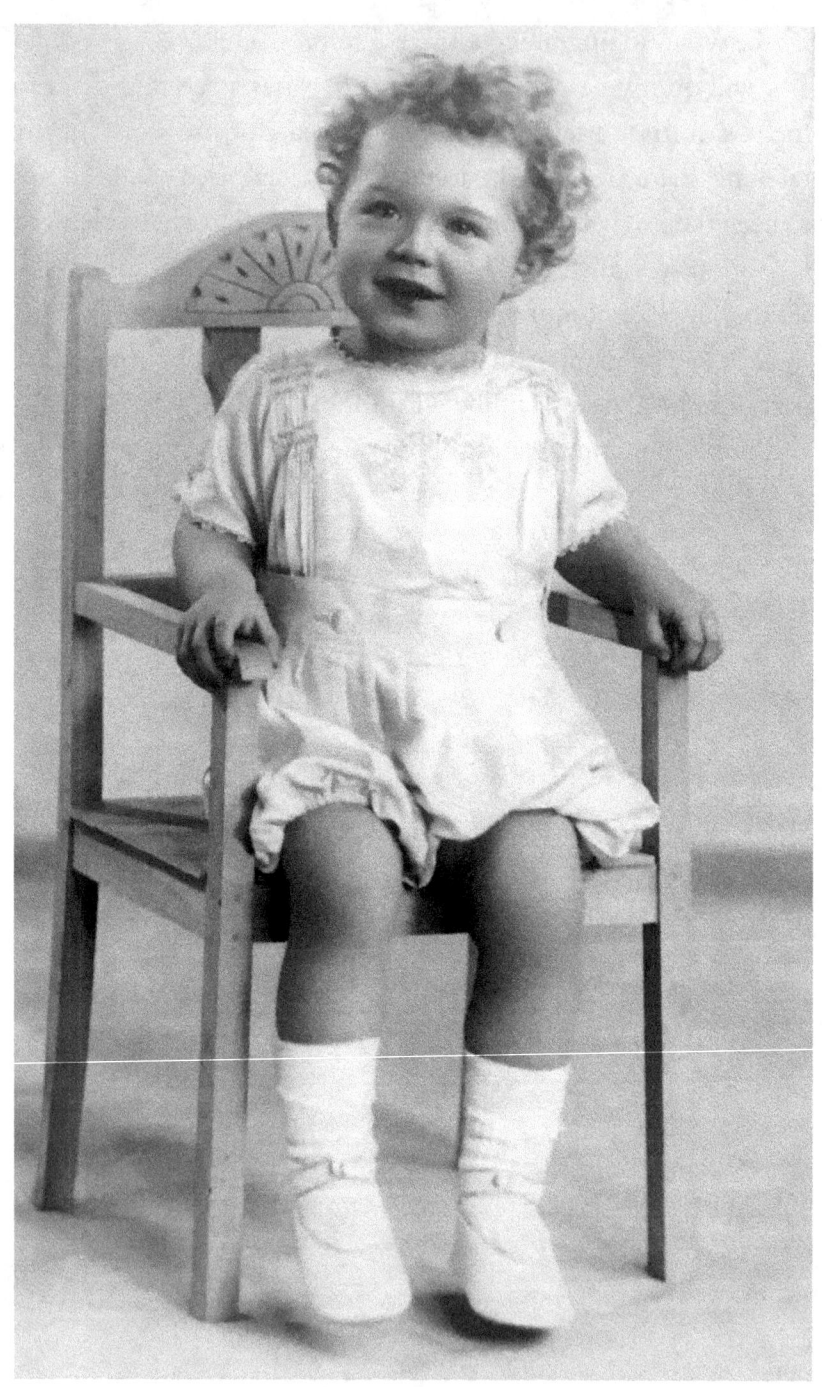

*Jack*

## Chapter One
## In the Beginning
## 1925–1935

Our story begins in the town of Nowra. Nowra is about 160 km south of Sydney, on the Shoalhaven River. Nowra was first officially recognised in 1852 and declared a town in 1885. The region around Nowra developed into a thriving farming community with dairy farms and state forests.

The name Nowra was first written by Europeans as NOU-WOO-RO and is an Aboriginal word for black cockatoo.

In 1861, the first Melbourne Cup was run and won by Archer, a horse from Nowra. He was trained by Etienne de Mestre and ridden by John Cutts. The trainer, jockey and horse travelled by steamboats – Nowra to Sydney and then Sydney to Melbourne. Archer won consecutive Melbourne Cups in 1861 and 1862, a feat not repeated until 70 years later by Peter Pan.

Perhaps when Jack spent almost a year with his grandparents in Nowra, this history permeated through him, and evolved into his passion for racehorses.

Jack's parents, David Worthington Woolridge and Thelma Merle Sawyer (known as Merle) were married at Mosman, a suburb of Sydney on 21 January 1925. After their wedding, they lived in Nowra, where Merle's parents lived. David was a pastry cook and had a job in the Nowra bakery. They lived a happy, comfortable life in a cottage in Kinghorne Street. Merle's parents lived nearby; they had a small sawmill in their large backyard.

Nowra can be a miserable place during the winter months, and the night of 20 August 1925 was cold, wet, windy, and dismal. This was the night Merle went into labour with their firstborn. Fortunately, the Elston Private Hospital in Plunket Street was just around the corner from their home and baby Jack was born there at 2:10 am on 21 August 1925, delivered by Dr Foy.

David and Merle baptised their son at the Church of England church in Nowra. They baptised him John David but somehow, he was always called Jack. With white-blonde curls which hugged his head and tumbled onto his forehead just above his mischievous grey-blue eyes, Jack was a beautiful baby.

In 1925, the population of Sydney was about 1,000,000; a Federal election was held; and it was the first year of compulsory voting. The currency was still pounds, shillings and pence – a loaf of bread cost 4 pence; 1 litre of milk cost 5 pence; and a stamp to post a letter, 1 penny. The wage of a male factory worker was around 4 pounds a week; and about 2 pounds for a female.

In Jack's third year, his younger sister, Thelma, was born on 3 May 1928.

Jack's earliest memory – going for a ride in a car with his mother – also takes place when he was 3. The driver was not his father, probably a relative or friend showing off their new car, as in 1928 very few people were fortunate enough to have the wealth to buy a car. He remembers his mother lifting him onto the back seat of the car. This was a special treat for a little boy.

The following year, 1929, brought the US Wall Street Crash,

which spread rapidly throughout the world, igniting the global Great Depression. In Australia, unemployment skyrocketed, reaching a record high of around 30 per cent in 1932. Prior to the Depression, most Australians lived very well. Now, the effects of the Depression were felt throughout the country. Thousands of Australians suddenly faced the humiliation of poverty and unemployment.

This was in an era when men were the sole bread winners for the family, as girls were dismissed from employment when they married. With no government unemployment benefits, it was left to soup kitchens and charity groups to try to feed the many starving and destitute families.

In desperate search of work, people moved either from the city to the country or vice-versa. Limited as they were, jobs were viciously fought over, with massive queues snaking outside the building where the daily newspaper was printed, as men eagerly awaited the job advertisements to be pinned up on the news board at the entrance to the building.

When the boy came out to pin the pages of the newspaper on the board, the crowd pushed and shoved to try to be the first to see the vacancies. Then the race was on to the premises of the employers who'd advertised – the first person to arrive at their site was usually hired.

City and urban people planted gardens to produce fruit and vegetables, and in some areas, a barter system for sharing food was formed. Shacks were built on the outskirts of cities and along the foreshores, with some making their homes in caves, while others camped in tents in friends' backyards or at relative's farms.

In Nowra, Jack's family was also affected by the recession. As locals lost their jobs, there were fewer people with money to buy Jack's father's pies and cakes. So, David made the difficult decision to move his family to Sydney. Merle did not want to leave her parents in Nowra, but with relatives in Sydney, she and David were among the lucky ones, and they ultimately made the move.

In Sydney, they lived with Merle's sister, Ette, and her husband, Freddie, until David could find work. Freddie and Ette lived above their butcher shop in Kingsford, near where the Kingsford 9 Ways is today.

Once again, luck was on their side: David's brother-in-law Freddie had connections in the right places and David was accepted into the Police Force and posted at Daceyville Police Station.

With a steady wage coming in, David looked for a rental home for his family and found a suitable house at 37 Forsythe Street, Kingsford

A few months after they moved in, the landlords asked David and Merle if they would like to buy the house for £90 (ninety pounds). Unfortunately, they didn't have the money or the wherewithal to borrow money to buy the house.

The houses in Kingsford were on big blocks and everyone had a vegetable garden, fruit trees, chooks, a water tank and a 'dunny' (toilet). The dunny was a little shed with a sanitary pan which was placed at the rear of the little shed. In those days, there were no soft rolls of white toilet paper, only newspaper torn into squares and threaded on to a string which hung on the wall inside the dunny shed. The dunny pan was emptied by the dunny man either weekly or fortnightly. Everyone held their nose when the dunny truck came by, it was very smelly. No-one wanted to be a dunny man, it was a very unenviable job!

The Woolridge's backyard was a typical Kingsford backyard. Jack loved the chooks. He'd climb the tree that shaded the chook pen and perched on the branch, talking to the chooks; they were his friends. All through his life, he couldn't bring himself to eat chicken.

Some of their neighbours also had a 'quarter horse' in their backyard. The quarter horses were very popular and raced at the Kensington racetrack, situated where the University of NSW is today.

Jack's father didn't like the quarter-horse racing and said the racetrack should be housing blocks. Little did he know that a teenaged Jack would sneak away to the racetrack to watch the races.

As a child, Jack was busy and resourceful and like all the other boys in his neighbourhood, he built a billycart. The boys had billycart races down the big hill near his home, and of course, there were the inevitable crashes with the usual injuries of cuts and bruises, and sometimes a broken bone, but Jack was tough and managed to avoid too much damage.

Jack and Thelma attended Daceyville Public School. It was a tough school and every afternoon after school there would be an arranged fight on a street corner. Sometimes, the Police would turn up and give the boys a clip over the ear or a boot up their backside, sending them home with a threat that if they did it again, they would grab them by the scruff of their neck and take them home to their mother.

Big and strong for his age, Jack was respected in the neighbourhood, and he knew his way around a fight – he was never afraid, he knew how to look after himself. You had to be tough to survive Daceyville Public School.

The family attended the local Anglican Church, where Jack sang in the boys' choir, and was especially 'chosen' to mow the church lawns every Wednesday with a push mower. But he was not a willing partner to this arrangement and one Wednesday he decided he had better things to do, and didn't show up. The church vicar wasn't pleased and went to see Jack's father to find out why Jack didn't mow the lawn.

The vicar was anticipating Jack's father to be apologetic with a promise to punish Jack, but instead David told the vicar to 'P**** off!!!!'

That night, Jack's father had a warning for his son. 'Jack, you had better not forget to mow the church lawn next Wednesday, because I don't want that vicar coming to see me again.'

As Jack grew up, so did his city.

One of Sydney's most important infrastructure builds, the Sydney Harbour Bridge, was completed in 1932. It was a mammoth undertaking. The first sod of soil was turned on 28 July 1923, two years before Jack was born. John Bradfield of the NSW Dept. of Public Works directed the build of the bridge, designed by Dorman Long of Middlesbrough UK,

The building of the bridge coincided with the construction of a system of underground railways in Sydney's CBD and the bridge was designed with this in mind. The bridge has six lanes for road traffic, flanked on each side by two railway tracks and a footpath.

Load testing of the bridge occurred in February 1932, with the four rail tracks loaded with 96 steam locomotives positioned end to end. The bridge was declared safe and ready to be opened

Sydney Harbour Bridge is the sixth longest single spanning-arch bridge in the world and the tallest steel arch bridge, measuring 134 metres from the top of the bridge to water level. The main roadway across the bridge is known as the Bradfield Highway, and is about 2.4 km long, making it one of the shortest highways in Australia.

The official opening of the bridge was on Saturday 19 March 1932, and approximately 300,000 people attended. Jack was so excited when his parents told him they were going to the opening. His dad found a prime viewing spot where they watched as the official party moved towards the red ribbon strung across the roadway of the bridge. As the officials took up their positions, a horse galloped purposefully towards them. Its rider – Francis de Groot, in military uniform —approached, slashing the ribbon with his ceremonial sword and declaring the bridge open.

But de Groot wasn't part of the ceremony.

Immediately, he was pulled off his horse, arrested and his sword confiscated. He was taken away and the ribbon re-joined, with Premier Jack Lang cutting it with a flourish and declaring the bridge open.

In 1934, the family faced a crisis close to home, as Jack's mother became dangerously ill with high blood pressure. Back then, there was no treatment for high blood pressure, other than advice to avoid wine, meat, pastries, anger and sexual intercourse. The only accepted treatment was complete bed rest.

# Chapter Two
# Tom Sawyer Days
# 1935–1939

In 1935, the doctors told David that Merle had to have complete bed rest, free from children, so Jack was sent to live with his grandparents, John and Mary Sawyer in Nowra, and Thelma went to stay with an aunt in the Blue Mountains.

Jack travelled by train from Central station to Bombaderry. Jack's grandfather picked him up from Bombaderry railway station, expressing his surprise to see how big and tall Jack had grown. On their way home, Jack and his grandfather chatted.

'Where is the school, Grandfather?' Jack asked, as they passed through the town.

'You don't have to go to school while you are living with us, Jackie,' answered Grandfather.

Jack thought this was a terrific idea.

When they arrived, Nanny was waiting for them on the front porch. Nanny Sawyer was a lovely, happy, sweet little lady, with grey curly hair framing her soft face, and sparkling, mischievous eyes. Jack had the same mischievous eyes.

She was so happy to see Jack, she wrapped her arms around

him and gave him a big hug, exclaiming how Jack had grown taller than she was. She had been baking cakes and biscuits most of the day, knowing her grandson would be hungry after his long train journey. Nanny and Grandfather took him in and showed him his bedroom, then left him to unpack, which didn't take long as he didn't have many clothes. Besides, he was famished, and could smell the freshly baked biscuits.

He settled in smoothly to life with Nanny and Grandfather, happily spending his days with Grandfather Sawyer in the forest finding wood for the sawmill. Grandfather was glad to have the company and an extra hand to help lift the wood. Jack enjoyed running around the forest helping his grandfather and looking for duck's eggs to sell for pocket money. Most afternoons, his grandfather would meet a few mates at the pub for a beer and he would send Jack to go and play with the other kids on the footpath until he was ready to go home.

Jack had many happy memories of his time in Nowra living a 'Tom Sawyer' existence. Apart from helping his grandfather in the forest, he had plenty of time for fun with the other boys of the neighbourhood, jumping off a bridge into the river, swimming, fishing, and prawning with the Indigenous children.

After they caught the prawns, the Indigenous children made a fire on the sandy beach and cooked them in a billy can of water on the fire. Jack and his grandfather would sit on a log or on the sand with them and eat the freshly cooked prawns. The children shared their prawns with Jack and his grandfather, giving them a bucket full of prawns to take home to Nanny. Nanny was thrilled, she loved prawns.

During good weather, Jack and the neighbourhood boys built crude rafts which they sailed down the river and played football on the beach.

Jack's days in the forest with his grandfather taught him to be resilient and resourceful. He learnt how to find his way through the woods without getting lost, though he still managed to get into mischief.

One day, he saw stray greyhounds, and for some unknown reason, he started throwing stones at the dogs. How stupid! The greyhounds started to chase him, and he ran for his life. He said that was when he realised how fast he could run. It was a close call, and he resolved never to do that again.

On his walks to the river, there were fruit trees along the side of the road, so when he felt hungry, he picked fruit off the trees, and when he caught a fish, he would run home and proudly present it to Nanny, who would sing and dance and make a fuss over him. She was a lot of fun. She loved Jack and enjoyed having him in her home.

Nanny loved a 'tid or two'. A tid was a colloquial term for an alcoholic drink, usually a glass of sherry. There were times when she would have more than a couple of 'tids' and would dance and sing around the kitchen table clapping her hands. She was such a happy, lively little lady.

It was an idyllic life for boy of 9. No school and all this fun.

However, the fun ended abruptly. Towards the end of this blissful year, the Truant Inspectors came looking for Jack. Grandfather was admonished for not sending Jack to school and told that if Jack didn't go to school next week, they would be in big trouble.

Jack attended Nowra Public School until he could return to his home in Kingsford and his school at Daceyville.

During his first week at Daceyville, he was pulled out in front of the class and the teacher announced that Jack was the biggest boy in the class and the only one not going up to 6th class. This was his punishment for not going to school in Nowra for most of the year.

However, his 'Tom Sawyer' year in Nowra had no effect on his scholastic ability – at the end of 6th class, he sat for the NSW State Qualifying Certificate (QC), and topped the state.

'I am pleased to announce that the results of the QC have been received,' announced the Headmaster at the school assembly. 'And I am very proud to say that the boy who topped the state is at this school – Jackie Woolridge.'

This exam result gave Jack an opportunity to attend Sydney Boys High School (SBHS), a selective high school at Randwick.

SBHS was, and still is a prestigious high school, funded by the Government. SBHS is a member of the Athletic Association of the Great Public Schools of NSW. SBHS first applied for admission to the Association in 1894 but was not accepted until 1906.

While Jack was at SBHS, the schools in the Association competed against each other in Rugby Union, Athletics, Cricket, Rowing, and Rifle Shooting.

The year after Jack started at SBHS, life changed.

On 1 September 1939, Germany invaded Poland and on 3 September 1939 the United Kingdom and France and their empires declared war on Germany and as Australia was part of the British Empire, we followed Britain and declared war.

On 15 November 1939, the Australian Prime Minister Robert Menzies reintroduced conscription. Conscription at this time was the mandatory enlistment into National Service of all single males 18–41 years of age.

Australia suffered huge losses in WWI and so the general public had little enthusiasm for war, but, over time and following the fall of France in June 1940, there was a surge of volunteers whose sense of duty to defend Australia and the British Empire was reignited.

# TOM SAWYER DAYS 1935–1939

*Jack with his mother and aunty in Sydney*

At the start of the war, life in Sydney was much the same except for a rise in the cost of living and unemployment.

Before and after school, Jack worked for his Uncle Freddie and Aunty Ette in their butcher shop. He learnt to make sausages (six sausages to the pound), swept the floor, and delivered meat orders riding his bike. Butcher-shop floors in the 1930s were covered in sawdust, so that bits of meat and fat that fell on the floor were covered in sawdust, helping prevent anyone from accidentally slipping.

Aunty Ette spoiled Jack whenever she could. Every year she took Jack to the Royal Easter Show at the showground in Moore Park, near SBHS. The showground displayed their posters in Uncle Fred's shop window and in return, he received free entry tickets to the Show, which he gave to Ette and Jack.

Jack loved to go to the show, and he loved more than anything to go into the Jimmy Sharman tent and watch the boxing.

Ette and Fred treated Jack like a son. Fred would give Jack a large piece of steak for breakfast every day, as well as some money. Jack used the money to help buy his school uniform and sporting equipment for school.

Jack was popular at school, with a knack for making friends easily. There was a great camaraderie among the boys, and they had fun assigning nicknames to the teachers – the French teacher was 'Quack Quack,' and the Latin teacher 'The Morgue'.

One of Jack's friends from school, Dick Burnett, wrote a letter to Jack on Jack's 80th birthday, capturing the essence of the schoolboy Jack:

'Jack, you and I go back a long way, in 1938 we were two little 'wackers' (although Jack, you were never little), entering the portals of Sydney Boys High School, beginning our secondary education and attempting to prepare to make an impression on the world at large. We spent a lot of time together while you were becoming by 1942, the best cricketer, the best footballer and the best athlete in the school. It was no wonder I admired you, you were so 'cool' and of course not a 'swat'. Why you were not school captain I could never understand. Jasper Killip, our Headmaster, has a lot to answer for …'

As Dick shared in his letter, Jack excelled at sport, representing the school in athletics in the 100 yard and 200-yard dash and shotput (he held the school record for shotput for many years). From the age of 16, he played in the school's first 11 in cricket as opening batsman, and 5/8 in the Rugby A team. The school's football coach was Frank O'Rourke, an ex-international football player. The school recognised Jack's talent for cricket and the Headmaster arranged for one of the teachers, Mr Oates, to take

## TOM SAWYER DAYS 1935–1939

*Jack in the Sydney Boys High School 'A' Football Team photo.
He is the first boy on the right of the second row.*

*Jack in the Sydney Boys High School first 11 Cricket Team photo.
He is second from the left in the first row*

*Jack in the Sydney Boys High School Athletic Team photo.
He is third from the right in the first row*

Jack to Sykes Sports Shop to buy him a cricket bat. Sykes had the reputation for making the best cricket bats in Sydney.

He practised his skills in the backyard, throwing a tennis ball at the brick wall of the house and hitting the ball back and forth with a home-made cricket bat. To strengthen his arms for shotput, he would throw house bricks around the back yard to see how far he could toss them.

School sports were played at different school grounds each weekend, so Jack had to find his way to these grounds, usually by train, bus or tram. Occasionally, he would be lucky and offered a lift by one of his friends' parents. The cricket games were played over two days and at lunch time they were taken into a big dining hall, where lunch was served. One of the schools had cute waitresses dressed in black and white uniforms, which impressed Jack.

Sadly, Jack's parents couldn't go to the school sports events, as his mother was too ill, and so they missed sharing in his triumphs. This was a great disappointment for Jack. Merle adored her son and looked forward to him coming home each day, he would sit on her bed and tell her about his victories and adventures, no doubt with a touch of flair, exaggeration, and an exhibition of how he hit the ball, or caught someone out.

Jack's mother wanted the best for him and told Jack that she thought he would be a good schoolteacher and that he should think about teaching as a career. Yet during his interview with the school career advisors, they told him he had no apitutude as a schoolteacher and should think of another career path.

Poor Merle, she was so disappointed, she had her heart set on Jack becoming a teacher. It didn't worry Jack at all, though, as he had his eyes set on a sporting career – that was his passion, he lived every moment of his life for sport. Nothing else mattered.

Blessed with an outstanding memory, Jack managed to pass all his exams without much effort or study. This meant that he could spend more time on his sport, either competing or honing his skills.

Occasionally, Aunty Ette would give him a ticket to go to the movies. One year, sitting for the end-of-year science exams, he finished the paper in half the time so that he could go to the movies and see *Tom Mix and Some Men*.

He passed the exam.

I was never sure if *Tom Mix and Some Men* was actually a movie, or if it came from Jack's vivid imagination, so I did some exploring. I found out that Tom Mix (1880–1940) was a well-known American actor, writer and director who appeared in hundreds of films and established himself as the screen's most popular cowboy star, setting the standard for famous cowboys who'd follow, such as Gene Autry and Roy Rogers. His horse, Tony, also became a celebrity.

Jack's father, David, was very proud of Jack's achievements at school and was keen to go and visit his father 'Old Bill' Woolridge – he had not seen his father since he and Merle were married in 1925. This was probably due to family disharmony or dysfunction. David's father owned a pub and had married a barmaid and lived in Mosman, a wealthy harbourside suburb in the lower north shore of Sydney, about 15 km from Kingsford.

One Saturday, David decided this was going to be the day.

'I want to take you to visit your grandfather,' he told Jack. 'Put on your school uniform so that he can see how good you look.'

They had a long trek travelling by bus, train and ferry. Jack felt curious and excited. When they eventually found the address in Mosman, the house was large, with a beautiful garden. As they walked up the path, David looked at Jack and Jack looked at his dad, noticing his father's slight nervousness.

David took a deep breath and straightened himself up, hoping to look confident. He knocked on the door, and after what seemed like minutes, the door was flung wide open, revealing a tall, well-built man whose physical frame filled the doorway. He had a grey beard, messy straight grey hair and prominent grey bushy eyebrows. He wore a pair of grey serge trousers held up by a pair of braces worn over a well-worn white/grey singlet.

He looked straight at David and a glimmer of recognition swept across his eyes, then he turned to Jack. His gaze swung suddenly back to David with a defiant grimace, and a steely glare. In a loud, bold voice, he growled, 'Go away!' and slammed the door in their faces.

David and Jack looked at each other in disbelief. Well, that was that, there was no arguing with a slammed door. Jack was somewhat bewildered, and David was humiliated. David took a deep breath, hoping that it would help him pull himself together. And so, they silently turned around, and slowly, together, took the long weary trip home.

This excursion was a silent secret between David and Jack.

Jack couldn't understand why his grandfather reacted so sternly and inhospitably when he saw them standing at his door.

## Chapter Three
## **Turbulent Times**
## **1939–1946**

The war rolled on relentlessly, from 1939 to early 1941. Germany conquered or controlled most of continental Europe and formed an Axis alliance with Italy and Japan. On 7 December 1941, Japan launched a surprise attack on the USA, bombing Pearl Harbour. The USA followed with an immediate declaration of war against Japan and the European Axis powers quickly declared war on the USA.

On 9 December 1941, Australia formally declared war on Japan. Rapid Japanese conquests over much of the Western Pacific ensued. On 11 December 1941, the Australian Government called up single men aged 18–45 and married men 18–35 to join the army.

On 19 February 1942, Japan launched a bombing attack, with 205 bombers dropping 681 bombs in two separate raids, bombing Darwin, the ships in Darwin Harbour and the two airfields. The official death toll was 292, but survivors suggested the number to be more like 1,000, recalling the digging of huge mass graves and seeing barges loaded with bodies being towed out to sea.

The Japanese launched more than 100 air raids against Australia from 1942 to 1943. On 1 June 1942, three Japanese midget submarines entered Sydney Harbour and sank the HMAS Kattabul – a converted ferry – by torpedo, 21 sailors died. This was followed by a campaign to disrupt merchant shipping and over the next month, seven ships were attacked, sinking three and killing 50 sailors.

On 3 June 1942, the Japanese shelled Sydney and Newcastle suburbs. They failed to damage any significant targets, the main impact was psychological, creating a fear of impending Japanese invasion and precipitating the commencement of convoy operations to protect merchant shipping. It also boosted the intensity of patriotism among Australians and there was a surge in the numbers of volunteers for the war effort.

Rationing of meat, tea, coffee, sugar and footwear began in June 1942, although it never became as onerous as the rationing in the United Kingdom.

After completing the Leaving Certificate in 1942, Jack joined the long queues of young men seeking to enlist in the Royal Australian Air Force, but at only 17, he was told he was too young and to come back the following year, after he'd turned 18.

He looked for work and found a job in the Railways as a clerk. Jack had a good work ethic and quickly acquired the skills required for this position. His boss came to him during his second week, with a word of advice.

'Look, Jack, you are a nice boy but you don't have to work hard,' he said. 'Work like the other boys and have a smoke-o, you know, we don't want to upset them'.

So, Jack got the message to slow up or they would give his job to a slow worker. With unemployment high and jobs scarce, he knew it would be hard to find other work.

On weekends, Jack played first-grade cricket with the Randwick Cricket Club. They were impressed with his talent and suggested that with some extra training, he might be good enough for the NSW cricket team. This thrilled Jack, whose dream was always a career in sport.

But that dream was sidelined in 1943, when, after his 18th birthday, Jack enlisted in the Royal Australian Air Force (RAAF). He passed the medical and, this time, his application was accepted.

He started at Bradfield Park on 11 September 1943. Bradfield Park was a suburb of Sydney now known as Lindfield. During WWII, a station was built there to house RAAF and WAAAF (Women's Auxiliary Australian Air Force) units for their initial training as part of the Empire Air Training Scheme, to learn the basics of military life, and included subjects such as mathematics, navigation and aerodynamics.

It was here they sorted out the potential flyers from the groups of boys. It was simple: the tall boys were pilots, and the short boys were gunners and engineers. The women were trained for the Radio Direction Finding Stations, to guide aircraft home. The coastline of Australia was screened by radar 24 hours a day.

At the end of this initial training course, he and some of his fellow students went to a pub in Woollahra to celebrate the completion of the course. At this stage of his life, Jack had not had anything stronger than a glass of milk. By the time he left the pub, he was legless and fell into a puddle of water. How he got home, no one knows.

When his mother saw him, she was furious. 'You need a big smack, a 'Settlers' and a good lie down,' she scolded (Settlers was a popular pink headache powder).

On 8 December 1943, Jack arrived at Temora and joined the

10 Elementary Flying Training School (10EFTS). He loved flying and couldn't wait to get up in the skies and destroy the Japanese.

His flying career got off to a dramatic – and dangerous – start.

During training, he was involved in a plane crash in a Tiger Moth. He was on his first solo flight, when the plane lost a wheel after take-off – it was one of the two main wheels, the off wheel. As he came in to land, he looked down and saw the fire brigade and ambulance waiting for him.

Somehow, he survived the landing. The cockpit of the Tiger Moth is very cramped, so cramped that you sit on your parachute, and as the plane hit the ground with a terrifying force, his knee smashed into the joystick and his head and torso crashed on to the instrument panel. By the time the ambulance got to him he was a dazed and crumpled heap.

The medics pulled him out of the cockpit and mopped up the blood streaming down his face. They placed him on a stretcher and took him in the ambulance to the Medical Unit on the airfield. When they got him out of the ambulance, he jumped off the stretcher and declared in garbled words that he was okay, then lurched and wobbled off. One of his mates saw him and helped him back to his quarters.

Determined to show them that he was no wimp, Jack refused to see the medical officers. He desperately wanted to keep flying because he had joined the RAAF to fight for our freedom and democracy, not to be a patient in a hospital. It took him a few days to walk without significant knee and back pain. He also had a painful stiff neck, a blinding headache for a week and a few cuts and bruises, but fortunately no broken bones that we know of. He managed his injuries himself and just got on with the job.

He was at 10EFTS for six weeks.

On 7 March 1944, he was sent back to Bradfield Park, and

on 5 April 1944 was transferred to Point Cook to undertake a Telegraphist's course. Later, on 9 January 1945, he was sent to Townsville. From Townsville, he was sent back to Melbourne on 23 January 1945, to the Telegraphic Unit Headquarters.

He returned to Townsville, where a new adventure commenced: he boarded a ship en route to New Guinea. He loved the voyage and spent most of his time perched at the bow of the ship, gazing out at the water and enjoying the sea air on his face and in his hair. On 4 April 1945, the ship arrived at Jacquinot Bay.

Upon arrival at Jacquinot Bay, Jack recalled they were given a tent and told to go to the tent area and put it up. Jack's experience with tents was zero. With no clue, he gave it a good try and somehow managed to put it up, then put his rucksack inside the tent and laid out his bed sheet on the ground. When night came, he went into his tent and laid down on the ground sheet, using his boot for a pillow.

Something woke him, probably the wind in the trees, and then, chaos – the tent fell on top of Jack. The ruckus of Jack yelling and trying to find his way out of the collapsed tent woke everyone. The other fellows couldn't stop laughing and cracking jokes. When they'd settled down, they showed him how to put up his tent. He was the butt of camp jokes for a couple of days, but he was a good sport. Jack had a knack of making fun of himself and everyone liked him for it.

He was given a stretcher to sleep on, which was at least softer than the ground, and as time went on, he got used to living in a tent, and scavenged a few bits and pieces to make it comfortable. He found a lump of wood which made do for something to sit on, and strung some rope across one corner of the tent so he could hang-up his clothes.

It was always hot and wet, but they had to make the best of

their situation. Most things were bearable, except for the rats. Eventually, Jack had to wear his boots to bed because the rats were eating his toes, and he couldn't shake the little blighters off.

There was great camaraderie amongst the boys, who were all very young and most had never been anywhere before they joined the RAAF, let alone out of Australia. It was common for them to have nicknames; nicknames were a sign of mateship. Jack's nickname was 'Tubby'. His mates reckoned, 'When the Japs come, we'll be safe because they'd take 'Tubby' first.'

With only the bare basics at hand, the men washed their own clothes and were expected to keep the camp tidy. For food, they lived mostly on 'Bully beef' (beef jerky) and tinned peaches. Every week, the camp chaplain handed them two bottles of beer each, with the tops removed. They were also offered cigarettes. The beer was always hot, so the boys took the bottles to the river and placed them in the water to cool them down.

When they were not on duty, there was usually a game of cards going on somewhere in the camp, and with a good supply of cigarettes on hand, Jack joined the boys and learnt to play cards and smoke.

Meanwhile, they lived amidst incessant bombing raids. The palm trees were topless, just black, burnt stalks poking out of the white sand.

Jack had settled into the routine of the camp, when his life was suddenly turned upside down. Told he'd be relieved of flying duties, as he was considered 'too dangerous,' Jack was transferred to Telegraphic duties.

This was a humiliating and tragic change of fortune and it took Jack a long time to accept this decision, as he had a great passion for flying. But there was no time for self-recrimination, and so he replaced his passion for flying with a passion for Morse

code and decoding Japanese codes. Jack became very proficient in Morse Code and managed to crack some enemy codes, enabling the Australians to follow the Japanese movements.

The Jacquinot Bay camp was in the southern part of the island, and the men got to know the area very well. Instructed to check for Japanese snipers in the northern part, Jack and 'Pappy' jumped into a jeep and set off. With a few years on Jack, Pappy wanted to drive and they headed out of the camp and up the mountain track, which was more like a goat track.

After they'd travelled part of the way up the mountain, Pappy suddenly lost control of the jeep, which speared off the track, heading for a cliff. Yelling to each other, they jumped clear as the jeep crashed over the cliff, lucky to escape.

But a bigger fear loomed: they would rather die than be captured by the Japanese. There were rumours around the camp that the Japanese were struggling to get food supplies to starving soldiers, and were eating anyone they captured.

Eventually, after a long walk, they made it safely back to camp.

Jack always made friends easily, and one enduring friendship was with Mark L., whom Jack later likened to 'King Rat,' referencing the 1965 film, *King Rat*, about the struggle to survive during WWII in an American Army camp. He said that whatever you wanted – from a bottle of beer to a haircut, or a jeep – you went to Mark. He was the go-to man who could find you anything.

Mark was also quite the entrepreneur who owned properties in the main street of Caringbah. He told Jack to buy property at Caringbah when he got back to Australia, but Jack didn't follow Mark's good advice. He also told Jack not to go to work: 'If you go to work, you miss all the good deals,' maintained Mark.

After the war, Mark and Jack kept in touch.

Jack's memories of the camp were also enduring, especially the darkest days.

It seemed that it was always raining and when it rained, it was torrential – inches of rain in a matter of minutes, mud everywhere. After one of these storms, Jack was walking along a track when suddenly he found himself sinking in a mud hole. Sinking deeper and deeper into the hole, he yelled out for help. Eventually, someone turned up but they couldn't pull him out; the mud held him like glue, sucking him in, and for the first time in his life, Jack felt helpless and frightened.

By the time someone found a pole big enough to take the weight of a man and long enough to go across the mud hole, only Jack's head, shoulders and arms were exposed. The pole was laid across the mud hole and Jack tried to pull his arms out to grab hold of it, but with no solid ground beneath him, he couldn't get traction.

Bravely, one of the boys sat astride the pole and worked his way along it to reach Jack. As he drew closer, the rescuer's feet were in the mud hole and he lost the traction he needed, but he backed off a little and managed to pull his feet out. He lay along the pole and reached out for Jack's arm, which was covered in slimy, greasy mud and he lost his grip on Jack, almost falling into the mud himself. He regained his balance and wiped the mud off his hand onto his shirt and reached again, this time hoping to grab Jack's hand.

He called out to Jack to raise his hand as far as he could. Amazingly, he managed to grab hold of Jack's hand. He had a good grasp, and holding on with all his might, he pulled Jack closer to the pole. As soon as he was close enough, Jack grabbed hold of his rescuer's shirt and, now that he had something to hang on to, Jack managed to drag his other arm out of the slime hole.

The rescuer was now having a hard time staying on the pole, but he knew he just had to, so he hung on for dear life, trying to fight off the fear he felt in his heart. Jack managed to get a good grip on the pole now that he had his arms free, as his rescuer slowly and carefully wriggled his way along the pole, trying not to move or shake the pole. A cheer went up as the rescuer shakily stood up on solid ground.

By this time, there were about half a dozen men standing around watching the drama unfold. They split into two teams so that there were men at each end of the pole, and, working together, they managed to pull Jack out of the hole. As they pulled him out, another loud cheer went up.

Nightmares of drowning in mud would haunt Jack his entire life. During the night, he'd cry out and bang the bed. When awakened, he'd read until morning to settle his mind.

On a clear day, out of the blue, a nearby volcano erupted. There are 13 volcanoes in New Guinea, 19 in New Britain and 27 in the surrounding islands, some are active, and others are extinct.

'It blew hell out of the joint,' Jack remembered, and they had to make a dash for safe ground. When the volcano quietened down, they moved the camp to a safer site.

A highlight of Jack's time in the RAAF was when he was offered a significant opportunity to work with General Douglas MacArthur, the Supreme Commander of the Southwest Pacific Area. They worked together for about two weeks. Jack told me he liked working with General MacArthur, and found him to be a genuinely nice man.

Towards the end of the war, Government officials came to visit the boys in New Guinea and New Britain. They sat around on logs listening to the officials and were told that Australia was very proud of the wonderful job they were doing, and to show Australia's appreciation for their sacrifice, the Government was starting a Rehabilitation Scheme, and servicemen could apply for a University Loan to pay for a university course. The interest on the loan would be 2.5 per cent, and the loan was to be paid off after they completed their course and were working.

'What's the longest course?' Jack asked the official.

'Medicine,' he replied. This was Jack's lightbulb moment. 'That's what I'll do,' he thought. 'I will become a doctor.'

On 7 May 1945, Germany unconditionally surrendered at Reims.

Jack was moved to Morotai, one of Indonesia's northernmost islands, on 14 June 1945, then the following month to Balikpapan in Borneo, the site of the last major Australian ground operation of WWII.

The Japanese unconditionally surrendered on 15 August 1945, but the document of unconditional surrender was not formally signed until 2 September 1945, on board the USS *Missouri*.

There were great celebrations and relief, but not for Jack, whose homecoming was delayed when he was ordered to stay and mop up.

This would go down as the most unpleasant time of Jack's life. He was on his own (he had only just turned 20), the place was desolate and lonely, all his mates had gone home. Jack was tasked with packing up and sending on any military paraphernalia the RAAF had left behind.

One of the most harrowing jobs was the burying of body parts he found.

He eventually arrived in the port town of Lae on 17 January 1946, and from there was sent 80 km east, to Finschhafen on 20 April 1946 to depart for home. He arrived in Australia at Bradfield Park on 7 May 1946, and was decommissioned later that month.

Jack's next chapter was about to begin.

# Chapter Four
# Jack and Jill
# 1946–1954

Jack's family were so happy and relieved to have him back home. His father cooked roast lamb for lunch to celebrate, Jack thought nothing had ever tasted so good. Roast lamb was always his favourite meal.

On his second day at home, Eric, a friend from SBHS, phoned him to say welcome home, and asked Jack if he would like to go to Luna Park.

It had been a long time since Jack had had any fun and he needed a distraction from his memories, and so he agreed. They met at Luna Park late in the morning. Eric and Jack were eager to enjoy the day and raced into the park, heading straight for the Big Dipper roller coaster.

The ride was mind-bending, rapidly changing speed and direction and taking them onto an elevated track and then down terrifying descents and back up steep inclines, descents and sharp turns. Jack relished the accelerated sense of excitement and exhilaration, which reminded him of his electrifying days of flying.

They had a wonderful time on the rides. On one of the rides, they met two girls and invited the pair to join them. It was a perfect day, the sun was shining, and everyone was enjoying themselves. The girl who paired up with Jack was a vivacious blonde nurse, Jill, who worked at Crown Street Hospital for Women, where she had trained. It was the first time Jack had spent any time with a girl.

Jack and Jill became friends.

Jack was accepted into Medicine at the University of Sydney, commencing at the beginning of 1947. He began looking for work while he was waiting to begin the course. At the time, there was still a lot of unemployment and not much choice in jobs, especially for someone without a skill. He eventually found a job at the nearby glass factory, putting tops on bottles.

Following a stroke, Jack's mother was paralysed down one side and needed someone to help her with her eating, doing her hair, putting her clothes on and helping her bathe. Between them, Jack, his father and his sister, Thelma, shared the care.

Jill became Jack's constant companion and as their relationship deepened, Jill opened up to Jack about her family history. Jill had a dysfunctional start to life. When she was two weeks old, her mother disappeared, never to return, and Jill's father, a farmer in the Grafton area, did his best to look after her, but it was more than a man could manage. He called on his two spinster sisters, Muriel and Agatha, to help take care of the newborn baby.

In 1924, Jill's mother passed away. During Jill's precious six years of life, her mother had not once returned to claim her abandoned baby. Jill's aunties Agatha and Muriel had fed and bathed her, and nurtured and loved her, telling her Bible stories and singing lullabies to her in a caring environment.

In February 1947, Jack commenced Medicine alongside more than 1,600+ other medical students at the University of Sydney.

He had a very busy life working, helping to look after his

mother and studying medicine. He said he found it easier to teach himself at home most of the time as there were so many students in the year, the rooms were always overcrowded.

One of the after-effects of the war, apart from the post-traumatic stress disorder (PTSD) and terrifying nightmares, were the attacks of malaria. Whilst in New Guinea, Jack had been taking anti-malarial medication but ceased the medication upon returning home. Jack's first attack occurred on a tram on his way to university when he suddenly developed a fever, shakes and sweats. He managed to get back home and saw the local GP, who diagnosed malaria. He was quite ill, but once on medication he recovered. More episodes followed, and, fortunately, eventually subsided.

On 20 December 1947, Jack (John David Woolridge, age 22) and Jill (Bernadette Nerrida Gwendoline Gillett, age 29) were married at St Mary's Cathedral in Sydney with a reception at the City Tattersalls Club. Jill paid for the wedding and her Aunt Muriel bought Jack a black dinner suit for the occasion. (Jack wore this dinner suit to the many auspicious occasions he attended throughout his life). After the wedding, they lived in a small flat in Woolloomooloo, and Jill became Matron of Crown Street Hospital for Women.

Meanwhile, the University of Sydney managed to sift out the struggling students and reduced the numbers dramatically each year, so much so, that in Jack's final year of medicine, only 165 out of the 1,600+ students passed the final exams.

Jack was one of the successful students.

The following is the University Year Book description of John David Woolridge:

*'Jack joined the faculty after three years' service in the Islands and immediately surrounded himself with many friends because of his easy-going, happy-go-lucky attitude. His academic career has been an enigma to his friends because, although he is constantly seen playing cards or the horses, he still manages to come near the top of the year.*

*Early in his career he had represented Sydney High School in both cricket and football, but nowadays he spends most of his time either studying the life-cycle and habits of the white leghorn, or travelling to and from his new home at Miranda.*

*We predict great success for Jack because of his great integrity and boundless good sense.'*

New Year's Eve 1952 proved auspicious for Jack. That day, he received his university results, learning that he'd topped the state of NSW in medicine with HONOURS (MB BSc (Hons)). He spent the day at the pub celebrating his results, *and* the birth of his first daughter, Judith Monica. Jill had given birth earlier that day.

In 1953, Jack was offered the plum position of Resident Medical Officer (RMO) at St Vincent's Hospital and held that highly prized post for a year. He travelled by train to the hospital each day, and earned 5 pounds a week.

Next, he was offered the position of Clinical Assistant in 1955. The following year, he became a Visiting Medical Officer (VMO) as an Assistant Physician at St Vincent's Hospital.

While Jack worked at St Vincent's, he often assisted the surgeons in the operating theatre, and while they worked, they talked about other things. He developed an affinity with one surgeon who was an avid racing fan and a member of the Australian Jockey Club (AJC). Their conversations invariably centred around horses and racing.

*Jack's Graduation Day (holding Judy)*

The surgeon offered to nominate Jack for membership to the AJC. This membership was highly prized among Sydney's high society and, because you needed two members to nominate you, membership was tightly held. So, when Jack's nomination was accepted, it was a very memorable moment in his life.

# Chapter Five
# Sutherland to Scotland
# 1955–1961

On 4 January 1955, Jack and his family moved to Sutherland and Jack joined Dr Eric Miles' General Practice, working part time so that he could continue with his positions at St Vincent's.

Dr Miles' practice was located in a building in Belmont Street Sutherland. The building was owned by Dr Tom Miles, Eric's brother. It was a very popular General Practice with at least six doctors. When Jack joined, they were Dr Rod Fisher, Dr Harry Soper, Dr Jerry Douglas, and Dr George Miller, as well as Dr Eric Miles and Dr Tom Miles. Not only did they see patients all day, they also had appointments after dinner from 9 – 11pm, so that patients could enjoy their evenings, catching a movie or having dinner, prior to visiting their doctor.

Dr Miles relied heavily on Jack due to his expertise in electrocardiography (ECG). When Dr Miles had a home visit to a patient with chest pain or shortness of breath, he would ask Jack to come along and carry the ECG machine and then conduct and interpret the tests. ECG machines in the 1950s were cumbersome and heavy, weighing around 10 kg. An ECG was a very involved procedure, the patient lies on the bed while the doctor places metal electrodes on each limb, and each electrode is held in place by a rubber strap. Then 6 rubber bulbs with a metal suction cap are placed across the left side of the chest at specific sites. The limb straps and the chest bulbs are each connected to the ECG machine by a lead. Once this procedure is completed the doctor then switches the appropriate buttons and the ECG machine then prints out a graph. The patient does not feel any sensation and just has to lie still and breathe normally. The whole procedure would take 5 to 15 minutes depending on how co-operative the patient is.

The most challenging house calls in Dr Miles' practice were often allocated to Jack, and the most difficult ones were up the river at Woronora. With no bridge for access, the only way to arrive was by boat, and the tide had to be below high tide, so that you could find the rock steps, the only access to go ashore.

The calls were often to treat injuries from domestic violence, and there were also calls for children who needed their tonsils removed, as well as women giving birth. He removed children's tonsils at the patient's home, where the child would lay on the kitchen table, and the mother assisted. Babies were delivered in the bedroom, with the husband or a relative assisting.

Jack also consulted patients from his home; he used a bedroom as his consulting room and the waiting room was on the veranda of the house. Jill helped where she could, particularly with new mums and breast feeding. When there was an epidemic of measles or other infections, he would be out most of the night.

There were no mobile phones in the 1950s.

General Practictioners in the 1950s were multi-skilled, performing the work of surgeons, obstetricians, gynaecologists, orthopaedic surgeons, dermatologists, etc. They could remove your appendix or tonsils, deliver babies, plaster broken limbs, and stitch up gaping wounds ... they did just about everything.

But the world of specialising was dawning.

In 1956, when Judy was 3, she became ill. During her mystery illness, her legs became weak and she was continually falling over and, before long, she could not walk. Poliomyelitis was ruled out. Jack took her to many doctors, who gave varying diagnoses. Unfortunately, a definite diagnosis was never agreed upon. After a while, she was fitted with callipers to help her walk. Despite this, she was a happy child and very bright.

That same year, Jack decided to move to Kirrawee. He purchased a ¾-acre block of land adjacent to Kirrawee Railway Station. Jill designed the home and Jack found a local builder. Two years later, the family moved to their new home. Jack and Jill were green thumbs and together, they created a beautiful garden. There were fruit trees and large gardens filled with masses of beautiful rose bushes. Jill's blooms were sought after – she provided red roses to government officials for overseas VIPs, and the family fridge was often filled with flowers.

As a very popular GP, Jack too was sought after. It was common to see long queues of patients waiting to see him, and he frequently went above and beyond the call of duty. If he had an ill patient, he would drop into their home, free of charge, to check on them, sometimes every day until he was satisfied that they were recovering.

(Jack's mother passed away in 1957.)

In April of the following year, The Sutherland Hospital (TSH) at Caringbah opened and the Hospital Board appointed four doctors: Dr Noel Kinny as the Chief Medical Officer, and three Honorary Medical Officers – Dr Don Wurth (General Surgeon), Dr Harry Kee (Urologist) and Jack, a General Physician.

The first patient at TSH was a man admitted at 9:30 am on 21 April 1958, and placed under Jack's care. Jack visited his patient each day, usually early in the morning, but was troubled by this man's presentation – a diagnosis evaded him, and this bothered Jack. He sat on the bed chatting to the patient, hoping to find a few clues, when Dr Kee walked by.

'I don't know what's wrong with this chap,' Jack said to Harry.

With a quizzical smile, Harry looked at Jack, and then across to the patient. 'He has thyrotoxicosis,' he told Jack. Dr Kee had noticed the patient's bulging eyes, a sign of Graves' disease, the most common cause of hyperthyroidism, an autoimmune disorder. Harry was a thorough gentleman and a delightful person who with three words took the wind out of Jack's sails for a minute or two. Jack soon recovered and so did the patient, with the appropriate treatment.

The medical world was changing, and Jack was eager to move with it. More and more doctors were specialising, some in surgery, others in orthopaedics, dermatology, ophthalmology, urology, anaesthesiology, and some, as general physicians. Doctors wanting to further their careers and specialise travelled to the United Kingdom or the USA, working and studying in universities and university hospitals.

Jack had an ambition to become a member of the Royal College of Physicians in Edinburgh. He thought about how this could become a reality and designed an innovative plan involving the General Practice where he worked. He approached Dr Eric Miles with his proposal: each doctor in the practice would contribute from their wage each week to a fund which would support one of the doctors while they studied for membership into a specialty. Only one doctor would go per year on a rotational basis starting at the beginning of 1959. Jack was the first to take advantage of the scheme.

He applied for a position with Dr E B French in the Department of Medicine at the Western General and the Eastern General Hospitals in Edinburgh, with the aim of sitting the membership exams towards the end of 1959. His application was accepted.

He arranged to take sabbatical leave from Sutherland Hospital and then had to find a way to get the family to Scotland. He had heard about doctors working on ships for their passage to the United Kingdom, so he made enquiries and found a job as a ship's doctor on a cargo ship, the Sydney Star. Jack's duties were to look after anyone on the ship who was ill or had an accident. He was to consult each day from 8 am to 12 noon. How easy this would be compared to his long and busy days! It would be like a holiday.

The young family packed up, rented out their home and boarded the ship in Fremantle, Western Australia. When they boarded, the captain told Jack they'd spend a few days in Fremantle, as they had 'repairs' to attend to. After talking to the crew, Jack realised that these 'repairs' were a ruse to give the sailors a chance to go ashore and visit girlfriends. Apparently, the captain sent a message to his company saying that they had engine trouble and needed repairs.

A few days later, they were on their way to Mauritius. Jack said it was nice to get off the ship for a while and find their land legs. The ship then proceeded to the Gulf of Aden and on to the Red Sea.

About midway through the Red Sea, one of the crew developed acute appendicitis, and needed an urgent appendectomy. It was night-time and they were a long way from a port. The ship was not equipped with an adequate room for surgical procedures, so Jack asked Jill to give him a hand to prepare and disinfect a room ready for an operation and to be his assistant throughout the operation.

Searching for some sort of table to operate on, he summoned the crew, and they found several card tables. Jack instructed the crew to tie them together to create a makeshift operating table, and to secure the tables so that they didn't slide across the floor with the movement of the ship.

Then he instructed the cook to find a large baking dish and fill it with water and put it on the stove to sterilise the instruments. Next, he showed the First Mate how to drip the ether while he operated. They were all set to go, and the patient (who had been given a good dose of rum) was brought in. The card tables were covered with a clean white bed sheet and the patient was helped onto the 'operating' table.

Jack settled the patient and once again showed the First Mate exactly how he was to drip the ether, and as soon as the patient was unconscious Jack proceeded to operate with Jill as his assistant. Jack was almost finished when he looked up and saw that the First Mate was so busy watching what Jack was doing, that he was pouring the ether over the patient's face.

'Stop, stop, stop, what are you doing?', Jack yelled at the First Mate, who looked up in a state of confusion and shock. Jack had to quickly finish the operation, and revive the patient. He survived. Everyone was delighted with the outcome.

When the ship arrived at Port Said, the crew went shopping and came back with a big bunch of flowers for Jill, and the First Mate took Jack ashore to a bar for a drink. They ended up at a brothel. Jack told them he wasn't going into a brothel and turned away to leave. As he did, he heard a loud thud on the pavement behind him. Turning around, he saw a man crumpled on the pavement – he'd been thrown out of the first-floor window. According to the

First Mate, he was one of the Sydney Star crew. The First Mate and one of the injured man's friends picked him up and the four of them squeezed into a small taxi which took them back to the ship. Jack spent the rest of the day stitching and patching him up.

After a few more port calls and 'delays' to accommodate romantic flings for the crew (apparently sailors do have a girlfriend in every port!), the ship arrived in France. Some of the crew had arranged to meet their wives here and the wives joined the ship. Jack recalled it was amazing how the sailors suddenly changed into saints in the blink of an eye, strolling round the promenade hand in hand with their wives and looking all lovey-dovey.

They soon arrived in the UK and the family made their way by train to Edinburgh, where rental accommodation had been arranged for the family at the hospital, and Judy attended a school nearby.

Jack worked very hard, he did nothing but study, go to university and work at the hospitals. There was no time to go out for a coffee, to lunch, or to the park. Jack told me that during his time in Edinburgh he did not have time to read a newspaper, as he had a mountain of text books to read, understand and commit to memory. He read carefully and if he came to a word or sentence he could not understand, he would not go on until he'd fully grasped it.

He often became exhausted and would lie down and listen to Jill read the medical books to him. He was so very committed and determined to accomplish his challenging ambition to pass the Royal College of Physicians membership exam within the year.

He loved Edinburgh, declaring it a great place to study because the weather was so bad that there was nothing else to do but hit the books.

Jack had a huge respect and admiration for his teachers, Dr E B

(Ted) French, Dr Matthews, and Dr Bill Price. Not only were they his teachers and mentors, they also welcomed the family into their homes. Jack had a special relationship with Bill and Mary Price. Bill was a General Physician and Mary, a General Practitioner.

Jack was intrigued by Dr Ted French, a master tutor who taught Jack to question everything. 'Why is this so?' he would challenge Jack, or provoke him with, 'Why do you say that?'

With his brilliant mind, Dr French inspired and excited Jack every day, demonstrating an exemplary work ethic, working day and night over a sick patient, yet as soon as he had a diagnosis, he would lose interest. He was challenged by the unknown but when he'd unravelled the mystery, his interest vanished. Jack developed the same deep curiosity and determination to find a diagnosis, but instead of losing interest when the diagnosis was made, Jack's care of the patient was always a continuing journey.

Jack revelled in his time in Scotland, and found the Scottish people to be most charming. Some, though, were direct and blunt, as demonstrated one day when Jack went to the Pathology Department and asked if he could look at pathology slides of a certain disease that he was researching. 'Ye no welcome!!!' was the response, and he left rather perplexed. In Australia this was not an unusual request and access would have been given.

Another quirky snapshot of Scottish life occurred when Jack was on a bus travelling to the university, and the bus made an unscheduled stop. 'Dog wants off!' the driver announced, and patiently waited for the dog to get off the bus and do a wee, and hop back on the bus, when he then resumed his route.

The Scottish idea of a picnic was also intriguing. Heading out on a picnic, you drive to a destination and park the car. If the weather is fine, you roll down the windows and sit in the car and enjoy your picnic. If the weather is inclement, you leave the windows up and enjoy your picnic in the enclosed car, no doubt with foggy windows. We are so spoiled in sunny Australia.

After a year of hard work and long study hours, Jack passed all his exams and was now a Member of the Royal College of Physicians, with the letters MB, BSc (Hons) and MRCP after his name. His dedication to his studies and work, combined with his self-denial of rest and recreation, were not in vain.

During their stint in Edinburgh, Jack took Judy to many specialists, hoping for a diagnosis. However, he was denied answers and her disability remained a mystery.

In early 1960, Jack and the family flew home in a Comet 4 Series airliner from London to Sydney.

The Comet Jet was the world's first commercial jet airliner, making its first commercial debut in 1952. However, within a year of entering airline service, three Comets were lost, two from metal fatigue and the third from overstressing of the airframe during severe weather. The Comet was extensively redesigned and the Comet 4 Series debuted in 1958.

Jack was aware of the history, but with his adventurous outlook, he felt confident flying home in the Comet Jet.

The route from London to Sydney was nicknamed the 'Kangaroo Route', and in the late 50s and early 60s, it left from London, with fuel stops at Zurich, Bahrain, Karachi, Calcutta, Singapore, Darwin and then finally arriving at Sydney. The multiple fuel stops were due to the Comet 4's limited range, and stops could vary, depending on the airline and weather conditions, an entire flight could take 36–60 hours, sometimes longer.

However, the flight home was not quite what Jack had expected, it was long and exhausting. They were delayed overnight in Bahrain for aircraft repairs, and had to disembark and sit in an un-airconditioned airport, in blistering, humid heat. Judy recalls there were four nuns travelling on their flight, and in the 1950s, nuns wore the distinctive black and white garment called a 'habit'. Judy said the nuns' heavy clothing was saturated with sweat.

After travelling for three days, they eventually arrived at Sydney Airport, where a large gathering of family and friends were waiting to welcome them home.

Their joy soured when they arrived at their house to find it had been almost destroyed by the tenants who had rented it for a little over 12 months.

Jack set to work finding accommodation for the family. With nothing available in the rental market, the only option was the Caringbah Hotel, where they lived for a few weeks while they searched for somewhere to lodge during the rebuild of their home. Jack decided to buy a unit in Cronulla where they lived until their home was ready.

With their home rebuilt, Jack continued to practice part time from his home as a General Practitioner, and commenced a part-time practice as a General Physician with rooms at the Wyoming Medical Centre, Caringbah.

He might have been back on home turf in Sydney, yet more changes were afoot for Jack.

When he'd arrived in Scotland, Jack's main interest was gastro-enterology. However, over the course of his studies in Edinburgh, this changed, ushering in a passion for cardiology. No doubt this was due to Dr French and Dr Price's enthusiasm for cardiology, together with their insatiable quest for knowledge in the field. Lit up by this exciting atmosphere of curiosity and knowledge-seeking, Jack developed a voracious passion for cardiology.

A few months after his return to Sydney, the phone rang. The caller was Professor Ralph Blackett from the Prince Henry Hospital (PHH) and Prince of Wales Hospital (POW).

The conversation went like this:

'How are you Jack, what are you doing?'

'I'm watching *Tarzan*,' Jack replied.

There was a pause, then Professor Blackett chuckled and said, 'Ohhh!!' before adding, 'They tell me you're pretty smart and I wondered if you would like to come and work with me?'

Jack accepted Professor Blackett's invitation to become an Honorary Physician/Cardiologist at PHH and POW, and the Royal Hospital for Women, Paddington (RHW). This position required him to attend daily ward rounds, consulting and organising patients' treatment with the Residents and Registrars; Grand Rounds with Professor Blackett once a week; plus, a weekly Outpatient Clinic; and Department of Medicine Meetings held one night each month.

His commitments at Sutherland Hospital and his consultation appointments in his rooms at Caringbah had to be interpolated around his new commitments as an Honorary at PHH and POW hospitals.

He retired from his job at the general practice.

To Jack, the Honorary position at PHH and POW felt like an improbable opportunity. He would now be interacting with the top echelon of medicine. Memories surfaced of being a youngster at Sydney Boys High who dreamed of a career in sport and was told he did not have the aptitude to be a school teacher.

The PHH, POW and RHW are Public Hospitals and 85–90 per cent of patients he treated there were public patients, and 10–15 per cent were private patients. The public patients were treated in an honorary capacity, in other words, the patient was not charged for the visits, nor did the hospital pay Jack for his time. It was all gratis (free of charge).

However, in the case of private patients, Jack could charge the patient for the consultation. Upon discharge from hospital, public patients attended the hospital's Outpatient Clinic (also gratis), and the private patients were seen in his private rooms, either in Caringbah or Macquarie Street, where they were charged for the consultations.

Jack had arranged to rent a room in Macquarie Street to facilitate his private patients who lived in the city or in the eastern or northern suburbs, who required follow-up appointments after their discharge from PHH and POW. He attended the Macquarie Street room for half a day each fortnight.

To be offered an Honorary Medical Officer position at these hospitals was considered a great honour and a sign to the outside world that your skill and expertise are acknowledged and recognised by the medical fraternity.

Jack's day started with rounds at TSH at 7am, or sometimes earlier if he had a large patient load or a patient who needed extra time. It was not unusual for him to have a total of 40 or 50 patients in the hospitals. The RMO and a Registrar would accompany him on ward rounds and these doctors would follow through with Jack's instructions for medication and medication changes, pathology tests, X-rays, referrals to other specialists, make discharge arrangements, etc.

Jack saw every patient every day without fail, seven days a week. He finished his rounds by 10 am and would then go to his rooms at Caringbah and consult until 5pm, and once a fortnight he would consult for half a day at Macquarie Street, then go to Caringbah till 5pm. After 5pm, he went to see patients at PHH at Little Bay. Only then would he go home.

However, if he had a patient who worried him at TSH, he would go back to check on them. Two afternoons a week, he had an Outpatient Clinic to attend at one of the hospitals. He also attended Department of Medicine meetings at TSH and PHH as well as teaching sessions for the Nurses and RMOs. These were all held at night.

Jack's consultation room at Caringbah was in a building named 'Wyoming.' His room was one of seven in a wing of the building on the first floor. Each room was rented out in sessions, one session being half a day. There were 11 doctors and one physiotherapist using these rooms. The doctors were all specialists: Jack, a General Physician, three surgeons, two dermatologists, an ophthalmologist, an orthopaedic surgeon, an anaesthetist, a gynaecologist/obstetrician, and a pathologist.

Jack consulted at his Caringbah room for five sessions each week during 1961.

At the Caringbah rooms, there were two secretaries on the front desk taking care of phone calls, appointments, cleaning, sterilising, banking, and chaperoning female patients.

I was one of the secretaries.

# Chapter Six
# Sue's Story

I was 15 years old when I commenced working at Wyoming on 8 August 1961.

Before I go any further, I will introduce you to my childhood story, so that you are aware of my unlikely journey to my first job at Wyoming, Caringbah.

My job at Wyoming opened the door to an extraordinary lifetime adventure and introduced me to the incomparable world of medicine. It gave me the opportunity to enter this wonderful world through the back door. As the years went by, my education widened beyond my wildest expectations, and my achievements were due to Jack's confidence in my intelligence and to his masterful teaching and mentoring, his quiet patience and exceptional intellect.

**My Family History**

My parents Ruby and Irving Goodfellow were married in 1945. I was born in Bowral, in the Southern Highlands of NSW, later that year.

My father, Irving Goodfellow was born at Moss Vale in 1918, to Richard and Elizabeth (née Irving). He was the sixth of eight children: Stanley, Harold, Thelma, Elizabeth Una, Muriel Edna, Irving, Gordon, and Richard. Irving attended Avoca School from April 1924 until December 1931. When he left school at age 12, he worked on the family farm, 'Ferndale,' at Avoca, one of the most beautiful areas in the Southern Highlands, with glorious, gently rolling green hills and imposing trees scattered throughout. The land was very fertile and grew everything abundantly.

Throughout the area, there were vegetable farms, dairy farms and beef-cattle farms.

During the depression, relatives of Irving's family, who lived in the city, came to the farm and camped in tents in the paddocks close to the family home. Everyone worked on the farm; fertilising fields and planting crops and vegetables, mending fences, milking cows, feeding 'poddy' calves (young calves who are being bottle fed), feeding the pigs and chooks, weeding the vegetable garden or catching rabbits to feed their families.

The women cooked, cleaned and mended clothes, worn-out clothing was remade into children's clothing, nothing was wasted – every button, every zipper and metal clasp were saved and re-used. This generation would live the rest of their lives unable to bear the thought of waste. For entertainment, they all gathered around the piano, singing along while my father's mother, Elizabeth, played the piano, she had the ability to play the piano by 'ear', that is playing the piano without written music. Irving enjoyed singing. Other forms of entertainment included listening to the radio, playing cards and playing tennis.

Irving and two of his brothers enlisted in the army during WWII. Irving became a member of the 7th Light Horse CMF and then he was transferred to the 19th Battalion AIF at Goulburn on 16 July 1940, where he spent the next six months training at Wallgrove, Ingleburn and Bathurst.

Stanley enlisted on his 30th birthday in 1940 and was posted to the Australian Army Medical Corp. He was detailed to the 2/3rd Casualty Clearing Station. On 20 December 1940 Stanley left Sydney by ship for the Middle East and was sent to Greece.

Gordon was the second youngest in the family and he enlisted on 15 December 1941. In February 1942 he was detailed to North Head Sydney, then in August to Illawarra. In September he was moved to Queensland prior to embarking on a ship taking him from Townsville to Milne Bay on 25 April 1943.

On the 3 February 1941, Irving boarded the Queen Mary bound for Singapore with members of the 8th Division.

At the fall of Singapore, his Commander told the 8th Division, 'Every man make a break for himself'.

The following is a newspaper report from *Smith's Weekly – Sydney Edition* on Saturday 21 March 1942 which gives you an idea of the conditions and the decisions the men were faced with.

> *'Eight of us made a break through the Japs to the harbour. We found no boats other than barges and junks which were quite impossible to get away in, as the Jap planes were on top. We took a RAF truck and drove madly round to Keppel Harbour and found a pilot launch, but the motor was no good. Our mechanics slaved over it and at last got it to work. Some of us dashed off in the truck for petrol and found an abandoned petrol dump. We took a case of bully beef on the lorry and were bombed for hours before leaving the wharf.*
>
> *Smoke from Singapore helped us and as it was late in the day, night brought us a little respite. We had to go round and round in a circle till day break, and all that night we could*

hear the sound and see the flashes of gun fire. Saturday saw us hiding round one side of the island while planes escorted Japanese warships into the main harbour. By dodging around the island we were not seen but two bombers gave us a scare.

Well, we travelled about 845 miles in the launch, finding 15 tins of petrol in another launch, drifting somewhere near Sumatra. When we got there, we found the Dutch Controller and we were put on an island boat named 'Indragirl.'

The Japs had convoys and ships in Banka Strait and so we had to go round them to Banka Island and were machine-gunned by Jap troup-carrying planes. From there we risked the minefields to Java.

Arrived in Batavia and the consuls there would not have anything to do with us, according to the corporal from our boat who went ashore. He could not find out if there were any AIF units on the island. Dutch officials then told us that a ship was sailing for Australia in two and a half hours. We rushed down to the wharf and got aboard and were well-treated there.

In due course, we arrived in Fremantle and instead of being heroes for having escaped from Singapore, we were and still are – treated like deserters. Some boys from other units of the AIF came in a boat straight from Singapore. They were, on landing, put under arrest and spent three days in gaol being allowed only one shilling a day. We were a little luckier as we were not arrested. There are at least 30 of us now and every dirty job in the camp falls to us. Instead of being given a rest and sent back to our own state NSW we are almost prisoners – washing up for the sergeants and officers and doing work in the kitchens for men who haven't been in the fight yet.

Is this the way men should be treated in their own country who have been fighting the Japs since they declared war? We *all want a couple of weeks leave. We have only had five to ten days' leave in one year in Malaya and think we are entitled to a brief rest. Then we'll gladly and willingly help others to know how the Japs fight. We are all experienced men and know from hand-to-hand fighting their weaknesses and tricks. But the military does not seem to want us. We cannot even draw the money that is on our paybooks.*

*Three more Australians and four Englishmen have just arrived, and they have been put under open arrest.*

*But why? Don't they want men to escape from Singapore? Or are they afraid of what they'll tell their people what Australia should know?'*

Dad refused to talk about the war. It was a forbidden topic in the family for the rest of his life. Many decades later, an acquaintance told us Irving had escaped from Singapore with a few mates. They found a fishing boat which was in a parlous state and the engine in disrepair with no sign of life. So, Irving, who had spent his early life on the family farm and knew how to fix machinery, managed to revive it. They had to find fuel without being captured, so they searched and discovered some old tanks of fuel outside one of the Japanese camps. They successfully removed the fuel without being caught and loaded it on to the fishing boat and escaped. They were picked up by a cargo boat somewhere in the Indian Ocean and arrived in Fremantle on the SS Warigola on 3 March 1942. When they arrived in Fremantle, there was no welcome reception, instead they were charged for being deserters.

The war had a devastating effect on my father.

Over the next seven months, he received treatment for a long-standing injured knee. He was promoted to Corporal and detailed to training camp staff and discharged on 28 September 1943.

He returned home to his parent's farm and worked on the farm growing vegetables and taking them by truck to the markets in Sydney.

He met Ruby at a Blue Gum Girls' dance at the Avoca Hall in the Southern Highlands near his family farm.

The Blue Gum Girls was a local group of girls who wanted to do their part to help the war effort, so they made special treats for the soldiers travelling on the trains which usually stopped at Moss Vale Railway Station for water or fuel. They also held dances in the community halls for the local soldiers and their friends.

My mother, Ruby Jean Batton, was born in 1923 at Barmedman, the seventh child to Mark Elliott Batton, b. 1887, and Ruby Ellen Kent Haines, b. 1885. Mark Batton and Ruby Haines were married at Yahl South Australia on 12 March 1913.

Ruby's siblings were Dorothea (Dot), James (Jim), Constance (Connie), John (Jack), William (Bill), Gwendoline (Gwen).

The following is the story of my grandparents' journey from South Australia and their arrival, and their early days in Moss Vale. This is an excerpt from *Off We Go to Adelaide*, written by Narelle Bowern, with help from Pam Hodge and others.

> 'Mark and Ruby Batton first lived at Barmedman. The property was situated between the school and the railway line. The school was a typical two-room, one-teacher country school. The farm produced wheat, dairy, fruit and vegetables.
>
> Barmedman is a small rural town located 457 km west of Sydney and 30 km north of Temora on the road to West Wyalong. It is famous for two things – its therapeutic mineral pool, and two large wheat silos in the town, holding 1.4 million bushels and a sign of the district's economic focus.
>
> In 1924 the family moved to Moss Vale. Connie [Ruby's older

*sister] described arriving by train in the middle of winter, at about 2.30 am [the ages of the children at that stage would have been Ruby a babe in arms, Gwen 2 yrs, Bill 4 yrs, Jack 5 yrs, Con 6 yrs, Jim 8 yrs, and Dot 10 yrs]. The stationmaster had a fire going in the waiting room and they stayed there until it was light. They had a mixed farm, with dairy cows, pigs, an orchard and vegetables, at the end of Beaconsfield Road in Moss Vale. According to Connie, they lived happily there. On Saturday, the neighbours would come over and they would play cards or sing. There was always plenty of food. However, during the Great Depression, they were unable to sell the produce from the farm. Vegetables transported to Sydney would be dumped and a bill sent back for the freight. Men would travel on the train (which ran past their property) and jump off to ask for work. There was no work, but Grandma Batton would always give them a meal. Connie described walking back from the town with her father (about 3 miles), having bought some meat for the evening meal, and he said to her, 'That was my last shilling'. It was then that the family moved into Moss Vale and had a business at 527 Argyle Street, buying stock feed on a cooperative basis, and selling stock, machinery and furniture. Connie worked in the office as Secretary. He [my grandfather] ran this business until about the late 1950s, when he was struck by a car on his way home and was badly injured. This was the first time he had ever been near a doctor or a hospital. When he recovered, he used to walk every day down Argyle Street. But evidence of his serious head and spine injuries remained for the rest of his life.'*

During the war years, my mother Ruby belonged to the Blue Gum Girls, and it was at one of the Blue Gum Girl dances that set the scene for Ruby and Irving to meet. She told me that another girl, Poppy, was flirting with Irving and she decided she would win this handsome young man over. Mission accomplished!

In the early days of their marriage, my parents lived above a petrol station in Argyle Street Moss Vale. Dad worked on cars and trucks in the garage, and there were two petrol bowsers on the street kerb, where vehicles would pull up and re-fuel. I remember it being a dirty place to live; there was nowhere to play outside as it was a working garage with cars and trucks everywhere and the ground was covered in black grease.

Later, we moved to a house with a grassy backyard next to the showground, which was a great improvement. However, it was noisy, as the showground housed greyhounds and there were greyhound races twice a week, so we had barking dogs, night and day.

Dad went into business setting up a company, selling dairy equipment and products to dairy farmers. He was away for days at a time, travelling from farm to farm throughout New South Wales, selling milking machines etc. My mother managed life on her own most of the time, and had two sisters, Gwen and Con, who lived nearby. They were a church-going family, so this gave Mum the company and social interaction with her sisters and friends. The ladies from the church organised cake stalls, and concerts, and provided cups of tea with hot scones and delicious sponge cakes filled with jam and cream, for those attending church for christenings, weddings and funerals. They also sang in the Church Choir. The Church community was like one large happy family. Everyone knew everyone else and if anyone was in trouble, needing help or a meal, or someone to mind their children, there were always plenty of offers of support.

I have a special memory of the christenings at the church. When babies were christened, they were placed in a beautiful white wooden rocking cradle, festooned with exquisite white lace-trimmed sheets and pillowcase, covered by an intricately crocheted basinet coverlet. The cradle had ribbons attached to it and all the little children were called up to the cradle and were given a ribbon to gently rock the baby. We were well supervised so as to avoid any high-spirited rocking.

On 8 October 1949, Mum's sister Gwen, my favourite Aunt, was married, and she chose me for one of her flower girls. I was 3 years old. I thought I was a princess, in my pale-yellow organdie floor-length dress with puffed sleeves and matching gloves and a Dutch-styled bonnet. My cousins Helen and Roslyn were also flowergirls.

Aunty Gwen gave us a gold bangle as a memento of the occasion. I had never seen a gold bangle before. I kept touching it just to make sure it was real, and took great pleasure in showing everyone my bangle, it was my greatest treasure. Then, misfortune claimed me.

A few weeks later, I woke up one morning to find that my bangle was no longer on my wrist. I was shattered, I looked all through the bed, under the bed, under the mattress, I searched every inch of my bedroom, but it was nowhere to be seen. I was absolutely crushed; my beautiful bangle was my one and only treasure. I cried myself to sleep that night.

As a young child I had an eye condition called strabismus (squint) and wore glasses from the age of 4. My fondest early childhood memory was my mother taking me to see an eye specialist in Macquarie Street, Sydney.

I remember being so excited standing on the platform at Moss Vale, waiting for the steam train. I loved the noise of the chugging and the steam hissing out of the engine.

We climbed up on to the high step of the train and walked

into the carriage to find a seat. The carriage had green leather seats surrounded by beautiful rich brown polished wood. How I enjoyed smelling the fragrance of the leather and wood. It was a long journey, and I loved every minute. I was mesmerised by the passing parade of trees and paddocks, horses and cows, hills and gullies, and birds in flight.

When we arrived at Central Station in Sydney, we caught a bus to Macquarie Street and walked to the office of the eye specialist. The Doctor checked my eyes and talked to mum. Then we travelled back to Moss Vale.

Just after I turned 4, my parents placed me in a boarding school, Koyong Private School in Suttor Road, Moss Vale, not far from home. I must have been a terrible child! No one told me why I was sent away to boarding school at such a young age, and as a young child I assumed this was normal. It was a small school with students from kindergarten (children as young as 3 yrs old were accepted as boarders) through to 5th year (Leaving Certificate). The Leaving Certificate was the final year at school and students were usually aged 17. The school opened in 1915 and closed in 1952.

The following is an excerpt from:

*Koyong*
*Day and Boarding School for Girls*

*Moss Vale*
*1915–1952'*
*© Koyong School Ex-Students Association 2012.'*

'*Koyong was operated by a mother and daughter, Mrs Bertha Mein and Miss Hetta Mein. They purchased the building early in 1915 and arrived by train one day in June 1915.*

*Koyong Private School*

*They opened the school on 12 July 1915. The property was described as having 8 rooms, an attached kitchen, a pantry and a bathroom; a stable with 2 stalls, a weatherboard coach house, a small wash house and a chook house and was on land of less than 3 acres.*

*Mrs Bertha Mein married Andrew Mein in 1888 in Melbourne and Hetta was born in Nathalia in 1889. Mrs Mein's marriage was short lived, and she divorced probably in 1893. Andrew Mein died in 1894 from accidental drowning.*

*Sometime after that, Bertha and Hetta moved to Sydney and Bertha opened a Kindergarten and named it Tintern. Hetta attended Shirley School, Edgecliffe.*

*During this time at Shirley School, Hetta probably trained as a teacher, as prior to 1905 most teachers were trained on the job as pupil-teachers and began their 4-year course between the ages of 13 and 16. During school hours they taught a class full time, and after hours for an hour or so were instructed in teaching method and content.*

*Hetta's training at Shirley School probably explains the quality and style of teaching at Koyong which was based on experiential learning (learn by doing, rather than book learning), open-air schooling, self-discipline, and concern for the whole child.*

*The children at Koyong were encouraged to be aware of those who were less fortunate than they were and to be actively involved in supporting needy children, this was done through the Ministering Children's League and the Red Cross.*

*In the school's prospectus it stated that the school course includes Scripture, English Language and Literature, History, Geography, French, Latin, Science, Mathematics, Needlework, Class Singing, Drill, Brushwork, and Riding lessons may be arranged. It also stated that the school prepared pupils for school and musical examinations, that Boarders would be given every opportunity of healthy outdoor exercises and sports – Tennis, Net-ball, Cricket etc. and open-air classes would be taken when the weather was suitable. Koyong had sleep-out dormitories (enclosed verandas). It stated also that the school has its own cows and poultry, and vegetables grown in gardens on the school site.*

I remember my first morning.

Mum came into my bedroom, calling out, 'Suzie, Suzie, wake up, it is time to get up.'

I rubbed my eyes, and as I slowly opened them, I caught a glimpse of the little old brown suitcase sitting on the floor, with the lid open showing the world my few precious clothes, and then I remembered last night, when mum and I were packing my clothes into the suitcase ready for today.

Mum's words came rushing back to me, 'You are going to

school tomorrow and you will live at the school. Mummy and Daddy will come and pick you up during the school holidays.' Now, to a 4-year-old, none of this made sense, all I knew was that my nightie was packed in that bag, and I would not be home tonight.

I looked up at Mum and cried, 'I don't want to go to school,' and my little body trembled, and tears cascaded down my cheeks.

'Come on Suzie, be a good girl, we have to get you dressed and have breakfast and then we will walk to the school,' she responded.

I rolled over and reluctantly sat on the edge of the bed, letting my feet tentatively reach for the floor. I didn't want to put the strange clothes on, I wanted to stay at home with my mummy.

Mum started fussing, she had a wet washer ready to wipe the tears from my face and began to dress me. 'Okay, now we will put your shoes and socks on.' We had been practising tying shoelaces for the last week and I thought I was clever learning how to put the laces around my fingers and make a bow.

She brushed my hair and put a bobby pin in to hold the hair back off my forehead and said, 'Now put your glasses on and we will have breakfast.' With my eye problem, I had to wear glasses with a patch over one eye.

We went into the kitchen, and I sat on a chair at the wooden table. My little brother came running in, crying out that he was hungry. Mum had a big pot on the wood-fired stove with rolled oats bubbling away. She served out three bowls of oats and poured a little Golden Syrup over the oats in each bowl.

When we finished eating our bowl of oats, she wiped our faces with the wet face washer, Mum picked up the suitcase and called out for my brother and off we went. We dropped my brother off at the neighbours and started on our walk to the school which was just down the road, about a five-minute walk, but I didn't want to go, and started dragging my feet. Mum took hold of my hand and sang me a little song to take my mind off my impending unknown.

When we arrived, I looked at the white picket fence and gate, it looked menacing. As I peered past the gate, I saw a huge building with a ground floor and first floor. Mum put the suitcase down on the footpath, she could see that she needed two hands to open the gate. As she pushed it open it gave a squeak of protestation, and then as she closed it, it gave a whimper of a creak.

We walked up the path and steps to the front door. The door was imposing and had a gold-looking door knocker in the middle at about Mum's head height, and a round gold-looking door handle at the height of Mum's waist. She knocked loudly and at the same time looked down at me with a reassuring smile. I wanted to turn around and run back home, but as I turned, I could see that menacing gate was securely closed.

I could feel the butterflies flying around inside my stomach. It took ages before someone opened the door, it opened slowly and squeaked almost as much as the gate. We were greeted by a large smiling lady with curly grey hair. She had a big pimple-looking thing on her nose which held my gaze, until I noticed she had a couple of missing teeth. Her rotund body was wrapped in a big dirty white apron which tried to cover her long, dark floral dress that danced around her black stockinged legs and her black lace-up shoes.

'Hello,' she said cheerily. 'You must be Mrs Goodfellow. Come on in, you can sit in the sitting room, and I will go and find the Headmistress, Miss Mein.'

Off she waddled down the dark forbidding hallway. The sitting room had a lounge which was a tad faded. There were three other various chairs of the same vintage scattered around the room. The windows were covered in long dark, green velvet drapes which were tied back, and kept out most of any daylight or warmth from the sun, and the room had a slightly musty smell.

About 10 minutes later, another lady and a young girl came into the room. The lady introduced herself to my mother, and then she turned to me and told me that the girl with her was my 'Buddy' and the buddy would take me and my belongings to the sleeping quarters. The school had a 'Buddy system' where each of the older girls was responsible for one of the younger boarders.

My buddy showed me where I would sleep that night, a small bedroom with a huge-looking bed. My buddy placed my little brown suitcase on the chair in the corner and then took my hand and told me she was going to show me around the school. I would not see my mum for many months. I wanted to cry because I could not imagine my life without my mother, but my buddy had a firm hold of my hand and walked quickly and I had trouble trying to keep up with her.

I still vividly remember my first day and night at Koyong. My buddy stayed with me for the rest of the day showing me where my classroom was, where the toilets were and where we went for meals. I didn't feel like eating, I felt like I had worms in my stomach.

After the evening meal of bread, dripping and melon jam which I couldn't eat because I felt so sick, my Buddy took me to my bedroom and helped me change into my white nightie. I looked at the bed, it was so high, as I stood next to the bed, I could rest my chin on the soft pinkish eiderdown which lay over the bed. She took me to the bathroom where there was a bucket to use for going to the toilet as the toilets were outside toilets. At home, we always had a potty under our bed for doing a wee before bed or during the night.

She brought me back to the bedroom and I said to her, 'I don't think I can climb up onto the bed.' She laughed and quickly helped me climb up, pulling the bedclothes up so that I could snuggle into bed. She tucked me in and told me, 'Now don't you cry tonight because if you do you will be in trouble, and I don't want you to get into trouble.' Well, I did cry, I wanted my mummy, but I made sure no one heard me.

I struggled to settle into the school routine and struggled with the uniform, first the white blouse with little buttons, and then the tie. Would I ever learn how to tie that blessed tie? I had to ask my Buddy to help me, she gave me a lesson. Then came the navy serge skirt, tan laced shoes and socks. When it was cold, we could wear a woollen navy jumper and on formal occasions, we had a blazer, a Panama hat in the summer time and a felt hat in winter with gloves. Every Sunday we wore full school uniform including hat and gloves and marched from the school to the St Johns Church in Moss Vale, approximately 1.2 kilometres from the school.

The food, oh! Breakfast was rolled oats, nothing like what Mum makes, these rolled oats had great chunks of sticky gooey oats that choked you and were hard to swallow and there was no sugar or treacle to sweeten it. Lunch was the main meal of the day and was usually a stew, and on Sundays a roast, that was the best meal of the week. The evening meal was bread and dripping and melon jam. Oh! How I longed for the delicious blackberry jam Mum made.

The next day, I was moved into a dormitory where there was a line of six camp stretchers in the sleep-out (the enclosed veranda). Now an enclosed veranda in Moss Vale in winter is a very cold place to be. I still hate the cold.

One of the rules for the younger children was that if you went to the toilet during the day you had to take your buddy and report to them if you had done a wee or a poo. The toilets were outside and were smelly pans which were emptied by men in a big smelly truck. One day, I had not done a poo all day and was given some disgusting medicine. The teacher told me to hold my nose to try and stop the taste of the medicine, but it didn't help, I could still taste the revolting medicine.

The next morning when I woke up, I was in a bed of poo. Can you imagine how I felt? I was terrified, bewildered and distressed at the mess and smell. I started to cry, 'I want my mummy.' It was so bad, everyone was screaming and pointing at me and holding their noses and crying out, 'Smelly poo smelly poo …'

I was trundled into the bathroom and cleaned up with freezing cold water, and punished for a week: I had to sit on a chair in the corner all day and no-one was allowed to talk to me. The other girls looked at me and whispered to each other, pointing their fingers at me and running away giggling. This was the worst time of my little life; I want my mummy. I cried myself to sleep for the next few days.

They never gave me that disgusting medicine again and no-one wanted to be my friend. I think I was the most unwanted girl in the school. Life was hard enough as it was, having to wear glasses with a patch over one eye and with my buck teeth, I was always an easy target.

I soon learned to entertain myself. I would find a picture book to try and teach myself to read, or I would go and visit the animals and talk to them, asking them if they would be my friend as no-one else wanted to. I wasn't going to let those nasty girls upset me.

The days slowly rolled by into weeks, and the weeks rolled into months. My saving grace was that I enjoyed the classroom, it was my comfort zone, where I could feel less lonely and where the other girls could not tease me. The classroom was where I could bury myself in learning, and I had fun with myself, making a game of trying to learn quickly so that I came first in the tests.

Later in the year, on a lovely sunny day, I was in the play yard enjoying the warm sun on my face, when a couple of older students came over to me and showed me a plate of brightly coloured lollies. I suddenly felt happy because someone wanted to come and talk to me and show me their lollies. I hadn't seen a lolly close up before; we didn't have lollies at home.

I stared in wonder at the beautiful colours. They looked delicious. The girls asked me if I would like one, and as I hadn't had a lolly in my short life, they told me how lovely it would be, so I took one with great anticipation and quickly popped it into my mouth.

I froze, what was that disgusting taste in my mouth? I gagged and spat it out and ran to get some water to try and wash the 'lolly' out of my mouth. The older girls laughed and said, 'Don't worry, it's only dirt.' They had made the 'lollies' from dirt as a joke on the younger children. I never wanted to eat another lolly in my life. They ran away laughing. They thought it was such a great joke to play on all the little ones at the school.

Koyong was closed in 1952, and in 1953 I started 2nd Class at Moss Vale Public School (MVPS).

The transition from a private boarding school to public school was traumatic. I remember one day during an art class, I felt overwhelmed and started crying. My teacher Miss Hole was so kind and understanding, telling me to put my head down on the desk until I felt better.

After that moment of kindness from Miss Hole I started to feel as if I belonged and enjoyed my days at school. I was learning not to take any notice of the naughty children who wanted to tease me and now I had my little brother with me, he was my little minder. He'd just tell them to go away, and they usually did, although a couple of times he ended up in a fight. I was lucky, I had my little brother and schoolwork was easy for me.

We lived about 1½ km from MVPS, and walked to and from school each day – we didn't mind, as most of the children either walked home or caught a bus. The children who caught the bus usually lived on farms on the outskirts of Moss Vale.

I remember during that first year when I was in 2nd class, we had an outbreak of nits, and one of the girls in my class had nits in her hair and her parents shaved all her hair off her head. The poor girl! I couldn't imagine what it would be like having no hair. I felt so sorry for her. The school told the parents she was not to come back to school until her hair had grown to cover her head. I don't remember her coming back to school.

In 1950, the Menzies Government introduced free milk to all school children. The milk was delivered in small glass bottles with a foil lid, packed in crates which were left in the school playground for the morning break. The bottle size was probably about 200 ml. All the children lined up to take a bottle. I have always had a great dislike of milk, whenever I drink milk, I become very nauseous, so I would give my bottle to someone else.

Occasionally the kids would tell me it had turned sour from sitting in the sun for so long. But I am sure there were many disadvantaged children who benefited greatly from the school milk program. (The program was abandoned in the 1980s).

In 1953, when I was 7 years old, I had an eye operation at the Sydney Eye Hospital. When I was admitted, the nurse said they didn't have a children's ward and that I would be placed in an adult female ward. It didn't matter because all the old ladies fussed over me. Following my operation, I had both eyes bandaged and couldn't see and someone had to feed me.

I felt very special, I had never been fussed over so much.

When the bandages were removed a few days later, I had double vision which was unpleasant and made me feel sick. On the day I was discharged from hospital my father came with my mother and drove us home. The drive home was a bit scary as it felt like the buildings were falling across the road. It made me feel so nauseated, so I closed my eyes and slept all the way back to Moss Vale. The double vision slowly disappeared over the next few days.

Unfortunately, I still had to wear glasses, how I hated them. The boys in my class would call me 'four eyes' and 'bucky.' All this teasing tended to make me avoid a lot of contact with kids. A couple of the girls were not as cruel. I wanted to be friends with everyone, but found out early in life that you can't, that I was better off entertaining myself.

My little brother Richard was 18 months younger than me and always in trouble. He decided at an early age that he wanted everyone to call him Rick. I hated it when he got the cane or when he was in a fight with other boys. There were always fights after school. When he got the cane, it was always 'six of the best'. I cried for him.

Rick had severe asthma. When he had an asthma attack you just wanted to breathe for him, you could hear him trying desperately to get air into his lungs, he struggled so much. When the doctor came, he gave Rick an injection of adrenalin which seemed to help him through his attack.

Life in the 1950s in a small country town was very simple. Before we had an electric refrigerator we had an ice chest. The ice man drove around the town in his little truck selling large blocks of ice for ice chests. Also, the rabbit man came around once a week selling rabbits.

We had a vegetable garden, fruit trees and chooks in the back yard. This was the usual backyard in Moss Vale. All our food came from the garden, or relatives' farms, except for the flour and sugar which came in big bags and were kept in a dry, cool cupboard.

Our meals were simple; breakfast was rolled oats sweetened with brown sugar or golden syrup, lunch was a vegemite or jam sandwich, and our evening meals were mostly stews or baked mutton neck chops with vegetables. However, the best meal of the week was Sunday lunch after church when we had a roast leg of mutton. Our meat was always mutton, we didn't have lamb or beef until the 1960s. If we had dessert, it was mostly boiled rice with sultanas, or rice custard, except on Sundays, when we had apple pie or blackberry pie and, on our walk home from church, Mum bought ice cream as a special treat to accompany the pie.

But the best treat of all was Christmas lunch, when we had roast chicken with roast vegetables smothered in gravy, followed by Christmas pudding with threepences (little silver coins worth three pennies) hidden inside the pudding, which was covered with custard. The meal was accompanied by homemade ginger beer.

The worst part of this delightful meal was that Dad had to kill the chook. This was a grisly, bloody scene. He went to the chook pen and caught the slowest chook and carried it to the woodheap where there was a chopping block. He put the chook on the block and chopped its head off with his axe. The poor headless chook was released, and it ran around the back yard until it bled out and died. Then the poor chook was thrown into the laundry tub filled with hot water to soften up its skin so that it was easy to pluck the feathers out. I could not watch; it was too gruesome, and the smell was nauseating, but Rick enjoyed every minute of the whole event. And then it was mum's turn, she prepared the chook for roasting in the oven.

Throughout the 1950s, nearly every family went to church. On Sundays, the town was very quiet except for families walking or driving to the churches. On Sundays, all shops were closed except for one milkshake bar, which was where mum bought the ice cream, and there were no sports or other activities. Hotels and clubs were also closed.

During blackberry season, Dad occasionally took us for a drive into the bush to find the blackberry bushes. We were all given a billycan or bucket and Dad told us to be careful as the snakes like living in the blackberry bushes and the blackberry bushes have lots of nasty thorns.

When our billycans were full, we picked and ate as many blackberries as we could, they were delicious. We ended up with blackberry stain all over our hands and around our mouth and lots of scratches from the thorns on our arms and legs. Mum made delicious blackberry jam and blackberry pies.

When dad thought the conditions were right, he took us mushroom hunting during the wet autumn weather. We hunted for field mushrooms; most were the size of your hand and had a white/cream scaley cap with pinkish-brown gills on the underside. Some of the mushrooms were the size of a dinner plate. Dad loved mushrooms!

These outings picking blackberries and mushrooms were always lots of fun. Our drive often took us across a shallow river with a stony bed, where we stopped and had a picnic lunch and were allowed to splash and play in the river for a while.

Water was a very precious commodity. We had a 2,000-gallon water tank beside our house, which collected the rainwater off our roof, so we had to be very careful with our water use as this was our only water supply. Bath time was once a week, starting with the youngest member of the family and finishing with the adults.

The water was heated via a 'Chip' water heater. Later, when we moved to another house, there was no Chip heater, so Mum would heat the water in a large kettle on the stove and pour the boiling water into the bath tub, adding cold water to cool it down. She would add more hot water as the water got cold. Years later, we had the luxury of an electric water heater.

My mother's parents lived with us for eight years, from 1951 to 1959. My grandfather looked after the vegetable garden, fruit trees and chooks. He was a quiet man, tallish with a slim build and he walked with a limp and couldn't remember things. He had a nice face with big bushy eyebrows hovering over his eyes, and a mop of black wavy hair sprinkled with a few greys. My mother had been told by the doctor that grandfather had a clot running around his body and that was why he had intermittent memory loss. The doctor told her that this was probably due to the accident when a motor vehicle hit him while he was walking home from work. But I think, on reflection, my grandfather had dementia.

My grandmother helped my mother cooking and mending. She was a beautiful lady with white wavy hair, she was always neat and tidy and took pride in how she dressed. She had a wonderful sense of colour and would say to me, 'Blue and green should never be seen.' Her pet was a grey Persian cat which she loved; she would nurse it and sing to it.

Our family occasionally visited Mum's sister, Aunty Dot (Dorothea), Uncle Bert, and their three children Alan, Bob (Robert) and Helen. They lived at Albion Park. When we first visited, they lived in a house in the main street with a great big tree in the front yard, which we all loved climbing. Later, they moved to a dairy farm which was on a high hill just at the base of the Macquarie Pass.

Aunty Dot would always have a delicious sponge cake baked for our visit. It would be loaded with whipped cream and strawberry jam and iced liberally with passionfruit icing. She also baked biscuits, usually jam drops that just melt in your mouth. Whenever we visited Aunty Dot's family, there always seemed to be mountains of food.

The drive down Macquarie Pass was always a nightmare, as we all suffered from car sickness so there were frequent stops on our way down. Occasionally the car water tank would boil and explode, and Dad would have to park the car on the side of the road, and go and find water to fill the water tank which had spewed its water onto the road. He soon learnt to take water in a can for our trip, ready for the boil over.

We also visited Mum's brother Jim, who had been in the Navy during the war and sported the obligatory sailor's tattoos on his arms. Jim was married to Norma, and they lived in Glebe in a two-storey terrace house which was very narrow and dark, very different to the houses in Moss Vale. Jim and Norma had five sons: Keith, Robert, Colin, Barry and Victor. Keith was my favourite. I found five boys a bit overwhelming.

Uncle Jim was a good-looking man, always with a smile, he had a very happy disposition and would entertain everyone with his magic tricks. I guess with five noisy boys, he developed his magic to keep them entertained, as they did not have a backyard and played out on the street. Later, the family moved to a home in Five Dock.

The visits to our aunts and uncles were memorable occasions.

Life in a small town was quiet. There were no organised sports for children, and if you had a bicycle, you were one of the lucky few. You were even more fortunate if you had a horse to ride. However, for most of the children, there was nothing much, just a skipping rope, hopscotch, or marbles. There were no scooters or playgrounds, so the summer school holidays seemed to drag along.

But at the beginning of the summer school holidays of 1954, Mum and Dad surprised us with exciting news: 'We are going camping at Seven Mile Beach!' How marvellous. We had visited our relatives when they were camping, and it looked like a lot of fun.

Dad borrowed a canvas tent (I'm not sure where he got it from), a very basic canvas tent with three walls and on the fourth side it had a loose flap for entry – it was very well-worn, fraying around the edges, nothing like today's tents. There was no floor covering except for a couple of old mats Mum had brought from home. Dad had built two double bunks for the children to sleep on, and a bed for himself and Mum.

For me, this holiday was paradise, I could swim every day, go fishing on the beach, and there was a Christian Mission tent on the beach where I could go and meet up with other children. The Christian Mission organised games and taught us songs and read the Bible to us. It was so much fun. I was sad when it was time to go back home.

Just after I turned 14, my brother Stephen was born and I was sent to stay with Uncle Bill (Mum's brother) and Aunty Alice who lived in Dee Why in Sydney for all of January. They had three children: Jennifer, Phillip and Linda. They were a lovely family, and I had such a nice time; one of my special memories was prawning in the lake at night with lanterns. I didn't know what a prawn was until then. We had nets to catch the prawns and when we had caught enough, Uncle Bill lit a fire on the beach and cooked the prawns in a pot filled with water. When they were cooked, we let them cool and ate some and took the rest home.

Rick's asthma was getting worse. Whenever he had an attack, I remember sitting on my bed listening to him gasping and trying to breathe and wishing the doctor would hurry up and come and give him an injection of adrenalin. The doctor suggested that Rick most likely had allergies to some of the grasses and pollens in the area.

The asthma attacks were becoming more frequent and the doctor told Mum and Dad that if Rick continued to live in this region he would die. He advised they move the family to a home near a beach so that Rick could swim frequently, which would help his lungs recover. In a seaside environment, he would not be subjected to grass and pollen allergens.

Mum and Dad took the doctor's advice and moved the family to a beach environment for Rick's health. Dad had been operating his milking machine business from premises in Sussex Street Sydney, so as far as his business was concerned, the move would not be a problem. We moved to Cronulla in April 1960 into a rented house just across the street from South Cronulla beach. I could not have been happier. I said to Mum, 'Why would anyone want to live in Moss Vale when they can live here?'

We went to the beach most days until it was too cold. Stephen was a baby and I loved taking him for a walk pushing him in a stroller. I was often stopped by people who wanted to admire the beautiful baby. He had white flaxen curls and a happy smile, he rarely cried. Most people made the mistake of thinking he was a girl (Stephen would hate me saying this).

From the moment we moved into Cronulla, Rick thrived. He now rarely had an attack of asthma, and if he did, it was mild.

As our move to Cronulla was mid-year, I had to quickly find a high school. Cronulla High School had just been built and they were only taking Years 1 and 2, and Rick was lucky enough to start school there. As I was in 3rd Year, I had to look elsewhere; Caringbah High and Endeavour High had not been built, Gymea High School and Port Hacking High School said they were full and could not take anyone, and I ended up at Jannali Girls High School.

They fitted me into whichever classes had room for me, so I was squeezed into the compulsory Maths and English classes, and then slotted into classes that had room for one more student. These subjects were Biology, Geography, Business Principles, Typing, and Art.

I had studied Geography at Moss Vale; the others were all new subjects. This would mean that I was starting almost halfway through the year of the Intermediate Certificate year with four new subjects, so I had a bit of catching up to do.

I travelled to and from Jannali by train each school day, which I quite enjoyed. Making friends was hard because all the girls had established friendships, but I was lucky there were two girls, Wendy and Rhona, who took pity on me and became my friend. I think they too were outcasts.

Rick thrived and quickly made lasting friendships. He spent a lot of time in the water swimming and surfing, and his asthma continued to improve. After a few months we moved to a rental house in Croydon Street just down from Cronulla Police Station, and close to the railway station.

Not long after we moved to Cronulla, Dad's business failed, and he went into bankruptcy. This must have been a devastating blow for him, as he was a proud man. I remember him telling me that he was looking for a job and went to the Hooker Real Estate Agency asking for a job. They said there were none, but he wasn't put off, asking them, 'If I manage to bring someone in who buys a home will you pay me a commission?' They agreed.

He used to stand outside the office and when someone stopped to look in the Hooker window, he would chat to them and find out what they were looking for, and that was how he made sales. Hooker offered him a job – still commission only – and at night he studied for his real-estate exams. This was how he started a successful real estate business at Brighton-le-Sands, due mainly to his determination, fortitude, courage and tenacity.

He started to play golf and lawn bowls and made friends easily. He seemed happy with his life.

Dad bought a block of land in Woolooware Road, Cronulla which had a garage on it and moved the family into the garage.

The garage was a large brick shed, about the size of a large one-car garage. It had a concrete floor, one window and a garage door in the wall end near the road, and a house door near the other end. Inside was empty except for a deep cement laundry tub and a toilet, what a luxury. Dad built a shower recess which was a square walled recess, a bit like a shallow Roman bath, measuring about a metre by a metre and 20 cm deep. We had a refrigerator and stove and one small kitchen cupboard. The laundry tub substituted for a kitchen sink and baby's bath for Stephen.

Dad created a small bedroom, by building a wall at the other end of the garage, which became a bedroom for himself, Mum and Stephen in a cot. He put up our camping double bunks in the next room which was a communal sleeping/lounge room/eating area etc. We each had a small cardboard box for our clothes and treasures, and the boxes lived under the double bunks.

By the time we moved here, I had left school. Dad told me that I was to leave school and go to work as the family needed the money. As I was still only 14, he had to write a letter explaining why it was necessary for me to leave school. Mum was pregnant with her sixth child, and I think she was grateful for my company and my help. She desperately missed the companionship of her sisters and friends in Moss Vale. It must have been a very difficult time for her.

We cooked, cleaned and did the washing and ironing together. We searched all the ads in the newspapers and junk mail for all the specials on sale and then walked to Cronulla to shop. All our clothes and shoes were hand-me-downs or bought from an op shop.

On Sundays, we went to church at the Cronulla Methodist Church in Surf Road. Mum and Dad attended the morning service and I chose to go to the 7:30 pm service, which was popular with teenagers. My sisters Robyn and Bonnie attended Sunday School and I was a Sunday School Teacher for the kindergarten-aged children.

I belonged to the young people's group who met once a week on a Friday night, and I made friends with most of the people in the group. It was so nice to be accepted. The Youth Group was a wonderful teenager's social club with a very capable youth leader, Russell. The Youth Group occasionally performed concerts and, once a year, we went to a Youth Camp at Bundeena. Mum and dad joined a Couples Club, which they seemed to enjoy, and it was a good way for Mum to make new friends, but I sensed that she still felt isolated.

Stephen was still only a baby and needed constant supervision and as there were no fences around our corner block, Mum occasionally put him on a long rope and tied him to the clothesline and let him play with his toys out in the fresh air, as there was very little room for him in our garage/home. He was an easy child, never any trouble.

During Mum's pregnancy she was under the care of Dr Alec Macintosh and he arranged for her to go to Jacaranda Maternity

Private Hospital when she went into labour. Fortunately, Jacaranda Hospital was about two blocks away from our 'home'.

The Matron of Jacaranda Hospital, Sister Irene Haxton was well liked and respected. She gave every new mother a jacaranda seedling, and the Sutherland Shire is sprinkled with the beautiful purple-flowering jacarandas during October and November. Each jacaranda tree commemorates the birth of a baby born at Jacaranda Maternity Hospital. What a wonderful tribute to Sister Haxton.

On the day Mum went into labour, she asked me to wash all the baby clothes in preparation for the baby's homecoming.

The baby was a boy and Mum named him David James. He was born with serious breathing difficulties and was urgently transferred to Sutherland Hospital, where he died a few days later. Everyone was sad, Mum was grief stricken. A funeral and burial were held at Woronora Cemetery. I am not sure who attended, maybe it was only Mum and Dad? It took Mum a long while to get over this heartbreaking loss.

While we lived in the garage, Dad had a project-home built on the block. It was a typical 1960s red brick, doubled-fronted home, with four bedrooms, one bathroom, lounge/dining, a kitchen and the laundry off the back porch. After living in a garage for a year or more, this was like five-star accommodation.

In the 1960s, Australia was experiencing an 'economic squeeze' and there were far more job seekers than jobs. Every week, I checked the local newspaper for job vacancies. Unfortunately, I had no skills and so there were very few opportunities for me.

Dad asked me if I would like to go to an auction sale with him. As auction sales are fun, I was happy to go. I saw an old typewriter and asked dad if he would buy the battered Royal typewriter for me. He bought it for two shillings.

I had been taught the basics of typing at school and so I thought

I could practice typing at home and this would give me a skill. My practice was copy-typing from the library books I was reading at the time. After many weeks of practice, I managed to eventually increase my typing speed to an acceptable 30 words per minute, which I hoped might help me find a job.

## Chapter Seven
## Meeting Dr Wooly
## 1961

I applied for many jobs without success. Then, one day I received a letter in response to an application. I had applied for a receptionist position with Dr David Sugerman in Hurstville. His letter told me that my application was unsuccessful.

About six weeks later, I received another letter from him, saying that he had passed on my application to a group of doctors in Caringbah who were looking for a junior receptionist. The receptionist for this group contacted me and arranged a time for me to come for an interview.

Feeling very nervous, I asked Mum to come with me to the interview. As I waited, Mum patted my hand to give me courage. After about ten minutes, the doctor called me in to his consulting room and invited me to sit down.

We sat opposite each other across his large, old wooden desk, which was not a desk, but a beautiful oak table. Looking up, I noticed he had an amiable face, which calmed my nerves a little. His hair was not straight, it had a little curl here and there, and was a sandy colour tinged with ginger and strands of grey. His eyes were intelligent with a twinkle. He was immaculately dressed in a dark grey suit, white shirt and an unremarkable tie.

Dr Ackary introduced himself, and asked me my name, my age, where I lived, and about my experience. Could I type?

There wasn't much to tell him. I told him I'd left school the previous year after completing the Intermediate Certificate, that I could type, lived at home with my family, and taught Sunday school at the Cronulla Methodist Church. That was the end of the interview. He showed me to the door, letting me know that someone would be in touch.

I went out to Mum, and she kindly took my hand in hers and we left to catch the next train back to Woolooware.

The next day, I received a phone call telling me that I had the job and that I was to start on the following Monday at 8:30 am. I'd be working five-and-a-half days each week (that is, full time Monday to Friday and Saturday mornings), and was expected to wear a white uniform and white lace-up shoes.

My starting wage was seven pounds a week (one pound is equal to two dollars). In those days, it was enough to buy a pair of shoes, which is what I did with my first pay. My father was so dismayed that I would spend most of my pay on a pair of shoes, that he instructed, that from now on, I was to give mum half my wage for board. Some weeks that was all she had in her purse.

One Sunday at Sunday School at the Cronulla Methodist Church, I discovered Dr Ackary's youngest son was one of the little boys in my class.

Life has turning points, and later in life, on reflection, I could see that this was the beginning of my amazing pathway in life.

The senior receptionist was a lovely English girl, Claire. She was kind to me and taught me everything I needed to know, which was

## MEETING DR WOOLY 1961

a lot, as I knew so little about office procedure. We developed a good working relationship. There were 12 doctors in the group – Dr John Ackary, a gynaecologist and obstetrician; Dr Trevor Allen, a dermatologist; Dr Adrian Cousins, surgeon; Dr Richard Loudon, ophthalmologist; Dr Gilbert Lynch, surgeon; Dr William Lyons, orthopaedic surgeon; Barbara MacCulloch, physiotherapist; Dr Leo Musso, dermatologist; Dr David Sugerman, pathologist; Dr David Woods, anaesthetist; Dr John Woolridge, physician; and Dr Don Wurth, surgeon.

I started my job on Monday 8 August 1961, and it was on this day that I was introduced to Dr John Woolridge. It was about 10 am when he came in. He was a daunting sight, at least 6' 2", of medium build, with a mop of light brown, very curly hair, and when I say curly, it was a mass of tight curls hugging his head and framing his forehead.

He walked with purpose, looking nowhere but at the floor in front of him, obviously deep in thought. There was an aura of sadness about him, which I would later understand. His shoulders were slightly rounded as if he were carrying the worries of the world. He was quiet and looked shy and nodded as I was introduced. To a 15-year-old country girl, he looked intimidating.

For a while I was the 'go-to girl', making tea and coffee, running errands, going to the banks, buying cakes for afternoon tea, tidying the waiting room, sweeping the floor and disposing of the rubbish, until I learnt the office work.

I settled in very quickly and enjoyed my job immensely. There was a perpetual parade of patients and doctors, and the phones rang incessantly. We were constantly busy greeting patients, answering phones, typing accounts, writing receipts and making cups of coffee for the doctors. Each doctor had their own account and payment system and we reconciled everyone's payments each day. We also had to clean the consultation rooms and waiting room and sterilise their medical instruments.

One of our more unusual duties was as a chaperone for one of the dermatologists, Dr Musso. He was an odd-looking man, most likely in his 60s, about 5'8', with a stocky build. He always wore the same crumpled light-grey suit, with a white shirt and a dark tie. His hair colour was every shade of grey and straight as sticks. No matter how much Brylcreem he plastered on, or how often he tried to flatten it, his hair refused to stay flat.

He had a round cherub-like face with chubby cheeks and grey eyebrows that were so thick, bushy and unruly, they overshadowed his eyes. He wore a pair of rimless glasses which sat on the end of his small nose, so that when he spoke to you, he would drop his head down and peer at you over the top of the glasses.

Whenever he consulted with a female patient, he stood in his doorway and called out in a thunderous voice, 'Miss Goodfellow – chaperone please,' and so I would go into his consulting room and try to stand as unobtrusively as I could while he talked with and examined his patient.

A bright respite each day was a visit from the postman. His name was Pat and everyone in Caringbah knew 'Pat the Postman'. He was a little man, probably about 5'5', and wore a postman's uniform with a peaked hat and carried the mail in a large dark-brown leather bag with a cross-body strap, which looked heavy and awkward.

He was the most obliging man, always offering to buy our postage stamps, and so when we needed them, we gave him an envelope with the money inside and a note on the front with a list of our requirements. I don't think I ever saw him with anything but a happy face. His smile filled a room, showing his nicotine-tinged teeth.

## MEETING DR WOOLY 1961

*Pat the Postman*

We were always busy. Our official work hours were 9–5 Monday to Friday and 9–12 on Saturdays. However, we were always there early, sometimes 8 am and we rarely left at 5 pm. Sometimes I would be there till 10 pm. We were not paid overtime.

Claire did the wages and during the 1960s, Australia had Income Tax Stamps. At the end of every month Claire calculated my tax which was then paid in cash at the Post Office and you were given tax stamps to the value of the money paid. Then the stamps were glued into your personal Income Tax record sheet. At the end of the financial year you sent your Income Tax record with your Income Tax Return to the Australian Tax Office.

In early 1962, one of the surgeons pulled me aside and said that the doctors were very pleased with my work and suggested that it would be a good idea to learn shorthand. The surgeon explained that Dr Woolridge would be needing a secretary soon but that he'd need someone who could take shorthand and type his reports.

I followed the surgeon's advice and enrolled at Gymea TAFE and attended classes one night a week. It wasn't long before I was taking notes in shorthand.

A few months later, Dr Woolridge asked me if I would like to be his secretary.

Of course I said, 'Yes.' I was thrilled to have the opportunity and my fear of him was dissipating. I now found him to be a pleasant person to work with. He was now consulting four days a week and together with all his hospital commitments, he was exceedingly busy, working very long days.

In turn, this meant that I was busy, and needed an office to work from. Fortunately, the doctor who interviewed me was closing his Caringbah practice and his room became vacant. Dr Woolridge rented this room for my office. Conveniently, it was adjacent to his consulting room. Another girl was employed to take my position at the front desk.

Working alongside Dr Woolridge, I realised that he was not only kind and caring with his patients, he was also highly intelligent and always researching diseases and illnesses, searching for cutting-edge research, medications, innovations and new ideas.

I realised there was so much to learn and I discovered that I had a great thirst for knowledge, and fortunately I found I had the ability to absorb information. I enjoyed the challenge which gave me a sense of fulfilment and responsibility. Working with Dr Woolridge was demanding and exciting.

He had an astounding memory; he could remember patients' details without their records, and even 40 or 50 years later, he could recall their medical history, how many children they had, where they lived, who their neighbours were and how many cats and dogs they owned.

He was interested in everyone, and would treat everyone as if they were the King of England, regardless of their station in life. Butcher, baker, a trash man, a bank manager, priest, or Prime Minister, it made little difference to Jack, they were all treated with respect and humility. In conversation, he would always try and find common ground, whether it be the cricket, football, horse racing, gardening, or where to catch the best fish, so that they felt comfortable and at ease with him. He allowed them to feel as though they were talking to an old friend who was their confidante, and so the story of their troubles and symptoms flowed easily.

He often sat next to his patients, rather than on the other side of the desk, and when they were distressed, he would comfort them. Patients loved him, they were all his 'best friends,' and they would bring him cakes, jars of homemade jam, chutney or pickles, apple pies, home-made wine and beer, the fruit off their trees, fresh fish they had just caught, or tomatoes from their garden. They wanted him to feel he was part of their family and somehow demonstrate their love and respect for him, and for him to enjoy the fruits of their labour.

# Chapter Eight
# Invitation to the Ball
# 1963–1969

In Edinburgh, Jack had been introduced to Dr Desmond Julian, who in the future would be recognised as the pioneer of the revolutionary Coronary Care Unit. During one of their meetings, Dr Julian shared his idea of the revolutionary Coronary Care Unit (CCU). Jack remembered their conversation, and in 1961, as the head of the Medical Department of The Sutherland Hospital, he tried to engender some enthusiasm for the idea of this revolutionary CCU.

It wasn't well received. The hospital had only been opened in 1958 and was considered a new hospital. No-one wanted to think about making changes in a new hospital. He ignored all the negativity around him and pushed ahead, checking out other hospitals' Coronary Care Units and from his review, he sketched up plans for what he believed would be an appropriate and fitting Coronary Care Unit for TSH.

He heard that Dr Julian had immigrated to Australia and had designed the first Coronary Care Unit in one of Sydney's hospitals. Jack contacted Dr Julian and told him he had been planning and designing a CCU for TSH and asked if he could use some of his design elements. Dr Julian agreed.

And so, Sutherland Hospital's first Coronary Care Unit was conceived, designed and later delivered, thanks to the enormous efforts of the Ladies Auxiliary who raised some of the funds.

The CCU design had 15 beds with a central nurses' station surrounded, in a circular fashion, by patient cubicles with glass partitions. This would allow nurses and doctors to view the patient from the nurses' station or anywhere else in the unit. Each cubicle would be fitted with monitoring equipment which transmitted information to the monitors in the central nurses' station.

In 1964, Jack and his friend and colleague, general surgeon Dr Gilbert Lynch, discussed their plans to move, as they both needed more room than they had at their present location. They'd heard that the lawyers were moving out of the other wing on the first floor, so Jack and Gilbert decided to move there together.

They arranged for a builder to fit out the area to their specifications: two consulting rooms, a reception desk and a waiting room. The rooms were tastefully lined in a honey-coloured timber panelling. The builder, a Dutchman, was a true craftsman.

Moving day was huge, but there was an air of excitement which seemed to ameliorate our exhaustion. It was thrilling to arrive at work for the first day in our smart, yet elegant, new office.

Dr Gilbert Lynch's secretary had been working from home, but was now based in his new rooms. His secretary was an older lady with two adult daughters. She and I worked together in the reception area side by side, but independent of each other.

Jack embraced new knowledge. He'd been introduced to stress-exercise ECGs in Edinburgh and was keen to use it in his practice.

Though the procedure had improved since his Edinburgh days, it was still awkward and bulky.

To do a stress test, a resting ECG would be taken, then the ECG machine leads were detached from the limb straps, and the suction bulbs were removed. The patient would put on a shirt and Jack would take them to the stairs, where they'd run up and down until they could do no more. Quickly, Jack would take them back to lie on the examination bed, re-hook up all the leads and suction bulbs, and take another ECG recording.

The resting and post-exercise ECGs would be compared, looking for changes which could indicate coronary artery disease. The sight of Jack and patient with the rubber straps flapping around, climbing up and down the stairs was rather comical, but with an element of risk.

After a few months, Jack decided there had to be an easier way of exercising and discovered the two-step exercise box. He briefed the Dutch carpenter, who built one for him. The box was about 80 cm wide and 1 m long and the steps were 20 cm high, and about 30 cm deep, with one step up then a second step up to the top platform, then down the other side to a step. The patient would go back and forth over the two-step box.

Now that the whole test could be done within Jack's consultation/examination room, it removed the element of embarrassment for the patients, and the possibility of a patient falling down the stairs. Now, Jack could exercise his female patients appropriately.

The following year, Jack introduced a treadmill into his practice after learning about the results of a 1963 study by cardiologist Robert Bruce, who designed a protocol for stress ECG testing using a treadmill. This became known as the Bruce Protocol.

The addition of a treadmill and the Bruce Protocol greatly improved the implementation of the stress ECG test and the sensitivity and specificity of the ECG interpretation.

Jack's reputation was growing exponentially. Patients with

baffling cases were often referred to the highly regarded general physician/cardiologist. When they presented, he persisted until he had a diagnosis, this tenacity was undoubtedly Dr Ted French's legacy.

Cardiology was an exciting, evolving specialty, incorporating new surgical procedures, investigations and medications. Doctors were learning to understand coronary artery disease, which then produced better methods of treating the disease. Professor Blackett and his team were a great influence.

Jack's reputation as a teacher and mentor was also climbing. He was regarded as one of the best and the Resident Medical Officers all vied for the opportunity to work under Jack. He was also sought out by the Registrars (Senior Medical Officers in Hospitals) for tutoring when they were sitting for their Membership exams.

Though much in demand, Jack found time to indulge his interest in horse racing. Occasionally, circumstances turn into opportunities, and a sequence of events turned into opportunity for Jack after he treated a patient at PHH.

The patient was Billy H, a horse breaker. Billy was a knockabout sort of fellow of average height, with a round head and round torso sitting on top of a pair of bowed legs, the trademark of middle-aged horsemen. His hair was honey-brown with a trace of red, and an unruly cowlick fell across his forehead. He had red-apple cheeks and twinkling eyes masking occasional flashes of sadness. His demeanour told you he'd lived a hard life.

Over the course of his recovery, Billy and Jack chatted about horses and Jack's love for horse racing was stimulated. He told Billy he would love to buy a racehorse, and Billy said he had a good friend, Doug Lonsdale, who was a horse trainer at Randwick. He arranged for Jack and Doug to meet one Saturday, following a

## INVITATION TO THE BALL 1963-1969

meeting Jack had at Prince of Wales Hospital (POW). Doug's home and stables were in Hay Street, adjacent to POW, and by chance that day, there were horse sales on at the Inglis' Thoroughbred Sale Complex, just up the street from where Doug lived.

Going to the thoroughbred horse sales at Newmarket was always an exciting experience, as I'd learn. On sale days, the whole complex would be abuzz with buyers, sellers, horse handlers, agents and on-lookers who wanted to experience the atmosphere.

Doug took Jack to the sale and introduced him to this other world which would come to play such a momentous part in his life. They toured the complex, looking at the yearlings and greeting some of Doug's mates. Doug asked his mates if there were any nice fillies (a young female horse), and they were taken to look at a couple.

They eventually purchased a filly for Jack. She was by Gallant Knight and out of a mare named Torna. Jack paid £475 guineas (guineas were equal to 475 pounds plus 475 shillings, which now sounds so strange). The filly was sent to Billy's Londonderry property to be broken in. Back home, Jack asked Judy to name the filly, and after a lot of fun thinking up all sorts of names, they came up with Cri Cri, which is the name of a small rose.

This was the beginning of Jack and Doug's lifelong friendship, which was undemanding and unpretentious, and allowed Jack to be relaxed and enjoy their common bond – a love for horse racing. It was also the inception of Jack's incredible foray a few years later into the world of thoroughbred breeding.

While all this was going on, Jack's private life was an enormous struggle. Jill's bi-polar disorder became more difficult to treat after their return from Edinburgh and during the ensuing years, she required multiple hospitalisations. She had a number of treatments with electroconvulsive therapy (ECT), which involves passing a carefully controlled electric current through the brain. It affects the brain's activity and was thought to relieve severe depressive and psychotic symptoms. It was a short-term treatment for severe manic or depressive episodes, particularly when symptoms involved serious suicidal or psychotic symptoms, or when medication was ineffective.

During these challenging times, he and Judy looked after each other, living on frozen meals from the supermarket, and chocolate. Fortunately, Jack had organised a cleaner for their house shortly after their return from Edinburgh. The cleaner was a delightful man. Everyone called him Bassett.

He came once a week on Thursday afternoons. Bassett was a gem. He was not only an excellent cleaner but also a Mr Fixit, and a wonderful entertainer of children, delighting Judy with the games he entertained his six children with at home.

Judy's disability was an extra challenge, she had an ataxic gait with disequilibrium and poor depth perception. She used a walking aid to assist with her walking issues. Jill's Aunt Muriel, a retired schoolteacher, helped where she could. She adored Judy. Muriel was a delightful woman, probably in her seventies, tallish with a stout proud figure, and short grey hair framing her almost 'schoolmarm' face. But if you watched her for a little while, you would catch glimpses of softness in her eyes, which were hidden behind unremarkable glasses.

She didn't wear any makeup, that was not her style. Muriel was a spinster who didn't speak of her early life, but we knew that she and her sister Agatha looked after Jill as a baby and during her childhood and teen years.

Muriel apparently did have a boyfriend some time ago who unfortunately was killed in the war. She was a devout Catholic and went to church daily. The church was only a block away from her home in Rockdale, and occasionally, she invited the priest to her home for a roast dinner.

She kept active and would walk up the street every day, purchase one or two items and then walk home, stopping at the bus stop, where she sat and chatted to anyone who happened to be there waiting for a bus. When she had finished chatting, she wandered home. She looked after herself in an admirable manner: breakfast was always a 'dip egg' and toast, lunch was a sandwich and dinner was always a roast dinner or grilled lamb chops with vegetables.

During Jill's many hospital admissions, Jack would sometimes ask me to pick Judy up from school and help her with her homework, and on one these afternoons, Great-Aunt Muriel was at their home waiting for Judy. She made me a cup of tea and started talking about her friendship with Henry Lawson and her visits to Henry and Bertha Lawson when they lived in a small cottage near a river at Bargo during their short difficult marriage. She could recite many of his poems from memory.

Henry Lawson is recognised as one of Australia's important poets and writer of short stories romanticising the gold digger, stockman, drover and shearer and often illustrating the great Australian Mateship. Mateship is a concept which can be traced back to early colonial days when the environment was harsh and convicts and new settlers found themselves in situations where they closely relied on each other for all sorts of help. A 'mate' was more than a friend, it implies a sense of shared experience, mutual respect and unconditional assistance.

Muriel, a prim and proper spinster who loved the English language, was fond of Henry, even though he was known to be unpredictable, and an alcoholic. He often wrote to Muriel sending her draft copies of some of his stories, asking for her opinion.

Fortunately, Muriel lived close to Rockdale railway station and

# JUST JACK

Jack's home was right at Kirrawee station. This meant that Muriel could come and go, travelling by train whenever she was needed to look after Judy while Jill was in hospital.

My working relationship with Jack was respectful and, I hope, intuitive. It was a pleasure and privilege to work with him. He was never demanding, and his dedication, empathy and kindness towards his patients inspired me. He had a profound influence on my capabilities, always encouraging me. He never hesitated to teach me (in language that I could understand) about medical terminology, diseases and medications. Of course, there were times where I needed to consult a medical dictionary or visit the library.

By observing his manner with patients, I learnt to be kind and patient. 'They come to me sick, frightened and scared, which sometimes makes them cranky and angry,' he explained to me one day. 'And so, we should be gentle, kind and understanding.'

My priorities were to anticipate his needs and to try and ease his workload if I could, in some small way.

Some days, at the end of his consulting day at the Caringbah rooms, he would ask me if I would drive him to PHH and back, so that he could sleep in the car. I think he was very brave to ask me, as his car was a large Ford and I was only used to driving a small Vauxhall Viva. The first time I got in to drive his car, my feet could not reach the pedals and I had to move the front seat all the way forward. I'm pleased to say I learnt to adapt very quickly, and fortunately we had no mishaps.

His days were long and gruelling, and he expected so much of himself, always placing the patient's care and welfare above his wants or needs. He was also driven by an obsession to be the best. He wanted to be the best Cardiologist in Sydney.

Amidst this busy life, he somehow managed to find time to

co-author a treatise on McCardle's Syndrome which was published in the well-regarded Medical Journal of Australia in 1967.

A teenage boy presented to him at his rooms and after exhaustive investigations, Jack diagnosed McCardle's Syndrome. As it was such a rare condition, Jack decided to publish his experience. He co-authored with Dr N Corbett-Jones (MB, BS) who was the patient's referring GP, and Kenneth B Taylor (BSc Ph D) Institute of Clinical Pathology and Medical Research, Lidcombe, NSW. The article was well received.

McCardle's Syndrome is a rare disorder of energy supply due to a genetic defect which can cause exhaustion. This was the first article published on McCardle's Syndrome.

One day, a friend of Jack's, Dr Lou Levi, phoned. He said he had a proposition he wanted to discuss with Jack. Lou was an Ear Nose and Throat specialist and had been a friend of Jack's for many years. At one stage, they had jointly owned a trotter (a horse that trots and is trained for harness racing).

Lou was a unique doctor. He loved doing anything that was the opposite of what was expected of the medical fraternity. He frowned on etiquette and respectability, and yet he was well behaved and well mannered. He abhorred the uniform of the specialist – the neat dark suit, white shirt and tie, and clean polished shoes – and instead dressed in a casual style, usually baggy grey trousers with a white shirt (sans tie) with a grey woollen cardigan. His battered, unpolished shoes were laced up with string.

Instead of driving a car, he rode a motor bike. He revelled in being different and snubbed his nose at the 'toffs'. Lou was an Honorary Medical Officer at St Vincent's Hospital and The Sutherland Hospital. One day, he rode up to the security guard at the doctor's parking area at St Vincent's and the guard told him he could not park there.

'Why not?' said Lou.

'You have to be a doctor to park in the doctors' parking area,' said the guard.

Lou looked at him with a smile and said, 'I am a doctor and I work here! Now can I go in?'

Jack admired Lou for being his own person and they shared a passion for horses and for being slightly nonconformist towards the establishment.

Lou trained all his own horses; they were all trotters. He was determined to learn all the skills required to completely care for his horses. If a horse had a problem which required a skill he did not have, he would find someone to teach him how to master that skill. He became the consummate carer of his horses, including shoeing them and looking after their teeth, and when his horses raced, he was also the driver. He became so accomplished he published a book on the care of the trotting horse.

Lou and Jack met to discuss Lou's proposal. He told Jack a friend who was in real estate had told him of a property in Mulgoa which he considered to be a good investment. Lou said he didn't have the finances to buy it on his own and he was hoping he could find two friends to buy the property with him.

Jack knew the real-estate agent and had a great respect for his entrepreneurial skills. Lou took Jack to Mulgoa to have a look at the property. It was dark when they arrived, so Lou shone the headlights at the gate and said, 'There it is.'

Jack decided to take a leap of faith and go in with Lou. Together with a mutual friend, Brian, the three formed a loose partnership and purchased the farm with dollars and cents (the currency changed from pounds to dollars on Valentine's Day 1966). Lou offered to set it up with a few steers to chew the grass, and he knew someone who could look after them.

## INVITATION TO THE BALL 1963-1969

Early in 1967, one of the secretaries in the Wyoming building called in with the news that TSH was having a ball and that she was organising a table. 'Was anyone interested?'

I said I would love to go, but that I did not have a boyfriend at the moment, as I had just had a break-up and was now without an escort.

Then she added 'Ask Dr Wooly if he and his wife would like to go to the ball.' 'Dr Wooly' was a pet name for Jack used by the nursing staff and other hospital ancillary staff, and also by some of his patients.

I was in a period of my life where my years of transformation from an 'UGLY DUCKING' were well behind me, and at last I did not have to deal with persistent and intimidating teasing and name calling, I have not worn glasses since leaving school and my teeth were straight and white. I was enjoying being grown-up and having a job. I loved my work and all the challenges that came with it, and, I loved working with Jack.

I discovered that some of the boys at the Church Youth Group were being nice to me, and, one boy in particular who was a little older than the others, was being very friendly. He was a school teacher at the Sth Cronulla Public School and lived just up the road from our home. His name was Graeme. I thought he was quite goodlooking. He had fair hair and an attractive face with beautiful grey-blue smiling eyes, and was one of the few boys who had a car which made him even more attractive. His car was a small car, and it was a most unusual pale green colour. I felt very special driving around with him. Our friendship which was congenial and easy going, lasted about six months, this was when he told me that he was being transferred to a school in Nyngan, in central New South Wales. I missed him for a while, but the loss of his companionship was overtaken by my excitement of buying a car with my brother. We had decided to share a car together, I would use the car to go to and from work and Rick would use the car on the weekends. This arrangement suited both of us, and gave us both a delightful feeling of independence and adventure.

I enjoyed the Church youth group, because it gave me the opportunity of developing friendships and with that my self confidence and self-esteem grew. Each year the youth group put on a concert and the production that I enjoyed the most was 'South Pacific'. It was so much fun and a wonderful experience, giving me an opportunity to sing. I loved singing and was blessed with a voice that was easy to listen to.

Another Youth Group annual event was a fun-filled weekend youth camp at Bundeena. Plenty of fun and games and not much sleeping.

My life took an interesting turn when a girlfriend's family, invited me to come with their family to a holiday cottage on the Hawkesbury River, and they told me that we would be water skiing. I felt a bit anxious as I did not know how to water ski and I was not a good swimmer. I needn't have worried. I had the most enjoyable weekend learning to water ski on two skis. I was so captivated by water skiing that I made enquiries, and found a water skiing school at the Narrabeen Lakes.

Whenever Rick did not want to use the car on a Saturday or Sunday I would take myself off to Narrabeen and waterski all day. I met a boy there, his name was Jerry. He would have been maybe a year or two older than me, he looked about 5'8', was good looking, and he had a dark green MG sports car. Oh my goodness what fun, riding around in an MG sports car with a good looking guy. He wasn't a water skier, he was a friend of the water ski instructor and sat in the boat and watched others water ski, he said he wasn't interested in water skiing. I found that difficult to understand, as water skiing for me was the most exhilarating water sport I had experienced and I quickly became a very proficient skier on one ski, otherwise known as slalom skiing with one foot behind the other on the one ski. That friendship only lasted about three months but they were three months of fun.

During my annual leave I decided to attend classes at June Dally Watkins Deportment School. June Dally-Watkins started a personal-development school in Sydney in 1950 to train young women in etiquette and deportment. I guess I had some fanciful idea that this school could magically turn me into a beautiful model. Why I would want to be a model, I have no idea, nor did I know where that thought came from, but who knows what will happen. The advertisements sounded exciting. The classes were a lot of fun and I learnt a lot about how to make myself attractive, how to act appropriately and graciously, and to how to walk elegantly. After I graduated quite a few modelling jobs came my way, but I decided, after all, that a modelling career was not for me I preferred my life as it had been, working with Jack.

I enjoyed many outings with my group of friends, sometimes we'd go to the movies in the city, and occasionally we went ballroom dancing at Hurstville. During the summer weekends if I was at home I would arrange to go to the beach with my girlfriends, where we would stay for most of the day surfing and sunning ourselves in our new bikinis, which at that time were slightly risqué (the bikini in some parts of the world were banned in the 1950's). Sometimes, some of the boys who were brothers of the girls would come and join us. During the summers we would all be sporting a golden suntan.

I kept thinking about the ball, and wondered who I could ask to accompany me. I felt a bit self conscious about approaching any of the boys in the Church Youth Group. My quandary suddenly came to an end when the girl who was organising the table at the Hospital Ball, called in to tell me that her friend had a brother who would be happy to accompany me to the ball. Oh! how wonderful, I had just about given up hope of going to the ball. I was so delighted. How I love dressing up, and I love to dance.

I couldn't afford a dress so decided to make one. I am not a dressmaker in any sense of the word, and when I went to find a pattern, of course I chose the most difficult pattern in the Vogue Pattern Catalogue. The pattern was a strapless gown with a full gathered skirt which fell from under the bust line. The suggested fabric for the pattern was chiffon which is not an easy fabric for a novice to manage. Chiffon is a sheer fabric, so the whole dress would have to be lined, which is like making two dresses!

The colour I chose was vermilion with a touch of fuchsia, a mauvish-crimson colour. I loved it. And so, every spare minute I had was spent making my ball gown. Mum thought I was crazy, but I was very determined to complete my mission. The most difficult part of the dress was the bodice. As it was strapless, the lining was boned so that the bodice had structure and shape.

It took me hours to master this skill, but by following the Vogue pattern instructions, I finally completed the task of sewing straight channels in the bodice lining and then inserting a long, thin piece of plastic into the channel. Day by day, the dress took shape and finally became a beautiful glamorous ball gown.

Mission accomplished. Thank you Vogue for showing me how to make this gorgeous ball gown.

I felt so proud of myself and the excitement was overwhelming.

I mentioned to Jack that I was going to the Hospital ball and asked if he had thought about going. I was not sure what his reaction would be. At first, he was not keen, as Jill was in hospital, but as the weeks went by, he mentioned it to me a couple of times,

*Sue in in her home-made ball gown*

and then one day he said he thought he would ask Gilbert's wife, Judy, if she would like to go to the ball with him, as Gilbert was away.

Gilbert had been in Vietnam for the last couple of months as a member of a surgical team operating on the wounded soldiers.

The Vietnam War was very controversial. Most Australians felt we should not be part of the long, costly and divisive conflict between communist North Vietnam and the democratic South Vietnam. South Vietnam's ally, the USA, had asked Australia for support, as they feared the spread of communism. (Our first troops arrived in South Vietnam in June 1965 and their withdrawal occurred throughout 1971. The fall of Saigon to the communists occurred on 30 April 1975. During April, the RAAF Hercules transports carried out Operation Babylift, evacuating refugees and Vietnamese orphans, and then finally taking out Embassy staff on 25 April 1975.)

Going to the ball would be a good diversion for both Judy and Jack.

Judy accepted Jack's invitation.

On the morning of the ball, I had an appointment at the hairdressers. The hairdresser was known to me, he had asked me on a few occasions to be his model at hairdressing competitions. He enjoyed working with my hair, as it was long and thick and very easy to manage, making it easy for him to create hair styles which were dramatic and yet stylish.

I asked him for an 'up do' and this took all morning, but the result was rather special. I spent the afternoon getting ready, and by 7.30pm I was ready to go. I was madly excited and thrilled with my home-made dress, which turned out to be spectacular, and Mum was delightfully surprised at the end result.

My date for the night arrived, a young man probably in his mid-twenties, pleasant looking and tall, with sandy-brown, spiky-straight hair. His face was ordinary but in a nice way, and his eyes were wary. He stepped into our house, looking nervous. I introduced him to my parents and then we departed.

The ball was abuzz with people. Chatter and laughter filled the air. We found our table and introduced ourselves to the other four couples who had arrived earlier and were already drinking champagne. We sat down and my date ordered a bottle of champagne. My partner for the evening was shy and struggled with conversation. I guess if you are amongst strangers, it can be a bit intimidating.

The other couples on our table were secretaries with their husbands or partners. They all worked in 'Wyoming', and were familiar with each other, so they commandeered the conversation. When the music began, we started dancing, which was a reprieve from trying to make conversation. I love to dance and fortunately my partner knew how to dance. What fun, dancing and twirling around in my gorgeous gown I felt like I was a princess.

The supper came out at about 9.30 pm and was the usual mass-produced meal, nothing to get excited about.

A short while after supper, Jack came over to me and asked me if I would dance with him. Naturally, I said I would love to; I asked my partner if he would mind if I had a dance with Jack and he said go ahead. Jack took my hand and led me to the dance floor. As he gently held my hand, I felt embarrassed at how excited I felt, I had not anticipated this invitation to dance and wasn't expecting these emotions.

Oh, my goodness, this was the first time we had touched each other. I felt very flustered and self-conscious, I could feel myself blushing. We started dancing and it was if we had danced together all our lives. He gently guided me around the dance floor, I felt as if I was on a cloud as we laughed, chatted and danced. We danced through three sets of music, and then Jack took my hand and led me outside in the fresh air.

We sat on a bench looking at each other, both realising these were stolen moments, not to be repeated. We didn't talk, there was no need for talk, he gently took my hand in his for a moment and then realised what he was doing and slowly released his hold, his eyes sad and heavy, expressing the words he couldn't speak. Suddenly, someone else ventured into our little realm and we were thrown back into reality. We both remembered our partners and reluctantly returned to our tables.

On our way back, a professional photographer asked if we would like our photo taken. Jack did not hesitate. 'Yes,' he said. This photo is one of my greatest treasures.

Upon our return to my table, my date was obviously unimpressed and gave me a frosty reception. After five minutes, he said, 'I'm going home, do you want me to take you home?' I replied, 'Yes, thank you.' He drove me home in a steely, hostile silence. but I did not mind I had experienced something more precious, and I will store those moments in my heart for ever.

*Jack and Sue at the Hospital Ball*

## INVITATION TO THE BALL 1963–1969

The photos from the ball were displayed in the hospital foyer so that those wishing to purchase a photo could arrange it with staff at reception. Jack purchased three photos and he gave me two. The photos of Jack and myself caused a lot of speculation among the hospital staff – 'who was the brunette with Jack Woolridge?' My friend who organised her brother to take me to the ball never spoke to me again.

(On 1 October 1967, Jack's father, David Worthington Woolridge, passed away.)

Meanwhile, Jack's home life had become increasingly stressful, with crises after crises to deal with. Jill's illness deepened and Jack and Judy got by with the help of Aunt Muriel. I don't know how Jack kept his equilibrium, though there were times he resorted to the comfort of alcohol. No wonder he looked like he carried the worries of the world on his shoulders. And yet, no matter how hard things were at home, he still managed to be a compassionate doctor to his patients.

Jack's passion for horse racing was a diversion from all that was going on in the home. He needed a distraction and decided to go to the 1969 January Summer Sales at Newmarket to buy another horse. He and Doug looked at the catalogue together and they were looking for specific pedigrees. There was one pedigree that stood out to both of them. It was a colt by the stallion Just Great GB, out of the mare Lavena

The sale day arrived. Doug and Jack went along, feeling great anticipation. They were lucky there was little interest in the colt they had chosen, and Jack managed to buy him with very little opposition in the bidding. Doug and Jack walked the horse to Doug's stables and Doug told Jack he would send him to Billy the Horse Breaker, to break him in and follow on with the usual post-sale conditioning.

Jack gave Doug a list of names for the horse and asked him to go to the Australian Jockey Club (AJC) and name him. Doug phoned Jack later and said that all the names Jack had chosen were knocked back and he couldn't think of what to call him.

'I'm so p****.....off,' said Doug.

'Name the ***** horse any****thing...just give him a ****name..... just call him any****thing,' he ranted.

'Call him Just...****... Just... Jack.'

Doug said he nearly fell over when the name was approved. And so, Just Jack was accidentally named after Jack. Just Jack would be the catalyst for Jack's remarkable adventure into the world of horse racing and breeding.

Bernadette Nerrida Gwendoline (Jill) Woolridge passed away unexpectedly on 22 August 1969 at their Kirrawee home. This was a tragic and heartbreaking time for Jack and especially for Judy, who was only 15. Father and daughter moved from their Kirrawee home, which was now the beneficiary of a traumatic, tragic memory. Jill had tragically taken her own life.

They set up home in their Cronulla unit, the one Jack had purchased just after their return from Edinburgh. Well-positioned on the Esplanade, just a short walk from South Cronulla Beach, the unit was on the third level of a small block. With no lift, the stairs were a big challenge for Judy, each step was taken slowly one at a time, with Judy pulling herself up via the handrail, and carefully navigating as she has no depth perception . The garages were on the ground floor, so there were four flights of stairs to navigate.

# Chapter Nine
# A New Beginning
# 1969–1970

A month after Jill's unexpected death, Jack received an unusual phone call from a patient.

Mr W lived on the Gold Coast and had been a patient of Jack's for two or three years. He told Jack he had been very unwell and did not feel up to travelling to Sydney to consult with Jack and so proposed bringing Jack to the Gold Coast that weekend to consult with him. Mr W said he would pay all of Jack's expenses and that Jack could bring whoever he liked with him.

Jack told me about the phone call and asked me if I would like to go to the Gold Coast with him and Judy.

I loved the Gold Coast. I'd spent an occasional week there water-skiing and was a reasonably accomplished water-skier on one ski. Occasionally, I'd taught people to water ski.

I accepted the surprise invitation.

Mr W arranged for us to leave Friday afternoon and return Sunday evening.

Apparently, Mr W owned a lot of real estate, including a hotel which at the time was the largest hotel in Surfers Paradise.

# JUST JACK

Jack and I had to make changes to Friday's appointment list, moving the afternoon patient's appointments forward to Wednesday and Thursday evening, and arranging for Jack's colleague, Dr Ian Mackie, to do Jack's ward rounds over the weekend, and cover for him at the hospital till Sunday evening.

We flew up late on Friday afternoon, and as the plane was preparing to land, the flight attendant came over and asked us to wait until everyone was off the plane. We looked at each other and shrugged our shoulders. What was that all about? Maybe they thought it would be easier for Judy?

After the last one left the plane, we started to make our way towards the exit. As we walked through the door of the plane, we were stunned to see a long red carpet being rolled out from the steps of the plane to a Rolls Royce parked on the tarmac.

The driver was standing at attention beside the open rear door of the car. As we climbed down the stairs, a young girl and a young man, both dressed in Hawaiian-style clothes, appeared at the base of the steps. She stepped forward and placed a flower lei around our necks and he was playing his ukelele as they both sang a welcome song. Our bags were brought to the car and the driver placed them in the boot of the Rolls Royce.

We were very embarrassed and self conscious at all the fuss. 'This is going to be an interesting weekend,' I thought.

We were driven to Mr W's hotel and as we walked into the foyer, Mr W greeted us very fondly. A small man, about 5'6' tall, of thinnish stature, with greying straight hair, his eyes looked piercing as he examined Judy and I.

Jack made the introductions and Mr W instructed the desk clerk to give us the keys to their best suite. As it was getting late, he took us straight into the hotel's restaurant and we ordered dinner from the menu. Jack and I both ordered lobster mornay and Judy had chicken. When the meals arrived, Mr W seemed agitated. 'I'll have to speak to the chef,' he frowned. 'These meals are too large! Just eat what you want and if the meal is too big, leave what you can't eat on your plate.'

He was trying to make us feel comfortable, but did not realise how famished we were. We hadn't eaten since breakfast at 6 am that morning and have good appetites. We demolished the whole meal without any effort.

As we chatted, Mr W gave us an outline of an itinerary which he had organised for us. A car would call for us at 10 am and drive us to his office where he and Jack would consult.

His office was in a small demountable building on a vacant block of land. As we stepped in, I looked around and could see one of the walls was covered with street plans, real estate plans and building plans.

Mr W and his secretary, Helen, stepped forward. Helen was a tallish woman, well dressed and well groomed, with hair that looked like she had just stepped out of a salon. She wore a classic corporate suit in a soft pinkish-grey colour, with a crisp white shirt, but what stood out the most to me was her bold red lipstick. She had a stiff, upright posture, appearing very officious, and obviously in command.

Jack and Mr W disappeared into the office and Judy, and I sat in the reception area.

The phone was continually ringing, and Helen was fending off the calls. 'No, we don't sell fans,' I remember her telling the callers. I'm not sure what that was about as it was obvious that this was an office of a land developer, not an office selling fans.

Helen said that Mr W had arranged for us to attend a ball that evening, and I said we really couldn't go to the ball as we did not have suitable clothing. She said, 'Oh don't worry, I will take you shopping, and we will buy you and Judy a dress.' And so, we left the two men and she took us to an expensive small boutique where Judy and I chose a dress to wear to the ball. While we were trying on dresses, I wondered what Jack would think of all this. Helen insisted that Mr W pay for the dresses.

By the time we got back to the office, Jack and Mr W were patiently waiting for our return. We were taken back to the hotel and left to enjoy the afternoon.

We took advantage of the free time exploring the main street of Surfers Paradise, then returned to our room to put our feet up for a while. When we arrived back at our luxurious suite, there were three black dinner suits plus accessories waiting for Jack to try on. Nothing had been forgotten.

I had to come to the rescue of Jack with his buttons and studs and cuff links and bow tie. Once Jack was sorted I turned my attention to Judy helping her with her new dress and shoes, and then finally it was my turn, I was so excited to have a new dress. My dress was a white halter neck gown, and as I stepped into the sitting area I noticed Jack looking at me with an incredulous smile on his face and a gentle nod of his head as if to say 'Wow'. It is always fun getting dressed up and I love spontaneous events, they are often the best. The ball was held in the hotel which was very convenient for us.

We had a wonderful night, meeting interesting people, most of whom lived in and around Surfers Paradise, and enjoyed good food and good wine. The music was easy to dance to, and we enjoyed ourselves till midnight, then made our excuses and went back to our suite. It had been a long day.

We were sitting around in our night wear chatting about the day's events, when Jack suggested we have a midnight snack. It was a good idea as I was beginning to feel hungry. Because I had enjoyed the lobster so much the previous night I decided to order lobster mornay again – this was a big mistake.

A little while after eating my lobster, I started to feel extremely ill. I will not go into all the unpleasant details but suffice to say I did not sleep much that night. I felt sorry for Jack and Judy who looked after me and Jack tried to entertain us with his dissertation of events during the afternoon.

Jack was disappointed that he was unable to offer Mr W a diagnosis for his symptoms but promised that on his return to Sydney he would spend time researching and would give him a call to discuss any further thoughts he may have.

Mr W sent the car to pick us up at 10 am and we spent the morning at his home on the Nerang River. The home was a Californian Bungalow, it was the longest home I'd ever seen. Its setting was tranquil, amidst lush green lawns and trees strategically placed for privacy.

Mr and Mrs W greeted us and made us feel comfortable, leading us to a wonderful outdoor setting under a magnificent old fig tree. The table was elegantly set, with delicate, pale blue crockery laid upon an immaculate white linen tablecloth. It was obvious we were expected to stay for lunch. As we settled in, we were surprised to see Helen approach carrying a tray of cool drinks. It turned out that she also lived with Mr and Mrs W.

We enjoyed a most delightful lunch, after which it was time for us to depart for the airport and return home.

Around a month later, at the end of October, Jack invited my friend Pauline and I to go to 'the farm' at Mulgoa on the weekend. This was the property he'd bought along with his friend, Lou Levi.

My 'farm' expectations were enhanced by my childhood in the beautiful Southern Highlands, where farms are endowed with vivid green rolling hills and magnificent English trees embellishing the landscape. As we arrived at the gate of the Mulgoa property, I was startled at the unexpected barren landscape. I took in a deep breath to hide my surprise at the reality of the bareness.

The gate was rusty and broken, you needed a strong arm to lift it and drag it open. We drove up the driveway, which was just a dirt track forged into the ground by vehicles coming and going. The paddocks on either side were bereft of grass, and full of dirt, dust, thistles and tussock. The 'driveway' was full of potholes and led to an old dark-brown brick farmhouse which looked sad, very old, and unloved.

Jack parked the car outside the house, and we went in with our bags and found Lou's wife Wendy at the kitchen sink preparing lunch. She greeted us and told us where to find our bedrooms. When we emerged from the rooms after leaving our overnight bags on the floor, Wendy told us that Lou was outside and that he and the others were castrating three bull calves. We went outside to watch the event. Castration of bull calves is common and is either by a surgical excision and removal of the testicles, or by using an instrument called an emasculatome. Lou was using the surgical technique.

We didn't have far to walk, maybe a hundred metres or so. Guided by the yelling and shouting, we found Lou, another man and a couple of young boys who were trying to catch one of the bull calves. The calf had other ideas and led them on a wild chase around the yard. Eventually, after a lot of chasing and yelling, he was caught, thrown to the ground and securely held, so that Lou could proceed to operate.

Once the job was done and the calf released, it leapt into the air, letting out a squeal of protest and discomfort. Lou was splattered in blood and had a big grin on his face, obviously enjoying the surgical exercise. After washing his hands and face in the water trough, he came over and introduced us to his friend, 'Chook', who had been helping, and the two boys, Lou's son and a friend of his son's.

Lou told us later that Chook was a Sutherland Shire Council garbage collector. A strange little man of indeterminate age – he was probably in his 50s but looked 80 – Chook, was about 5'3', and when he smiled, he displayed a few teeth missing, and the ones that remained were horribly discoloured from smoking. A 'roll your own' cigarette perpetually dangled precariously out of his mouth, and when he mumbled 'Hello,' you expected the cigarette to drop to the ground, but somehow it stayed glued to his lower lip, bouncing along with every mumbled syllable.

Beneath his scruffy, old, tattered Akubra, Chook looked like he had spent his life in the sun. His face, arms and hands were deeply wrinkled, cracked and weather beaten. His clothes were well worn, discoloured work clothes, and his boots too were shabby and tattered, crying out for some polish to soothe the cracks in the leather. His face and eyes told you he had had a rough life. Lou had probably felt sorry for him and gave him some work on the farm for extra cash.

When Lou had finished castrating the three bull calves, he asked Chook if he would like to go to the McGrath Hill sales after lunch and buy three more bull calves. Chook appeared uncomfortable around strangers and I guess Lou gave Chook this chore as an excuse to be released from his discomfort.

Late that afternoon, Chook returned from the McGrath Hill sales, but he did not come with the hoped-for calves, instead he arrived with a canary and a cat.

'Where are the calves?' asked Lou. Chook didn't answer, but muttered and mumbled under his breath and hobbled away. He was obviously annoyed or cranky, or both, or maybe just embarrassed. We never found out why he didn't buy the three bull calves.

Over the course of our stay, my initial misgivings about the farm were confirmed. It was very run down, its fences old and decrepit and broken down in places, with little hope of keeping animals within their boundaries. The paddocks too were uncared for, and looked like they hadn't seen fertiliser for a decade or more.

We left the next morning after breakfast and went home via Pauline's home and then, to PHH and TSH. Jack and I talked and laughed about our unusual visit to 'the farm' and decided that from then on, it would be called 'the funny farm.'

I'm relieved the farm was a real estate investment and not a serious farming enterprise because it would have cost a lot of dollars to get the property up to scratch to farm it seriously.

Early in November, I told Jack that I was planning to go to Canada with Pauline. Pauline and I had been planning a Canadian working holiday. We'd applied for a work visa, and our visas had been granted. We had just paid our fare to travel by ship to Vancouver on 6 December 1969.

Jack looked a bit shell shocked.

About a fortnight before our departure, Jack asked me if I would go to dinner with him at the Bay Seafood Restaurant in Brighton-Le-Sands. This was an unexpected invitation. Apart from the night of the hospital ball, the weekend at Surfers Paradise together with Judy and the weekend at the 'funny farm' with Pauline, we had never been on our own together anywhere, except at work.

Our working environment was official and demanding, we were always trying to find extra time to fit another urgent patient in – there was never enough time in the day for anything other than work. This would be the first time we'd been out on our own together. I had very mixed feelings; I was apprehensive, I was excited, I was frightened, I was sad, I was nervous, and I had to admit to myself that I had a very special feeling for Jack. Maybe this was love?!

Since the ball, I kept remembering how I had enjoyed dancing with Jack and being so close to him. I'd felt a thrill go through my body that I had not experienced before and I felt guilty because there was an exciting energy between us and he could feel it too, but at that time he was a married man with a wife who was struggling with a mental illness, and a disabled daughter. We both knew we could not follow this out of bounds pathway. His loyalty to Jill was in recompense for how she loved and looked after him in their early days together. He had enough to deal with and I could not expect anything other than a broken heart. It was an impossible dream.

And so, when Pauline asked me if I would like to go to Canada with her, it made me think that I should give thought to going away to try and find another life. Pauline was also running away from a broken romance. I decided to run away with her, and we started making plans.

But then, over the last three months there had been a dramatic shift in Jack's life: Jill's death, our trip to the Gold Coast with Judy in September, followed by our weekend at the 'funny farm.'

Was this going to be a night where we say our final goodbyes privately to each other? Or was he going to say thanks for the memories? It was hard for me to judge what his intentions were.

We'd had a very straightforward and effortless relationship until the hospital ball. But even after the ball, we did not allow our emotions to compromise our situation. We both understood without verbalising the many serious ramifications.

Even so, I was excited at the thought of actually going on a date with Jack.

I had trouble trying to decide what to wear, I think I tried on 3 different dresses before I decided on the one. I wanted to look elegant and so I chose a duck-egg blue crepe de chine sleeveless, dress, which was slim fitting, and figure hugging without being tight.

I felt very excited, but at the same time I felt sad. We had worked together for more than eight years, Jack was a big part of my life, and suddenly reality hit me: in two weeks' time I would not see him again for a very long time, if at all. I felt a searing pain go right through my heart. How was I going to get through the night?

I was ready well before Jack was due, I checked my handbag a few times making sure I had everything I needed, tissues, lipstick, wallet, and more tissues. He arrived on time, came in and gave my mum a lovely hug and kiss, and shook hands with dad. He told me how gorgeous I looked, and as we left, he held my hand. Oh, how wonderful ... as he gently and affectionately took my hand, a tingle went straight through my whole body.

We arrived at the restaurant right on time at 8 pm and we were shown to a table next to the window.

We had a delightful dinner although, I must confess, I didn't feel like eating. Conversation flowed easily; we were very comfortable in each other's company. We talked and laughed about the ball and our weekends at Surfers Paradise and the 'funny farm.' Throughout the evening, I was very conscious of Jack looking at me in a very affectionate manner.

As we left, there was a chill in the air, and Jack wrapped his arm around me. He was so tall I easily snuggled in under his protective arm, my heart skipped a few beats and an exciting energy passed between us again. Just the touch of him gave me a beautiful feeling of protection mixed with excitement.

## A NEW BEGINNING 1969-1970

On the way home, he unexpectedly took a detour to the parking area along Botany Bay and parked the car. He turned off the engine and we sat together quietly looking at the bay and the stars in the sky. It was one of those clear, crisp nights when the stars shine so brightly.

We were each buried in our own thoughts, when Jack suddenly turned to me and said, 'I can't let you go, what will I do without you? I love you. Will you marry me?' Then he reached over and kissed me. Oh my gosh, I am sure I could hear bells ringing. Jack looked at me with a quizzical look, then broke into a smile.

'Are you serious?' I asked.

'Yes, very serious,' he replied. 'I have never been so serious in all my life. I have loved you from afar for a very long time, and it used to drive me crazy when your boyfriends would come to pick you up to go out, I wanted to be the one taking you out. I was so jealous.'

I looked into his questioning eyes, and I could feel the tears welling up in my eyes, I said 'I would love to'.

As we drove home, a thousand thoughts raced through my mind. What will my parents say? Their 23-year-old daughter wants to marry her boss, who is 20 years her senior, with a daughter who has a disability. And what would I say to Pauline, my friend who is expecting me to get on a ship with her and sail to Canada? Meanwhile, Jack was chatting away, telling me that he would take me into the city tomorrow morning to buy an engagement ring. Oh, my goodness! Can this really be happening to me?

For some time, I had been concealing and censoring my feelings, and there had never been any amorous gestures from Jack. The one and only time that there was any demonstration of affection was the night of the hospital ball, but we both extinguished those feelings, we knew it could not be, without saying a word.

I respected his marriage and commitment to Jill and had to bury my feelings. When Pauline suggested going to Canada, I thought it might be a good idea. However, after Jill's death, I started to wonder could I manage to go away and leave Jack. I really could not imagine my life without him.

When I arrived home, my parents were asleep, so I waited until morning to talk to them. I wanted to talk to them before my siblings started clamouring for breakfast.

I knocked on their bedroom door gently, and their early morning voices invited me in. I went in and sat on the edge of their bed.

'Good morning, Mum and Dad. I have something to tell you.'

They wearily sat up, with a look on their faces of, 'What is it this time?' I could not stop smiling, and said, 'Jack has asked me to marry him.' Well, that woke them up!

They sat up in their bed, blinked and shook their heads. 'Jack wants to marry you?' they repeated.

'Yes, he has asked me to marry him.'

There was a moment's silence, and dad said sternly, 'Have you thought about this, do you know what you are doing?' I know he would have been thinking about taking on the responsibility of looking after Judy.

'Yes Dad, I have thought about it, and I would like your blessing,' I responded. They both kissed me and gave me their blessing, telling me they were happy for me.

Jack arrived just after 9.30 am. He came in and walked straight up to mum and gave her a big hug and a kiss, saying, 'Ruby, you don't mind if I take your daughter off your hands?' Mum laughed and said, 'Please do.' He had a great big grin on his face, he was very fond of my mum. Dad had already left for work and so he missed this little exchange of pleasantries. Jack had already been to TSH for his ward round with the RMO.

He drove into the city and parked in a car park. He seemed to know where to go. I didn't have a clue as I had rarely been into the city by car, I had always come by train. Strolling the streets, I was wide-eyed admiring the beautiful old buildings, and then, as we approached the stores, I marvelled at the shop-window displays, refined clothes and shoes. Everything that day looked glamorous and I was in awe of the magnificent displays.

We arrived at our destination, Percy Marks Jewellers, an exclusive jewellery shop. As we walked in, I was aware of a palpable, quiet ambience of luxury that I had never experienced before. It was a bit intimidating. Immediately, a kindly grey-haired gentleman approached us, enquiring if he could be of assistance.

Jack's eyes met mine as he said, 'Yes, we would like to look at engagements rings.'

We were escorted to two dark-green velvet chairs in front of a large glass cabinet filled with trays of diamond rings. After we were seated, he pulled out two trays of diamond rings from the display and asked what style of ring we preferred. I was too shy to speak, so Jack took the initiative and said he liked a solitaire diamond.

Studying the trays of rings, Jack picked one and asked me, 'Do you like this style?'

It was a perfect, white-gold solitaire diamond ring, the sort of ring girls dream of. I murmured, 'I love it.'

The lovely gentleman, seeing my embarrassment, softly said, 'Why don't you try a few on and see what you like?'

I did just that, and had so much fun trying on all the different styles, that I soon started to relax and enjoy myself. Isn't it strange? We kept going back to the first ring – it was the one. The sales assistant suggested that we also choose the wedding ring so that they would fit nicely together.

We left the jewellery shop with a dark-green velvet ring box, the rings sitting snuggly inside. When we were safely in the car, Jack gently kissed me and said, 'I love you and I hope you will be very happy.' He took the engagement ring out of its precious velvet box and placed the ring on my ring finger. I couldn't stop looking at this elegant, exquisite ring. I felt so excited. Jack laughed as he watched me gazing at the ring on my ring finger.

We left the city and drove to PHH, Jack parked the car and went in to do a ward round. I happily sat in the car waiting, thinking about how and when I would tell Pauline, and what would I say? I thought I should tell her as soon as possible, as she would have to decide if she would still go to Canada on her own. As her fare could not be refunded at this stage, I thought I should offer to pay her fare if she decided to stay home.

I went to see Pauline and her parents the next day, and as it was a Sunday, I suggested I come to see her in the afternoon, after church. Pauline's parents' home was in McDonald Street Cronulla, which is on the bluff between south and north Cronulla beaches. The home was a stunning double-storey built in blonde brick, which was regarded as being a bit posh in the 1950s and 1960s. Pauline's father was a stockbroker, and her mother was a stay-at-home mother. They attended church every Sunday and both sang in the choir on Sunday mornings. Pauline had a twin brother, Donny, who had a daredevil nature. She also had an older sister, Beverley.

Pauline and I had a mutual friend, Elizabeth (Liz), who lived not far from me, and on the weekends, Liz and I would walk to Pauline's house and after we chatted to Pauline's Mum for a while, we would head off to the beach to surf and sunbake all afternoon, sometimes joined by Pauline's neighbour, Ros.

When I arrived at Pauline's house, I was greeted with the usual hugs and kisses. After we sat down, I jumped straight in and told them the news, there was no easy way of saying it, I just had to say it. They were all obviously very shocked and surprised. Pauline looked like she was going to choke, and then she jumped up and hugged me and we cried together. It was a very poignant moment.

In between the tears, I briefly told Pauline what had transpired and how I anguished over how I was letting her down. I said to her that I realised we had made our final payment which was non-refundable, and that if she decided to stay home, I would happily give her the fare money as I felt responsible letting her down at the last moment.

No doubt she was trying to digest all I had told her. I could see she was browned-off and I don't blame her – we had spent months planning and dreaming and saving. I could understand her disappointment.

However, she was determined to go. She wanted a change, an adventure and was still feeling the pain of the broken romance six months prior. I think her mum and dad, Dora and George, were very disappointed and worried for their daughter, which I could also understand. Pauline would now be travelling to another country on the other side of the world on her own, without a companion to share trials, tribulations and triumphs, and to give comfort when she felt homesick for the sun and the beach. One saving grace was that Pauline was a trained nurse and she had a contact in Vancouver, an Australian nurse, and there was probably a job for her when she arrived. Nurses naturally have a wonderful sisterhood which stretches worldwide

Jack wanted us to marry straight away. He saw no point in waiting; we both knew what we wanted, and there was no time to waste, there was so much to do. However, his friend, John, who had been trying, unsuccessfully, to match-make Jack with some of the nurses at the hospital, thought Jack should wait a while and play the field, and that I should travel with Pauline. Then, if Jack and I were still keen to wed, a few friends and my family could travel over to John's friends' home in Winnipeg, Canada, where we would marry a few months later, about March or April.

John is a great organiser and would enjoy arranging such an event. But Jack was not interested in John's plans. He had no intention of waiting, he wanted us to be together. I don't think John understood that Jack and I were soulmates, we were destined to be together as one. Nor did he understand that my family could not afford to travel to Canada, nor could my friends, and there is no way I would consider marrying without my parents attending, it would cause a great deal of distress and hurt, as we were a very close and caring family. So, Jack and I agreed to disagree with John, and we buried his ideas.

However, things did not go as I thought they would.

Jack invited me to attend the hospital Christmas party with him. Of course, I accepted with great pleasure. We were greeted by all and sundry, as word had gone around the hospital that we were engaged, and would soon marry. Drinks and music were flowing.

Later in the evening I was sitting at a table talking to some girls I knew well, when I happened to glance at the dance floor and was surprised to see Jack dancing with one of the Registrars. I did not think too much of it until I noticed that they were dancing in a manner that was making every one stop and take notice.

I escaped to the ladies' room and sat in a toilet cubicle sobbing my eyes out. After a while I thought I should try and make an exit without anyone noticing. As soon as I stepped back into the ballroom, Jack walked up to me with a silly look on his face.

'I am going home,' I said.

'Oh,' was all he said, realising that things were not good between us. He gathered himself together and walked out with me to his car. He drove me home, and on the way, I spoke up.

'What is going on? Are you having an affair with that Registrar? I can't marry you,' I blurted out.

'Oh, don't be so silly, I was just having a dance,' he responded.

'You sure were.'

After a lot of back chat to each other, we arrived at my home. Jack jumped out of the car and came around to me and put his arm around me and reconciled with me without saying sorry. It took me a while to forgive and forget, but I knew if I wanted to marry Jack I would just have to, and I made it happen.

We wanted a quiet and simple wedding with our nearest and dearest. However, I did want to be married in the Cronulla Methodist Church, as this church has always been part of my life. Happily, Jack agreed. He had no current affiliations with any church, but said he wanted to be married in a church, he didn't mind which one.

I phoned the minister and asked if there were any dates free in January for a wedding and he told me that the only date available was the last Saturday in January, Saturday 31 January 1970. He asked me what time and I suggested 4pm, and so our fate was set and the invitations could be printed.

I sat down with my parents to discuss where we should have a reception and Dad said that because there would only be about 50 people, we could have it at home on the front lawn. He knew where he could hire a marquee with a wooden floor and enough chairs so everyone could sit.

As word spread about our impending wedding we received many offers: my cousin offered to make and decorate the cake, my mother's friends from church offered to help with the catering, and a patient of Jack's generously offered Jack a gift of seafood for the reception.

As with most wedding preparations, there were moments of angst. My moment came from the left field. Jack told me that the Matron of Kareena Private Hospital, Matron Robison, otherwise known as Robbie, had told him that she wanted to be my Matron of Honour and to tell me that she had already bought the dress. I have to say, I was more than upset at this proclamation as I really did not know Matron Robison, she was just someone on my periphery. I was annoyed because she was taking away the thrill of asking my closest friend to take the honour. (We wanted a simple wedding with a small bridal party).

Jack was in a hard place, as Robbie had been a good friend to him, sometimes in his time of need, so he was keen to allow her this pleasure. I agonised on the issue for a day and decided to acquiesce, mainly for Jack and his soft-heartedness towards Robbie. I also understood that Matrons are used to giving orders and can be very assertive and she would find it hard to accept a knockback graciously. Neither Jack nor I liked wasteful confrontations.

But now this meant that I had the painful task of explaining the situation to Liz, my friend, who would have assumed that as she was my best friend, she would be my Bridesmaid. We'd been close friends for the last five years and had shared each other's ups and downs. I hoped she would understand and forgive me.

When I shared my situation with her, she was so gracious and understanding, what a special friend. She offered to take our wedding photos instead. Liz had a passion for photography and an expensive camera which everyone envied. Bless her heart.

And so, we finalised our wedding party. Robbie would be my Matron of Honour and Judy, a bridesmaid. Jack's attendants would be John, his friend, and my brother Rick.

## A NEW BEGINNING 1969–1970

My next issue was Judy's dress. I popped in to see Robbie at Kareena Hospital to talk to her about our arrangements and she offered to show me her dress. She lived in a small apartment at the hospital, so she took me upstairs to her apartment and brought out the dress, it was a simple long gown of orange/red crepe. I have to say, this colour would not have been my choice, but I would just have to get over it.

I would have no hope of matching a dress for Judy, so I decided that Judy would have a white dress with a trim under the bust of matching orange/red satin ribbon. I found a dressmaker who said she could make the dress for Judy in time for the wedding on the 31st.

Christmas had come and gone and I still had not found a wedding dress, so I was now determined, once the Christmas crowds were gone and my birthday was over, I would go into the city for a day and accomplish my mission of finding a wedding dress. The pressure was on. I went into the city by train, clutching a list of wedding shops to visit.

After hours and hours of looking at wedding dresses, I was becoming disheartened. Everything I liked was too expensive or not in my size. I wandered into yet another wedding-dress shop, feeling a bit faint hearted. This shop was different, it had wedding dresses for hire. I hoped this might be my answer. The only issue was that the dress had to be returned to the shop within a week, and I thought I could manage that. That decided, I perused the racks, and I was pleasantly surprised at the quality and the styles of the dresses.

At last, I found a dress I liked. It was a simple sleeveless Princess-style dress in white satin with a white chiffon cape, which looked so elegant. I asked about veils and the attendant said they didn't hire the veils, you had to purchase them. I wanted something very simple, but long and trailing, and the sales assistant found one that was just what I was after. It was really a one-stop shop as I bought a pair of wedding shoes as well. What a relief. I could barely wait for our day to arrive.

Our next mission was Judy's 16th birthday on New Year's Eve, which we combined with our engagement celebration with my parents, and our friends John, Meg, Pat, Peg, Ian, and Ruth. We celebrated together at Jack's favourite restaurant, Herman Lightfoot's Herman's Haystack at Sylvania. Herman was more like a celebrity restauranteur, and it was due to his most gracious, affable personality that his restaurant was so popular with everyone. Herman's Haystack was of timber construction and the roof was covered in hay to mimic a large haystack. The roof was mobile to allow it to slide open on tracks to reveal the wonders of the evening stars. (Unfortunately, this restaurant burned down in the 1970s).

The week before the wedding, Judy and I went for the final fitting of her dress. She looked beautiful and said she felt like Cinderella going to a ball. On the way home, we bought a beautiful pair of white shoes for her. We were happy and relieved because finding shoes for Judy was always a challenge. She was delighted as she hadn't had such a pretty pair of shoes before. We brought her dress and shoes home and put them ceremoniously into her wardrobe waiting for the big day.

Our day arrived, blue sky and sun. Everyone was up early and preparations were in full swing, people, food and flowers everywhere. Mum and I left the chaos and went to the hairdressers, Mum had the first appointment. When she was finished, she looked so beautiful and so young, I hadn't seen her look so pretty.

My long, thick hair however, took much longer, as I was being pedantic about how I wanted it styled. I arrived home later than

# A NEW BEGINNING 1969–1970

*Engagement Party at Herman's Haystack*

*Herman's Haystack*

I expected and was having late lunch when Liz arrived, dressed and ready for the wedding. She started snapping candid shots of everyone. The house was full of joyful chaos.

Everyone had jobs to do and there were a lot of people coming and going. My mother was doing an excellent job of co-ordinating everyone and in the midst of all this, Jack's patient arrived with boxes and boxes of seafood, prawns, crabs and lobsters, all in polystyrene boxes filled with crushed ice, we all gasped at the magnitude of his gift.

Time was rushing by. Suddenly, it was 2.45 pm, time for me to get dressed. Mum and Liz came into my bedroom to help. I had my make-up on, and I was already in my gorgeous new underwear. Putting the dress on would be a challenge. I put a silk scarf over my head so that I didn't smear any make-up on the dress or mess up my hairdo, Liz and Mum gently lifted the dress over my head and softly eased it down over my body and then carefully zipped me up and did up all the tiny little buttons. Then we came to the veil, which was a simple white nylon netting veil with no embellishments, tightly gathered at one end which had to be bobby-pinned into my special hair-do, high up on the back of my head.

Robbie (the Matron) and Judy were getting ready at Jack's apartment in Cronulla and his friend, John, was driving them and Jack to the church. John had a white Mercedes, which was perfect for the day.

At 3.45 pm I came out of the house to get into the car. We were using Jack's white Ford to take Dad and I to the church. A friend of Lou Levi's had previously volunteered to drive. Liz helped me into the car, lifting the dress and carefully placing it well inside the car, then she lifted the veil gently, arranging it on the shelf behind the back seat, and handed me my bouquet. She lent in and gave

# A NEW BEGINNING 1969–1970

*Sue with her father on our wedding day*

me a gentle kiss on the cheek and said, 'See you in church.' All our neighbours gathered around the car to see me leave my parent's home for the last time as Sue Goodfellow. They were all so happy for me and wished me well, many of them taking photos.

I remember arriving at the church, and feeling grateful Liz was there to help with my dress and veil. She took a few photos, and then Dad and I walked up the steps to the main entrance of the church. Dad looked at me and said, 'Are you ready for your new life?' I smiled and nodded, then we slowly walked down the aisle.

I looked up and saw Jack standing there, waiting for me, and I could feel the tears welling up in my eyes. He smiled at me with such loving tenderness. I don't even remember what music was playing as I walked down the aisle. I don't think I even heard it, my head and heart were full of Jack.

As I drew closer, I noticed his attire. He had chosen to wear his pale fawn suit with a white shirt and dark tie, then I looked at his feet he had black shoes and socks on. I had a quiet giggle to

*Our Wedding Day*

myself. He was never one for coordinating colours.

It was such a relief to have the ceremony and photos over and to be on our way back to my parent's home. As everyone arrived, they were offered a glass of wine or champagne. The guest list was limited to only our closest friends and a few relatives, and it was obvious that everyone felt happy for Jack.

However, we had one special guest, Muriel, Judy's Great Aunt, who had misgivings. 'It is too soon, and she is too young,' she told Jack a few days before the wedding. I think as Muriel observed the personal interactions between my family and Jack and Judy, that her heart may have softened a little towards me, as she began to understand my background. It was not long before Muriel and

## A NEW BEGINNING 1969–1970

I had a very reverent relationship which deepened as the years went by.

It was a happy day. Everyone loved the abundance of seafood on the tables.

After we cut the cake, I changed into my 'going away' outfit and we departed for the city. Our car had been spared the usual post-wedding decoration of streamers, white spray and a string of empty cans attached to the bumper bar, as the boys, mostly my relatives, had mistaken a guest's white Ford for Jack's car. The guest – an unmarried, elderly, refined gentleman – was not amused. When the boys realised their mistake, they had to quickly undo all their trimmings so that he could drive home without drawing attention.

We drove into the city and stayed one night at the Wentworth Hotel, so that I could return my wedding dress to the hire shop in the morning. We checked in and received our room key. Entering the room, I took a few steps in and spotted two single beds. I started laughing and said, 'Is this a joke, Jack? You want us to sleep in a single bed together? It will be a tight squeeze. Did John make this booking?'

He laughed and said, 'Well what are you going to do about it?'

So, I picked up the phone and dialled the front desk. I told them this was my wedding night and could they please find a room with a double bed? About 15 minutes later, we got the phone call to say that they had found a room with a double bed and a bell boy came up and we exchanged keys. At last, we could be on our own. It was a night where Jack could release some of the anguish of the last few years and I could fulfil my dreams.

The following morning, we returned the wedding dress and then drove south, heading for Merimbula, where Jack had a block of land he wanted to sell. Merimbula is about 530 km south of Sydney. We decided to break the journey and spend a night in

Nowra. We arrived early in the afternoon and after we checked in at a motel, Jack took me for a walk, showing me where his parents and grandparents had lived and where he swam and fished and went prawning with the Aboriginal children.

It was a delightful afternoon; the sun was warm and shone brightly and the water looked like it had been sprinkled with sparkling diamonds. Jack enjoyed reliving his adventures while living with Grandfather and Nanny Sawyer. The next morning, we set off early and arrived at Merimbula about 1 pm. We found a fish shop and enjoyed fish and chips wrapped in newspaper while sitting on the beach watching a man searching for worms for fishing bait. He had a long stick with an old stocking tied on the end of the pole, and in the stocking was the 'stink bait,' which is supposed to attract the worm. When the worm pokes its head up out of the sand, you have to be quick, and grab hold of its head and pull it out of the sand.

After our little sojourn on the beach, we headed off to find Jack's block. It was on a bluff overlooking the ocean, with spectacular views. Our next job was to find and talk to a real estate agent and put the block on the market. Mission accomplished. We stayed overnight in a delightful resort motel and the next morning drove back home to Judy, who was pleased to see us. We were away for three days, though it felt much longer. The next day, I moved my few precious possessions into their unit at Cronulla. What a wonderful day! This was a new beginning for the three of us.

# Chapter Ten
## An Around-the-World Adventure!
## 1970

Jack and Judy both needed TLC, they were both traumatised and emotionally scarred from the dramas and traumas they had shared over the previous ten years. I was concerned about Judy, only 16, and living through the painful loss of her mother. Your mother is always your mother, no matter what your experience has been, and no one can fill that space.

She needed something positive to focus on. I sat with her and had a chat and I asked if she would like to work with her dad in his office and learn to be a receptionist. She loved this idea. Judy couldn't wait for Jack to come home to share the news. As she was telling him, he looked up at me with a knowing look and a twinkle in his eye. We knew that working would keep her busy and give her vital interaction with people, keeping her mind on other things.

We also discussed buying her a car when she turned 18, another thing for her to look forward to.

And so, each day Jack would leave around 6 am, and Judy and I would go to work and come home together, with Jack arriving home sometime after 8 pm each night. We were thoroughly exhausted every day, and during dinner one exhausted evening, Jack told Judy and I that the three of us should go away overseas for a holiday. He had been talking to John, who was heading off to Canada in April with a group of friends. This inspired Jack and, with John's help, he began to plan our holiday. Jack was keen to return to Edinburgh and visit his friends there, and then meet up with John and his entourage in Canada. The trip was quite the spontaneous affair. John put Jack in touch with his travel agent and suggested to Jack that a cruise from Sydney to Hong Kong might be a good way to start the trip.

We left Sydney in late February 1970, aboard the *Oronsay*, sailing to Hong Kong. After Hong Kong, our 'Around the World' air ticket took us to Rome as our first stop, then through Europe and across to England, then to Canada, Hawaii and home. We would be away for almost three months. I still have the original invoice; the total cost for the ship and air tickets for the three of us was $5,500.

A week or so before we left, Doug told Jack that his racehorse, Just Jack, was due to start racing while we were away. Jack had been impatiently waiting for Just Jack to begin his racing career. He told Doug that he would phone him regularly and when the horse was racing, Doug could hold the phone to the radio so Jack could hear the call of the race. He gave Doug $70 to bet on the horse and Jack told Doug that he and Doug would share any winnings.

We had many hilarious moments during our journey. On our departure day, we invited my mum, dad, brothers and sisters to come and visit us on the ship before we raised anchor, and then wave bon voyage from the wharf. In the 1970s, this was a typical ship's sailaway. However, we were very naïve. In our dreams, we had a grand image of the three of us in a comfortable cabin with a balcony.

We were in for a shock. John, who arranged the booking, was mindful of the dollar and booked us into the cheapest cabins on the ship, which were in the bowels of the ship, without a porthole, let alone a balcony. To make matters worse, we had to use a shared bathroom down the hall.

John had booked Judy in a cabin with five other ladies. Fortunately, our cabin was not far from her, but still, it was disappointing for Judy, who was not used to being with strangers. Our cabin was minute, it had two single bunk beds with a very small wardrobe and probably measured 2 m by 2 m, including the bunks. There was barely room to move. When one was dressing, the other had to sit on the bed, out of the way. This was definitely not what we were expecting.

I don't know what my parents thought, but there was no room for visitors, so we took them on a tour of the ship until the call for them to go ashore. We said our goodbyes and they disembarked and waited on the wharf till the ship sailed away. The sail away was a beautiful experience, firstly waving farewell to my family with the strains of a band playing 'Auld Lang Syne' in the background and then sailing past the almost completed Opera House. After we sailed, Jack and I took Judy to her cabin and introduced her to the ladies. Fortunately, they seemed pleasant enough and helpful, time would tell.

During our voyage, we met interesting people and enjoyed sea life until we got to the China Sea, where we hit an enormous storm. The ship was pitching and lurching incessantly, and it was impossible for Judy to walk without falling. Some of the furniture had to be tied down, and it was not possible to eat in the dining room. I was so seasick I could not stay in the cabin, so I found a blanket and laid down on a deck chair, leaving Jack to look after Judy. I thought I would die.

There were quite a few others in the same distress but there was no comfort in sharing this unpleasant malady. Thank goodness Jack and Judy were OK. We eventually sailed through the storm and arrived in Hong Kong. I was so glad to get off the ship.

We docked at Hong Kong, and went through customs. Everyone's luggage was on the wharf and the customs agents were asking people to open their bags for them to examine, checking for drugs or contraband, I assume. When we found our bags, an agent was there talking in Chinese and gesticulating madly. We were trying to work out what he was saying, when, in frustration Jack quickly bent over to unlock the bags and as he did, there was a loud rip. His trousers had split open at the back.

Unfortunately, Jack did not have underpants on and unbeknown to him, he was exposing himself to all and sundry. I quickly took my jacket off and wrapped it around him, while trying not to laugh and annoy the customs agent who'd been questioning Jack about all the tablets we had in our luggage.

Jack tried to explain that they were for headaches and diarrhoea, but the language barrier made it difficult to communicate. However, I think the sight of Jack tied up in my jacket distracted them and they left us in peace to try and sort ourselves out. Jack had a suit on, so we took my jacket off and he tied his jacket around his waist and left the dock.

We looked around to see if we could find somewhere to buy Jack something to wear. Luckily, we found a shop nearby and bought Jack a lovely Harris tweed overcoat, perfect for the icy wind that was blowing. He was so glad to put that overcoat on – it became his favourite coat for many years. We caught a taxi to the hotel and settled in. We were all in the one room, and this is how we travelled for the rest of the trip, usually with Judy on a rollaway bed next to our bed.

Hong Kong was very different to anything we had previously experienced. Our hotel window looked out across hundreds of multi-storied buildings, some with little shanties on the flat rooftops where people were living. Some of the shanties were made out of cardboard and some incorporated bits and pieces of leftover building materials. Wherever there was a flat roof, there was a mini shanty town on the roof. I wondered if we had a little shanty town on the top of our hotel.

When we left to explore, we found the streets so crowded that we had a hard time making our way through, so we gave up, worried that Judy might get knocked over.

Jack had promised a patient, Mr Lee, who lives in Hong Kong, that he would contact him when we arrived. Mr Lee wanted to take us out to dinner, as he felt a deep debt of gratitude to Jack for saving his life. We met him for dinner the following evening.

Before we left for dinner, Jack gave Judy and I a lecture that we had to eat everything that was put in front of us, as to not eat it would deeply offend Mr Lee. He knew we would have trouble as we were going to a traditional Chinese restaurant, not an Australian-Chinese Restaurant. Oh, my goodness, I struggle eating Australian-Chinese food! I told Judy I would take a large handbag with a big bundle of tissues and a plastic bag, so that she and I could secretly dispose our unwanted food when Mr Lee was not looking. It was going to be a long night.

We managed the first course, shark fin soup. It sounds disgusting but was edible, that was if you didn't choke on the shark fins. Thank goodness we got it down, because soup would not go well in a handbag.

Then came the preserved duck's eggs. After being buried in the ground for more than three months, this delicacy was slimy and green/blue, enough to turn anyone off. We tried to cut the eggs with our chopsticks. Well, you can imagine, they were so slippery, we chased them all over the plate, Judy and I surreptitiously depositing morsels of the offending eggs into my bag. Thank goodness Jack and Mr Lee were in deep conversation. I think Jack got the drift of what we were doing, as he was sending us black looks.

The next offering was monkey's brains in a coconut shell. Oh No! How could anyone eat monkey's brains? Those poor little monkeys! Judy and I were gagging at the thought of it. My handbag would never be the same, it would have to be cremated.

Then came the chicken, at last something we can eat, we thought, breathing a sigh of relief. Well, that was until the plate was placed in front of us, with the chicken's head and feet staring up at us from the plate. Poor Jack, he was mortified with our behaviour.

When we got back to the hotel, I asked the concierge if there was an American restaurant nearby. He grinned and said there was one two blocks away. We were saved! Hamburgers, here we come. I was hoping Jack would forgive us by morning.

I suspect Mr Lee managed to overlook our childish behaviour, his many trips to Australia perhaps having softened his traditional stance, as he turned up in the morning, bright and cheerful to take us shopping. Our first stop was to a tailor for men and ladies. Jack was reticent, but I encouraged him to have at least one suit made, he ended up with three. Judy and I had two outfits each made, with matching shoes and bags.

Our clothes would be delivered to the hotel the next day. How do they do it, I thought? Everything was beautifully made, and the shoes fitted perfectly. I still have my two suits with matching shoes and bag. Mr Lee could see how happy we were with the experience and offered to take us to a silk warehouse, where we purchased magnificent silk fabrics, which we took home to be made up.

We were in Hong Kong for four days, always ever so grateful for the American restaurant nearby. When we packed to leave, our bags were bulging.

Next stop – Rome. Jack had a couple of 'tids' and some sleeping pills, and after take-off, he crashed, managing to stretch himself out across the seats, using Judy and I as his pillows. He had a great flight, and slept for six hours. This was my first flight and I felt nervous, but Judy was good company, and helped to calm me down. Jack and Judy had flown before, so they were experienced travellers.

Judy had been looking forward to Rome. Judy's mother was a Catholic and Judy was educated in a Catholic school, so Rome and the Vatican held special significance for her. Our first day was spent at the Vatican, in the Sistine Chapel and then wandering through the catacombs. On our second day, Jack woke up with a terrible flu, he had a high temperature with rigors.

I phoned the front desk to arrange for a doctor, but they said they didn't have a doctor on call. He was too sick to move, so I hunted through our medical bag to see if we had any suitable medications. Fortunately, we had some antibiotics and pills for pain relief so we dosed him up and spent our remaining days in Rome in our hotel room nursing Jack. By the fourth day, he was starting to recover, which was a relief as we were due to fly out the following day to Barcelona.

The day after we arrived in Barcelona was Palm Sunday which was an important religious day for Judy, and she asked Jack to take her to mass. That was okay, except several hundred thousand others had the same idea. The Catalonians must all be devout

Catholics. I really don't know how Jack managed but manage he did. They arrived back at the hotel exhausted.

We found language a big barrier in Barcelona, and we were glad to leave.

Our next stop was Paris, our mission in France was to grant Judy another wish and that was to go to Lourdes.

Lourdes is a small market town in the foothills of the Pyrenees, south of Paris. According to believers, the Virgin Mary appeared to Bernadette Soubiróus in 1858 and spoke to her in her native Occitan language, 18 times at Lourdes. The site has since become a major attraction for Roman Catholic pilgrims and the Grotto is a place where miraculous healings are said to occur.

Judy would be hoping for a miraculous healing, and we could not deny her this opportunity.

We rented a car from the airport to drive to Lourdes. The car was a compact Renault and we had fun trying to fit three large suitcases and ourselves into it. None of us knew how to speak French, although Jack said his schoolboy French was pretty good. Maybe it wasn't as good as he thought, as he couldn't understand the rental-car agent who was trying to give him instructions on how to drive the car and what the knobs and levers were for.

After some frustration, we realised we just had to work it out as we drove along. The instruction book was no help as it was in French. We had lights flashing and windscreen wipers going as well as cold and hot air blowing over us. Jack went to pull a red knob, and I said, 'Don't pull that, that's an emergency knob!' We later found out that it was the control for hot air, and laughed and laughed, because we were shivering from the cold. Now we had hot air to warm us.

Now that we had the car somewhat sorted, we set off looking for signs indicating the way south. More than two hours later, we were still driving around Paris – we had been driving around on a Parisian ring road. On the third time round, we decided to run for luck and take the next exit. We had no idea where this road would take us, and as we drove along Jack saw a Gendarme (Police) sign, so he pulled over. He thought he would go in and ask for directions to Lourdes.

He could see about six Gendarmes in the office all laughing and singing, eating and drinking. He walked up to the building and knocked on the door, but no one came to open the door, so Jack knocked on the window, but they had no intention of answering his knock. He gave up in disgust. We kept driving, and at last, we saw a sign which indicated that we had accidentally found our way south.

We were finally out in the countryside, the scenery was breathtaking, with beautiful, lush green fields, some fringed by lofty dark green trees, standing tall, reaching for the sky. The day was closing in, so we started looking for a motel for the night. As we drove along, darkness descended and we spotted a motel sign shining like a beacon. Jack pulled the car over onto the side of the road, believing that there was a breakdown lane.

Suddenly, the car was tipping over an embankment. I immediately grabbed the door handle and managed to suppress my scream of fear. I looked around at Judy whose face reflected her terror. We could feel the car quivering and rocking, Jack and I very slowly opened our doors ever so gently, one at a time, and ever so carefully inched our way out of the car, trying not to make any sudden movement that would trigger further sliding.

We couldn't risk getting Judy out, as her jerking movements would likely cause the car to slide or roll down, as the car was teetering on the edge of a steep embankment. It appeared that the weight of Judy and the suitcases in the back of the car was holding the car on the crest of the embankment. Poor Judy was terrified, and shivering with fear. Jack decided to walk across the paddock to the motel, which would be quicker than walking along the road. Fortunately, it was always his habit to carry a small torch in his pocket, obviously for this type of occasion, and so he was able to find his way across the paddock to the motel.

The walk took him about 15 minutes. He went into the bar and dining room area where he could see a few people gathered and somehow, in his schoolboy French, told them of our plight. He drew pictures to help get the message across that we needed a tow-truck to pull the car back onto the road.

While Jack was gone, I kept Judy as calm as I could, trying to distract her from her predicament, which wasn't easy. It was very cold, and we were freezing, but I didn't dare attempt to try and get back in the car, that could have been disastrous. I stood shivering beside the car on the upside next to the window of the back seat and talked to Judy through the window.

In around an hour, Jack was back, telling us about his experience, doing his best to make the story entertaining for Judy. About ten minutes later, the tow truck arrived. A man jumped out of the tow truck and started chatting away in French. We had no idea what he was saying but he had a very kindly face, which reassured us, and he began to secure the car to the tow truck. He got back into the tow truck and pulled the car back onto the road. We cheered and clapped our hands with delight, our drama was over. Judy cried with relief.

We were safe, we had survived. We spent a very comfortable evening at the motel, and were served a splendid meal. After dinner, we went to our room and snuggled in comfortable beds under lovely soft, warm, fluffy doonas. Fortunately, there was no damage to the car, and we were on our way early the next morning after a delicious breakfast of croissants and coffee. The croissants were the lightest, flakiest, buttery croissants that I have ever experienced. Smothered in their delicious home-made strawberry jam, they were even tastier. Yum…

When Jack asked the manager of the motel for directions to Lourdes, he kindly drew a map with arrows for us to follow. Our drive to Lourdes took most of the day and as soon as we arrived at our destination in the mountains, we looked for accommodation, which was not as easy as we had hoped.

After many knockbacks, we eventually found a small boutique hotel which unfortunately did not have a lift, just the narrowest of staircases, and our room was on the second floor. It was a challenge for Jack, who had to try and squeeze up the narrow stairwell carrying one large suitcase at a time. The stairs were especially difficult for Judy, but we managed, one step at a time.

By the time Jack carried three suitcases to our room, he was puffing and panting and ready to collapse. When he arrived, he declared, 'Next time we travel, it will be one change of clothing for each person in one small case.' Judy and I told him he can come with one change of clothing but that we would need two! We all looked at each other and fell on the beds laughing. Judy and I knew we couldn't do it, and Jack knew it too.

Our room was neat and tidy, but tiny. We had a double bed and a single bed, side by side, the window was small by Australian standards, with a roller blind, and when we looked out the window, we saw other buildings which looked very old and built with stone blocks which were discoloured with black soot, but there was a beauty in their stature.

We were lucky to have a compact ensuite bathroom with a small shower, hand basin, toilet and bidet. It was so tiny, there was only enough room for one of us at a time. Our suitcases had to be squeezed under the double bed as there was no room for them in the room. We had a restless night on squeaky beds which reminded me of the squeaky gate at the 'funny farm,' but we were warm, and did manage to get some sleep. Judy was excited, she was looking forward to her visit to the Grotto.

After we woke up in the morning, we attended to our ablutions one after the other, dressed and went to the dining room for our traditional French breakfast of croissants and coffee. After breakfast, we went back to our room and cleaned our teeth and packed a bag of necessities for our day. When we departed the hotel, we didn't quite know which way to go but hoped we might see people who might be heading to the Grotto.

Stumbling through the steep, winding streets, we were chatting away to each other, when a stranger came up to us and said, 'Hello, I think I hear an Australian accent.' He noticed Judy's disability and said, 'Are you here to visit the Grotto?'

'Yes,' we chorused, and then Jack added, 'We seem to be a little lost.'

It was such a relief to understand what someone was saying and to speak to a fellow Australian who, fortunately, was familiar with Lourdes. He gave us the directions we needed, 'but' he warned, 'be prepared for a long wait in the queue.' We thanked him with our deepest gratitude.

Lourdes was nothing like I imagined. It is a small town built on the side of a mountain, with steep and narrow streets lined with stalls and hawkers selling small bottles of sacred water, religious charms and thousands and thousands of porcelain figurines of the Blessed Mary, in all sizes from 3 cm to 50 cm, or bigger. To me, the street sellers were pests whose distracting presence crushed the sacred atmosphere.

Eventually, we spotted the end of the queue. Already there

were hundreds of people – in wheelchairs, on crutches, some with walking sticks and many, amazingly, being pushed on hospital beds – all going to the Grotto for a blessing and hoping for a miracle.

Hours later, it was finally our turn to enter the Grotto for Judy to have her blessing in the sacred water. It was a very spiritual experience for Judy. Sadly, she did not receive a miracle, but she was so gracious about accepting her reality. She remained joyful and optimistic about her experience.

The following day we departed Lourdes, heading to Cannes and then on to Nice for a rest. Well, that was the plan, but as we came into Nice the road was like a parking lot. So, after two hours sitting in the car and going nowhere, we thought we would have to have a change of plan. We'd noticed a railway station sign so we thought we would forego our two days in Nice, ditch the rental car and go by train back to Paris.

We were in for a shock. We were inexperienced travellers arriving in Nice during peak holiday time, without bookings. Of course, the train was booked out for three months. So, we retreated back to our car, but wait, where did we leave the car?!

It took a while of traipsing around the streets with Jack and I lugging our big bags (no wheels), but we eventually found our car – what a welcome sight, what a relief. I was so exhausted. Jack had recalled some of the landmarks which helped him guide us to where we had discarded it, and so, apologetically, we climbed back into our trusty little Renault. We re-joined the traffic queue and, inch by inch, we departed Nice.

After that episode, I thought I would be happy after all to come with one change of clothing. The suitcases were heavy, bulky and awkward.

We drove all the way to Paris and stayed for two days, sightseeing the usual tourist attractions and sometimes enjoying the

*Jack with the 3 large suitcases*

French cuisine. We had trouble with the snails and frog's legs, Judy wouldn't let them go past her lips. Jack wasn't much better than Judy – I was the only one who actually tried them. They were delightful days. We had a lot of fun strolling the streets and taking in the sights and Parisian atmosphere.

The next leg of our journey was by train to Amsterdam. When we went to the ticket office to buy our train tickets, we were told that there were only second-class seats available and it was on a first-come basis, in other words, grab the best seat as quickly as you can. Luckily, we found three seats together, facing each other. Poor Jack had to lift our three heavy bags up on to baggage racks above our seats.

The seats were comfortable leather and we enjoyed watching the scenery of rich fertile land and charming villages flashing past. At lunchtime, we headed to the dining car at the end of the train. We had to pass through a few carriages to get there, which wasn't easy as there was a fair bit of movement between carriages. Judy was fearful and very apprehensive and so we had to almost lift her across the connecting platform, which was a bit scary.

We were in the middle of lunch when the train made a stop at Brussels and a message relayed in French came across the loudspeaker. I asked Jack if he could understand. I don't know what made us think to question what was happening, I think it was another passenger who told us that the front of the train had been disconnected from the back of the train, and the front of the train was about to depart to Amsterdam.

Oh my goodness, our bags with our passports and tickets were on the train that was about to pull out of the station! We jumped up and quickly moved through the carriages until we came to the carriage which had been uncoupled. We got out onto the platform and the front of the train was ever so slowly moving out of the station. Jack and I grabbed hold of Judy and managed to help her onto the open gangway platform at the back of the last carriage, and as the train started to move, Jack and I jumped on board, trying not to fall on top of Judy.

When we were safely on board, we opened the back door of the carriage and helped Judy to her feet and found our way to our seats. Finding that we still had our seats, and our three bags accounted for, we gratefully sat down and breathed a sigh of relief. As we recovered and attended to our injuries, which fortunately were not serious, we started to see the funny side of our predicament. What began as a giggle soon became a full laugh of relief. Still, the serious side of what could have been did not escape us. Had we not managed to jump back on the train, we would have been in Brussels without our passports and tickets. A lesson well learnt: always carry your documentation with you at all times.

Our Amsterdam stopover was primarily to visit Anne Frank's

hiding place. Judy had read *The Diary of a Young Girl* by Anne Frank, and was keen to visit the house where Anne and her family had hidden. Our visit was an emotional re-awakening of the horrors of WWII, with one delightful surprise.

We were touring the home when a museum guide paused and gestured toward an elderly man who was quietly talking to some visitors.

'That is Anne Frank's father,' said the guide. 'You should feel very privileged because Mr Frank rarely comes to the museum.'

Experiencing Anne Frank's home had been worthwhile, but on the whole, we found Amsterdam underwhelming, although an afternoon boat ride, sailing along the canals, playing 'spot the windmill,' was another highlight.

We departed Amsterdam in a sombre mood.

Our next stop was London, where we had a few days of shopping and taking Judy to shows, fulfilling another wish on her list. Judy had studied elocution with a wonderful teacher, Jean who encouraged Judy to perform at Eisteddfods and successfully sit for examinations. Through Judy's friendship with Jean she developed an avid interest in live Theatre. Two of the shows which we took her to were the musical Evita and Agatha Christie's play, Mousetrap, which had been running since 1952 and is the longest running play in the world.

While we were in London, Jack phoned Doug the horse trainer, as he had promised, to find out when Just Jack was racing. Doug had managed to find a race that would fit in to our itinerary – he was racing two days later, at 3 pm Sydney time, which was 6 am London time.

Jack arranged to phone Doug at the time of the race. Doug placed the phone close to the radio so that Jack could hear the race and Jack relayed the call of the race to Judy and I. We were all excited, laughing and cheering, and unbelievably, Just Jack won! How exciting! We felt a little sad, however, that we were not there to see and experience such a moment. When you own a horse, what you look forward to more than anything, is being at the races when your horse wins. Doug said that he hoped Just Jack would race again in a fortnight, if the horse pulled up okay.

Judy had another request; she had been writing to a Catholic nun who had been a favourite teacher of hers at school. The nun was now at what used to be the Dover Priory, a monastery for men and women, and Judy told Jack that she would love to visit her, as the nun had been very good to her.

On a bleak day, we caught the train to Dover, a town and major ferry port in Kent, southeast England, approximately 120 km from London. It was so cold that we needed to wear all our warm clothes; jumpers, overcoats, beanies, scarves, socks and boots. Now, I have to set the scene for you, because you would not have known Jack was a very heavy smoker, his smoking was a direct consequence of his experiences during the war, and cigarettes were freely given out to the boys. And I, I am ashamed to say, also smoked occasionally.

Scientific evidence was emerging that cigarettes caused cancer and so we'd decided that we had to give up this dreadful habit. Today was the day that we designated to give up smoking, and because Jack had been a heavy smoker since his war days, he would find it very hard and a challenge. I, on the other hand, being only an occasional smoker, would not find it as difficult. Smoking is an addiction and many people who try to quit smoking quit many times before they succeed. You have to be committed and it was probably best that we did it together.

There was no heating in the train and as we neared Dover, I was shivering and grumbling about how cold I was. 'It's not COLD!' Jack snapped at me. 'Stop complaining.'

I had never heard him like this before, or ever after. We arrived in Dover and walked to the 'Priory' in angry silence. I was so upset, I didn't take much notice of my surrounds, but I do remember the Priory was a beautiful, ancient stone building.

We pressed the doorbell and were greeted by a nun dressed in the usual nun's habit of black and white, that is a black veil on her head, a white wimple covering her neck, a black dress reaching down to her black lace-up shoes, and a black scapula, or apron, to protect her habit.

Judy told the nun that she was from Australia, and would like to visit her friend. The nun appeared indifferent and escorted us to a reception room which was very clean and tidy with uncomfortable bench-like seating. On one wall there was a small window which allowed the daylight to sprinkle some hope into the room. I sensed a little apprehension in Judy, and I was not surprised as I felt from our reception that Judy's request may not be honoured.

After a long half hour, another nun arrived. She smiled graciously at us – you could feel the tension leave the room. She announced that she had come to take Judy to see her friend.

Jack and I went for a walk and had lunch in stony silence and then returned for Judy.

We left the Priory and arrived back at the station in time for our train back to London. Judy's presence was a remedy for our grey moods. She was happy and chatted nonstop about her visit.

After our few days in London, Jack and I managed to overcome our cigarette-withdrawal traumas and I think flying up to Edinburgh was a good tonic for Jack. Edinburgh was his happy place. We arrived in Edinburgh, once again without a hotel reservation, but this was how we were travelling, we hadn't pre-booked hotels at any of our destinations, which in retrospect was rather foolish.

When we tried to find accommodation, we were told that everywhere was booked out as there were three international conferences in Edinburgh that week. We ended up in a hotel on the outskirts of Edinburgh. It was a charming 'olde-worlde' hotel with tartan carpets and an old-fashioned, yet grand, polished wooden staircase which was the centrepiece of the entry foyer.

Jack enjoyed spending time with his teachers and mentors, walking through the corridors of time and looking into the future of heart transplants. Most of our time was spent as guests at their various homes, which was delightful. Their wives served cordon bleu creations, accompanied by the best French wines. I remember one comical scene at the home of Dr Ted French, whom Jack deeply admired and respected.

Jack walked into the room, I followed, then Judy. Dr French walked straight up to me, put his arms around me and said, 'This must be your beautiful daughter.' Jack and I laughed, and I said, 'No, I am his beautiful wife,' and turned around to embrace Judy. 'This is his beautiful daughter,' I said. We all laughed and Dr French apologised, handing me a champagne cocktail to defuse the moment.

We were sad to leave Scotland. We'd loved our stay in Edinburgh, visiting friends and driving around the countryside, delighting in the scenery of verdant rolling hills and monumental mountains tumbling down into the still serenity of a loch. Travelling further into the countryside, we'd marvelled at the imposing Grampians, stark in their nature and astonishing harshness, reaching up to the clouds, with not one tree in sight.

Scotland has a treasure trove of beauty.

'Goodbye Scotland, we love you and hope to return one day,' I thought.

Our next destination was Calgary, Canada, via London. Calgary was our meeting point, where we would connect with Jack's friends John and Meg, and their friends Pat and Peg, with their daughter Tracy. We were to meet at the Calgary train station, and travel by train to Banff, where we had accommodation at the Banff Springs Hotel. The journey was about 2½ hrs, and we were entertained by the passing parade of the splendour of the Rocky Mountains.

Banff Springs Hotel is one of Canada's Grand railway hotels and was built in the Chateauesque style featuring steep pitched roofs, with ornate dormers and gables. It is situated within the Banff National Park and the town of Banff is located in the Rocky Mountains range, 1,414 metres above sea level. Our large room was on the fourth floor and featured a wide picture window showcasing a magnificent snow-covered mountain.

Our time at Banff Springs was a lot of fun. All the waiters and housemaids were university students, who were there for a good time too, and so there was plenty of infectious laughter and hilarity. It was nice also to meet up with Jack's friends, who seemed just as delighted to see us. After we checked in and unpacked our bags, we went on a tour of the hotel.

Stepping outside to take in the surrounds, we were surprised to see about 20 adult men wearing little red Fez hats, riding miniature, motorised quad bikes, buzzing around the hotel driveway, chasing each other having buckets of fun.

'They are The Shriners,' explained the concierge. Intrigued, we learnt that they are a fraternity based on fun, fellowship and the Masonic principles of brotherly love, belief and truth, and have thousands of clubs around the world. They also raise funds and support 22 Shriner Hospitals across the USA, Mexico and Canada, treating children with orthopaedic problems, burns, cleft lip and palate, brittle bone issues, spinal cord injuries and other problems, with no charge for treatment. I reflected that when they do so much good, we should not criticise their childish frivolity on their small motorised bikes.

Every evening after dinner, the hotel organised a dance in the ballroom. These were a lot of fun, mainly because the university students were allowed to join in, setting the night alight.

Judy, Jack and I left our friends in Banff and caught a train to Vancouver, where we were meeting Pauline. Banff is about 1370 km north east of Vancouver, about 11 hours by train, via the most picturesque scenery of towering snow-capped mountains with a scattering of impressive fir trees.

I was thrilled that we could come to Vancouver to visit Pauline. Over the last few months, I'd missed her happy face and infectious laughter and our heart-to-heart chats.

We were staying in a hotel in the Vancouver CBD and arranged for her to visit us at the hotel. She came with a girlfriend, and we went to dinner together in the hotel's restaurant. We had a delightful night and Pauline reassured me that she had settled in well, was making friends and had a good job in one of the hospitals in Vancouver. My heart felt a little lighter for having this time with her and finding out that she had successfully made the transition to a new life.

We had three enchanting days in Vancouver, exploring the parks, the waterfront, and the unforgettable seafood markets with Alaskan salmon and huge Alaskan crabs on display.

On our last day, we met Pauline again to say goodbye, and then flew on to Hawaii, where we were meeting up with Jack's friends again.

Hawaii, oh how I love Hawaii! It was everything I imagined, plus much more: the balmy air, sunshine, blue skies, warm ocean, mesmerising Hawaiian music, the sweetest pineapples and happy faces. Our friends met us in Waikiki, where we were all booked into the same hotel. Another couple would be joining our group, Dr Alec and his wife Isobel. Alec was a polio victim and walked with the aid of two walking sticks and callipers on each leg. They arrived in the middle of the night.

We were awakened by a phone call sometime around midnight. It was John, telling us that Alec had seen a cockroach in his room, and told the front desk. The receptionist offered him another room, and when he looked at it, he said it was dirty and no better than the previous one. He phoned John and said, 'I am not staying in this hotel, it is dirty with cockroaches, will you come and help me move to another hotel?' John rang Jack.

John and Jack helped Alec and Isobel find another hotel. When Jack picked up Alec's suitcase, the handle fell apart. Jack told me he thought the suitcase looked more than 20 years old and it was no wonder it was falling apart. John carried the second suitcase, which was in better condition, and so off they trundled, with Alec leading the conga line down the road in the early hours of the morning searching for another hotel room. What a sight that would have been.

Isobel followed Alec, then John carrying a suitcase, followed by Jack struggling and fighting with the handleless suitcase, every now and again he would stop and reposition the case in his arms and, once or twice, he struggled to put the suitcase on his shoulder. Eventually, they found a suitable hotel, which was the third hotel scrutinised by Alec. However, when shown the room, it did not have an ocean view, so Alec requested a room with a view of the ocean, insisting that it should be the same price as the room without the view. He got his way! Jack got back at 3:30 am, absolutely exhausted.

That was not the end of the Alec saga. Every time we went out to dinner, Alec walked, as best he could, along the street, scrutinising every restaurant. If it passed his inspection, he studied the menu and checked the prices of the meals. He would always choose the cheapest restaurant.

Jack was not impressed with this charade. 'I'm not doing that again,' he vowed. 'We will find a restaurant and go on our own.' We did just that, and found it much more relaxing without the hassle of finding the cheapest restaurant.

This was the last leg of our journey and we had so looked forward to our time in Hawaii, which, to this day, is still my favourite holiday destination. We were determined to make the most of it.

However, after such a long time away we were also looking forward to going home.

*Jack and Sue in love*

## Chapter Eleven
## **Double Trouble**
## 1970–1974

At last, we were home.

We arrived late in the afternoon, utterly exhausted, so we left our bags unopened and fell into bed early – everything could wait until the morning. Jack was up just after 5 am and settled in the lounge room with a cup of coffee and a pile of mail, waiting for 7 am, when Doug the horse trainer was free to take phone calls. He was anxious to talk to Doug; during the trip, we'd heard that Just Jack had won three consecutive races! Jack was elated and looking forward to Just Jack's next race.

They had a long chat and Jack told Doug we would come and visit on Sunday. Doug lived in Hay Street Randwick, adjacent to POW hospital, in a small, painted-brick home, probably built in the early 1900s. As you walked through the front door, there was a bedroom on each side of the hallway. The hallway led to a small lounge room which was so dark you almost needed a torch to find your way through.

The windows were shrouded in dark emerald-green velvet curtains which I'm sure held 50 years of dust, and the furniture

– a wooden table with four chairs tucked under, and an ancient three-seater lounge – all covered with dusty sheets, indicating that the room had not been used for many years. The space smelt musty and forgotten, and choked you as you walked through.

Entering the small kitchen, I admired the classic Aga stove built into a brick alcove, taking pride of place. Along the left-hand wall, a cupboard housed the sink and a cold-water tap. On the other wall, a window looked out to the stables. Here, there was a small table and a chair, and this was where Doug's wife Pearl sat for most of her life, presiding over her domain, in her dressing gown, nightie and slippers, with her grey hair in curlers, chain smoking.

On race days, she would sit there listening to the races on the radio, bent over the racing section of the newspaper spread out over the table, and a small notebook in which she recorded all her bets. Earlier in the day she would have examined all the races and marked out her fancies and then asked Doug if he knew 'a good thing,' that is, who would win. She gave Doug her bets scribbled on a scrap of paper with the money and he put her bets on the TAB for her. Some days, she would have about 10 bets during the afternoon. She always liked to tell you how on the mark her bets had been. This was her world.

Their back door led onto an asphalt-covered quadrangle, flanked on two sides by horse boxes and on the third side, the feed room and a sand roll. Not a blade of grass in sight. The sand roll was spacious, about 4 m by 4 m, the floor thickly covered with sand, and completely enclosed, with a large barn-door entrance. Doug gave the horses a roll in the sand every day, which they love, it's like giving them playtime. As the horse entered the sand roll, it would prance around, whinnying excitedly, then suddenly drop down into the sand and roll from side to side, legs flailing around, for ten minutes or so. Then, it would abruptly jump up and Doug had to be ready to quickly put a lead on the horse and open the door. The horse would jump through the opening and then Doug walked the horse back to its stable.

While we were standing in the quadrangle chatting in the sun, Doug said he had some money for Jack from the bets he placed for Jack while we were away. Jack was expecting a couple of hundred dollars.

'No, no!' exclaimed Doug. 'It's *a lot* more than that!'

Jack looked surprised. Doug explained how he had put all the money – the whole $70 – on the first race, then all the winnings from the first race were placed on the second race, and then all the money won on the second race went on to the third race, which is how we'd ended up with a total of $25,000.

Now, Doug didn't like banks, he didn't trust them, so all this money was either under the mattress, behind the fridge, up in the roof, under the lounge, and goodness knows where else. He was hunting around and pulling out money from all over the place. We were in a state of shock or maybe amusement. Jack reminded Doug that half of this money was his. When Jack realised how much money there was, he said to Doug, 'Why don't you let me buy you a block of flats?'

No, Doug shook his head, he didn't want to do that, so we left him with his half share. Goodness knows what he did with it. He certainly didn't buy Pearl a dress, because whenever we popped in, she was still in her nightie, slippers and dressing gown, with curlers in her hair and a cigarette hanging out her mouth.

Our time of magic with Just Jack ended abruptly. Sadly, about two weeks later, a very distressed Doug phoned Jack to tell him that Just Jack was spooked by a car while they were walking along the road from Randwick Racecourse to Doug's stables, and Just Jack was knocked over by a vehicle. Doug was devastated. He couldn't understand how it could happen as he had walked Just Jack along this road every morning without any incidents. He had been walking horses along this road for years, just as other trainers had, and there had never been an accident like this before. Just Jack had to be put down. The whole camp was in mourning, we couldn't believe what had happened.

The Just Jack winnings, Jack decided, would go towards a block of land so that we could build a house for our family. John told Jack that there were waterfront blocks being auctioned at Lilli Pilli. We went to the auction and bought a waterfront block for $27,000.00. When we got home Jack said, 'I should have bought the three blocks.' I'm not sure that the bank manager would have agreed with him.

John suggested we talk to our mutual friend Pat. (Pat and his wife Peg had been with us in Canada, they were the other couple with John and Meg). Pat was a Master Builder, and we happily placed ourselves in his capable hands. He drew up plans for a three-level home on the steep waterfront block. The top level was a three-car garage, opening in to the bedroom level of four bedrooms and two bathrooms. The middle level was the main entry, kitchen, dining, lounge room and family room looking out over an outdoor pool. Then, the lower level was 'the dungeon,' which was a room built around a rock wall. It took a while to get the plans approved by Sutherland Shire Council, but eventually they were passed, and building started. How exciting!

The three of us settled into a routine of work, eat and sleep. We were a happy little family settling into life together. Judy was enjoying her work at Jack's office, and I felt proud of the way she was managing. However, life was about to change dramatically. In October I discovered I was pregnant. I phoned John's office and made an appointment to see him just before Christmas. He confirmed that I was pregnant with an expected birth in June 1971. I was a little bigger than he expected and he wanted me to have an X-ray in February, just in case it was a multiple birth. The wait was agonising, but we had distractions – there was Christmas, my birthday, then Judy's birthday on New Year's Eve, and horse sales.

We went to the Summer Yearling Sales at Newmarket, Randwick. This had become an annual event for Jack, who loved to go and inspect the yearlings with Doug. At this sale, there was a yearling of particular importance to them. It was a colt with a pedigree that interested Doug and Jack: the colt was by Just Great (Imp), out of a mare well known to them, Dispose. Dispose was out of the mare Lavena who was the dam of Just Jack, so you can understand why they were keen to buy this yearling.

Doug looked him over closely, checking his mouth, his legs and making sure that he walked up well balanced. They were excited because he looked so good. Jack bought this colt for $600, which was not a lot of money for a yearling. Doug and Jack walked the yearling across to Doug's stables and on the way, Doug's mate Bernie saw them, and as they walked past, Bernie yelled, 'What are you buying Doc, dog's meat?'

He was referring to buyers who buy the cheapest horses and sell them to the knackery for dog's meat. Doug and Jack laughed and went on their merry way to Doug's stables, where the colt would rest for a few days before being sent to Billy the breaker, who would break him in and pre-train him. After the pre-training, Billy would put him in a paddock at his farm to grow out. Doug went to Billy's place every month or so to keep an eye on him and when he thought he was ready, he would bring him in to his stables for training.

Jack asked Doug to name him, giving him a list of names that we liked. At the bottom of the list was Lazy Pat, named after our friend who was building our house. It was a little joke, because Pat was anything but lazy, rather, a very hard worker and a great friend. I hoped Pat took the name as a sign of our affection for him and that Lazy Pat would carry on the winning tradition of Just Jack. Time would tell.

During the pregnancy, I organised the office so that we would manage. Judy was mastering the reception duties and I would do all the typing and accounts at home. The letters were now being recorded on a Dictaphone and I brought all the account records home. The dining table was our home office.

I felt confident that Judy was managing the office and I was managing the letters and accounts with time to spare, so I thought I would study for the Leaving Certificate/Higher School Certificate to overcome my lack of education which overshadowed my self confidence. I applied, was accepted, and set myself up, spending half a day most days studying.

I was well and truly showing by the time the day arrived for my X-ray in March (it was not considered safe to take X-rays until the foetus was in the fifth month). I was feeling nervous, and after the X-ray, I went to John's office to wait for a result. I didn't have long to wait. John came in with a silly grin on his face, and the X-ray in his hand. He ushered me into his consulting room and put the films on the X-ray box and flicked the switch on, and there they were: two babies, one up and one down.

Oh my goodness, I had better sit down.

'Do you want to tell Jack, or will I?' asked John.

'I think you should,' I replied. 'I am feeling a bit queasy.'

That's when Jack strolled in to the room. His eyes went straight to the films on the X-ray box. He went pale and sat down. It was a shock for all of us. When you fall pregnant you naturally think of one baby, now suddenly everything had to be doubled.

In April, I arranged for a typist to take over the typing of Jack's letters as soon as I entered hospital, and I thought she could continue until the babies were a month old, and then we could reassess the situation. She told me she was an experienced typist with good medical terminology.

The latter stages of the pregnancy were exhausting. Apart from the sheer fatigue of lumping around this big bump, trying to sleep at night was almost impossible as I was so uncomfortable. Our unit was four flights of stairs up from the garage, and during the last couple of weeks, Jack would get behind me and place his hands low on my back to gently help me up the stairs.

By this stage, I'd realised that with twins, I'd probably not manage to continue with my school studies. So, I withdrew from my studies, which left me feeling loss and regret, but I had so much to plan for that there was little time to squander on the emotional abandonment of my studies. I have to save my precious emotions for the tasks ahead.

On 3 May after dinner, Jack was called back to the hospital and as he left, I told him I felt unwell, and it might be a good idea to know what ward he was going to in case I needed him.

'Let me look down your throat,' he said. I thought, why does he want to look down my throat? It is the wrong part of my anatomy. Anyway, I complied. He asked me to say *Ahhh*, then announced I looked okay to him. 'Don't worry,' he added. 'You have six weeks to go before the babies are due.' I couldn't make up my mind if he was being funny and making fun to lighten the situation, or if he was being serious. Surely, he was not being serious? There were times where his sense of humour was hard to follow.

He arrived home about 10 pm and I was getting ready for bed when my waters broke, and then it was a mad scramble. Jack and

Judy were falling over each other trying to get organised and find my bag. Jack phoned John and the hospital and then we left for the hospital. As we arrived, we were met at the front door by a wardsman with a wheelchair and blanket.

Our twin girls were born at The Sutherland Hospital with John the attending obstetrician. Jacqueline was born at 2:10 am and Sara at 2:18 am. The babies were six weeks premature and placed straight into humidicribs.

Jack popped in to see me during his morning ward round and I was in tears.

'Why are you crying? You have two beautiful babies.'

'I haven't seen them yet,' I told him, so he trotted off to find the sister-in-charge and they brought the babies in to me for my first look. They were beautiful, my heart was bursting with love. When I looked at Jacqueline, she had a sprinkle of curls on top of her head. Her name came to me easily, she was to be Jack's namesake, Jacqueline, then I looked at Sara, she had the sweetest little baby face with rosebud lips. I couldn't think of a name for her, it had to be something special.

She remained nameless for four days, which worried poor Aunt Muriel, who was anxious that I had not named one of the babies. I finally decided on Sara, which in Hebrew means Princess. They were very tiny babies: Jacqueline weighed six pounds and Sara weighed five pounds, 13 ounces, which was not bad for six-week premature babies.

John and the Sister-in-Charge, Sister Hampson, came to see me to check if I had any problems. As John walked into the room he had a serious air about him, he chatted for a while and then he pulled up a chair and sat down.

This worried me, this was not our easy going, friendly, familiar friend. He had a frown and fidgeted a bit, then he told me that

Jacqueline had bilateral talipes equinovarus, otherwise known as clubfoot, both her feet were twisted. The cause may have been the foetal position, or congenital.

Her little legs and feet were placed in plaster casts, which were to be changed every week for the first six weeks. At six weeks, the plaster would be replaced with metal splints and gentle massage. I was a bit shocked and the tears started to flow. My poor little baby! What if she couldn't walk, or have deformed feet all her life? Then I thought about Judy and what she'd been through. She now manages very well, I thought, I am sure this will work out.

On the fourth day in hospital, Jack told me that the girl I had arranged to do the typing resigned, she couldn't cope.

'Don't worry, just leave it all till I come home,' I said to Jack. 'I will do it when I get home.' When I made that bold statement, little did I realise what I was in for.

We were discharged from hospital on the tenth day, it was quite an event, with people everywhere wishing us well.

Our unit only had two small bedrooms, one for Jack and I, and the second bedroom for Judy. So, the lounge/dining became the babies' room. We were starting to run out of room. There were two cribs, a portable change table, a baby bath, bundles of cloth nappies, and a cardboard box filled with baby clothes. Then, on one end of the dining table we had all the office account records, a large old Royal typewriter and piles of paper.

Our lives would never be the same again.

We settled them into their bassinets. Jacqui was the sweetest baby, she just lay in her crib looking around. Sara, on the other hand, cried from the moment we stepped into the unit. Oh my goodness, what was I doing wrong?

We changed her nappy, we fed her, we burped her, we changed her nappy again. Was she too hot or was she too cold? Did she feel sick or have a pain? Was she terribly ill?

After an hour or so of unrelenting crying, I decided that there must be something terribly wrong with her. I asked Jack to get a baby doctor to come and see her. He obliged, calling his friend Dr Albert Mar, and Albert, bless his heart, amiably came to see if Sara was about to die of some mysterious condition.

He examined her carefully and then, with a knowing smile on his lips and a twinkle in his eyes, pronounced that she was normal, he could find nothing wrong with her. In retrospect, after having a little more baby experience, I think she probably had reflux, but this was never mentioned. Sara seemed to cry most of the time for five months, meanwhile, Jacqui was quiet as a little lamb.

The first week was bedlam. The babies needed feeding every two hours. I was breastfeeding and found the easiest way to manage two babies at once was to sit on the lounge room floor with my back against the wall and a pillow on each side of me with a baby on each boob. Oh my goodness, what a challenge! It was a nightmare.

By the end of the first week, I had had very little sleep and was so sleep deprived I couldn't think. I was struggling to fit in some typing, I had ten days of reports to catch up on, then there was the bathing, the washing, the cooking, and other house duties, plus all the dramas of building a house.

Judy's Great Aunt Muriel came to the rescue with a gift of a nappy service which delivered fresh nappies weekly and provided two buckets for the collection of the used nappies. Thank goodness for Aunt Muriel, what a saint. Another angel came in the guise of my mother, who arrived at my doorstep every morning at 9 am and left at about 3 or 4 every afternoon. What would you do without a mum?

During the first week at home, I had to take Jacqui to an

*Aunt Muriel known as Moo Moo*

orthopaedic specialist, Dr Skip Grant, for the change of her leg/foot plasters. I was driving a station wagon at this stage of my life, and for the first few weeks, the babies travelled in the back of the station wagon in one basinet, top and tailed, they were so small they easily fitted in the one bassinet basket, and I think they were comforted by being together.

After I arrived at Dr Grant's rooms (his office was in the same building as Jack's), I was greeted by the physiotherapist, Barbara, who took Jacqui and said to me that I should wait in the waiting room while she replaced the plaster. She told me mothers become very distressed and get in the way when their babies are crying.

I was so glad when it was all over, and Jacqui, bless her sweet little heart, looked at me with her beautiful eyes without a sound or a cry. When I left Dr Grant's office, I was greeted by some friends from the building, who all wanted to see the babies.

In the second week, I took the babies to a baby clinic, a service provided to new mothers. A clinic Sister weighs the babies to make sure they are making sufficient weight gains and help with any other crises.

The Sister was concerned Jacqui and Sara were not putting on weight and suggested that if they failed to make sufficient weight gains the following week, I should go on to a complement-feeding regime, which is breast feeding plus a bottle feed. I said I would rather do one or the other.

On my return the following week, they were still not making the appropriate weight gain, and so we agreed to put both babies on to bottle feeds. This made life a little easier as I could share the feeds with whoever was available to help. Feeding was hard work – because they were premature babies, they were very slow feeders, taking about an hour to drink just a few millilitres of milk.

I have never experienced such sleep deprivation in all my life. Whenever I had a spare minute, I fell asleep. It didn't matter if I was sitting, standing, or whatever. I survived on catnaps for the first five months, which was when Sara started to settle and sleep. Somehow, in the middle of the babies' routine, I had to fit in typing letters and keeping the account records.

Jack was amazing. He had to cope on little sleep as well, and when he arrived home, he was handed a baby with a bottle. Amazingly, the babies survived, and we survived.

When the twins were six weeks old, Jacqui's plasters were removed for the final time, and she was fitted with metal splints which were held in place by crepe bandaging. I was shown how to put the splints on and how to massage her tiny little feet, trying to straighten them out. She could now have a bath, rather than an all over body sponge, and she loved getting in the water. Her little feet were responding to the treatment and Dr Grant was very encouraging about her outcome.

Our babies were baptised when they were six weeks old, at the Cronulla Methodist Church. We asked the Minister if we could have the service at 2 pm on the Sunday, as Jack goes to the hospital in the morning, and it is the busiest time for me with the babies. He acquiesced and we invited my family, Aunt Muriel, and a few friends to attend this special occasion with us. It was a challenge getting everyone ready to get to the church on time.

I eventually caught up with all the typing and settled into a routine of feeding and typing, then bathing and feeding. After this feed, I settled the babies in their basinets for a sleep, then bundled the typing up and took it up to Jack while mum looked after the babies.

Our poor washing machine was in constant use. It was a new type of washing machine, which washed and dried the clothes. You put your wash on and when the wash was finished, it went into dryer mode. In my sleep-deprived state, I'm afraid I shrunk a few of the babies' knitted clothes. I should have been washing them by hand.

We moved into our house when Jacqui and Sara were seven months old. John's wife, Meg, courageously offered to mind the babies while we moved in. She did not tell me how she managed until 20 years later, when we were visiting John and Meg after they'd retired to the Gold Coast.

We were chatting about old times when Meg told us that when she looked after the twins, they were crying a lot and one of Meg's daughters, who was trying to study, said, 'When are those babies going home?' I guess she had a very tough day. How lovely of her not to complain or mention how she had tried to cope with two

*Our precious twins in their daddy's rocking chair*

crying babies. I was so grateful to her for looking after Jacqui and Sara that day as moving house is exhausting.

However, I was so looking forward to living in a house with four bedrooms and a study/office. Life would be so much easier, everything would have a place, we could use our dining room table for meals and sit on a lounge in the lounge room and our babies would have a bedroom.

Shortly after we moved into our house, Jack started to think about looking for a farm where he could spell his horses, and so when Jack was not on call at any of the hospitals, we would pack our little family into the station wagon and inspect properties.

Lazy Pat was to have his first race at Canterbury on 19 January 1972. I arranged for our friends Margot and Frank's twin daughters to babysit for us so that I could go with Jack to the races. Lazy Pat did not win but it was still a special day. Lazy Pat was set for another race on 9 July 1972, which he won. That was such a thrilling and exciting day!

In Spring 1972, we bought our first farm, at Exeter. The farm was a beautiful old property named Lohengrin and was the home of a Murray Grey Stud. The owner employed a farm manager who lived on the property with his wife. When Jack saw the Murray Grey cattle, he immediately fell in love with them. He talked to the farm manager Vince and asked him if he would like to stay on and manage the farm and set up a Murray Grey Stud, as well as look after the racehorses when they came for a spell. Vince was delighted and so was Doreen, his wife. Doreen adored our babies, who were now 18 months old and running around.

Vince was a genuine country cattleman with skin that had seen too much sun. However, he was always sensible and wore a broad-brimmed Akubra hat and long-sleeved shirts. Doreen was lovely, cuddly and grandmotherly. There was an instant rapport between the two families.

The property was situated on a country lane, no tar-sealed road here, just dust and potholes. There were two fibro homes on the property, but the crowning glory was a magnificent red bauxite gravel driveway lined with majestic torulosis pine trees sitting in a carpet of verdant green lawn. The torulosis were like sentries standing to attention in perfect symmetry along the driveway.

The driveway wound past Vince and Doreen's cottage, coming to an end at the old fibro house. The house was very unpretentious, a typical farmhouse without trimmings, giving it a sense of being unloved. The garden was unassuming and modest, with three huge liquidambar trees shrouding the house as you approached. As you drove past the house, you noticed a sprinkling of sasanqua camellia shrubs and a garden of bedraggled irises and gladioli huddled around its foundations.

The concrete path leading to the front door of the house was broken with bits missing, making it a trip hazard. 'Front door' was really a misnomer, as it looked more like a back door, and it was the only entry to the house. The path brought you to an open porch beneath a sad-looking trellis covered by a climbing clematis. The porch doubled as a mudroom, where everyone left their dirty boots and gumboots before they went inside.

Stepping through the entry, you walked into a biggish country kitchen – big enough for a table with six chairs fitting comfortably in the middle of the room. On the back wall of the kitchen stood a classic AGA wood-burning stove nestled in a brick alcove. This beautiful stove served as cooker and heater, and also heated water for the kitchen and bathroom.

Adjacent to the kitchen was the lounge, where a generous fireplace stood as the centre of attention in the colder months (at least eight to ten months of the year in this region). On the other wall, a small window looked out across the garden.

The hallway led to a bathroom and two bedrooms: one small, and the other, a large dormitory-style room which easily accommodated six single beds. The laundry was outside on the other side of the porch, a very basic affair with a cement wash tub and space designated for a washing machine.

Behind the house, a large, corrugated-iron shed housed the tractor, other farm implements and hundreds of bales of hay.

We named our property Inverness, after the beautiful city in Scotland, which appealed to Jack and his Scottish heritage. Our Murray Grey Stud was named the Inverness Murray Grey Stud.

Once we settled on the property, our priority was to find an appropriate paddock for Lazy Pat, who was to come to the farm for

# DOUBLE TROUBLE 1970-1974

*Our favourite bull 'Lusty' sitting like a dog in the paddock*

a long spell of up to one year. Vince suggested the back paddock, a nice quiet paddock with a dam and a stand of gum trees. Vince said he could check him each day and take him fresh lucerne hay.

Lazy Pat quickly settled into his paddock. Occasionally, Vince put a few cows (and an occasional bull) in with him to keep him company. Lazy Pat didn't seem to mind sharing his paddock.

Vince educated us about the Murray Greys and introduced us to all the influential people in the Murray Grey Stud world. We went to sales and purchased the very best bulls and cows. Within a short period of time, whenever Jack came to a sale, there was always a flurry to see who could entice him to bid.

It wasn't long before we had one of the best studs in NSW. Vince prepared the bulls and steers for all the important shows, starting with the local show, the Moss Vale Show, then the Canberra show, the Castle Hill Show and the grandest of them all, the Royal Easter Show. To country people, the Royal Easter Show is approached

*My father Irving with our show ribbons*

with great excitement and anticipation. It's where they meet up with their contemporaries, share a beer in someone's tent and catch up on all the gossip in the stud world.

To win a Grand Champion ribbon at the Royal Easter Show is like winning the lottery. It means that your stock with the blood line of the Champion is worth more money in the sale ring, and the stud receives a lot of free and valuable publicity.

To accommodate our family on the trips to the shows, we decided to buy a campervan. It was such a good idea. The days at the show were always long and hot, or long and wet, and with the campervan we had somewhere to wash, eat and rest. It was ideal – we had a small kitchen with a fridge and a stove, a table with bench seating, beds if we needed them and, most importantly, a toilet. It was like a travelling motel room, including closets for spare clothing and kitchen cupboards for plates, cutlery and food.

We were very self-sufficient. It made our trips to the showgrounds so much fun, and I was surprised at how well Jack drove this large vehicle.

That year, Jack, John and another friend, Bob (an Ear, Nose and Throat Specialist) had been meeting about their plans to build a medical centre to cater for specialists in the Caringbah area. They decided to set up a company, find a builder and borrow money.

John knew a retired builder, Bill Lawson. The wheels were set in motion, and the search began for the perfect site.

In the intervening time, it transpired Lazy Pat's long spell in the back paddock was just what he needed.

**# 1973 Lazy Pat won the Alexandra Graduation Stakes at Canterbury, 3200m. What an exciting day! Did we have a potential champion on our hands?**

Doug was very excited about Lazy Pat and predicted a great future for him.

Life was full and demanding. Jack's practice was extremely busy, and the farm was taking care of any spare time we might have had, plus two little ones, and another on the way!

At my pre-natal check, my obstetrician, John, scared the living daylights out of me.

'You are bigger than I expected,' he said. I think you need to have an X-ray to rule out another twin pregnancy.'

I felt ill. Fortunately, John was able to organise an urgent X-ray. There was great relief all around when John put up the films showing just one baby. Oh, Hallelujah! Waiting for the results, my mind went into overdrive, trying to imagine how I would manage twins again, plus two toddlers.

Rebecca was born on a winter's night in 1974.

As John would be away for the birth, he'd arranged for our

mutual friend, Dr David Richardson, to care for me. I saw David for a check-up and he told me I should be induced at TSH. I didn't mind. I would be very happy to unload this bundle.

All went well and Rebecca Ruby came into the world at 1:13 am. I had secretly hoped for a boy but how could I be disappointed? Rebecca was beautiful, and so easy; no crying, no plasters. After coping with two newborns at once, I suppose one would seem easy.

Jack had other things on his mind. Lazy Pat was racing on Saturday and he was full of anticipation. I was still in hospital and felt sad that I would not be with Jack, as Doug had told him Lazy Pat would run a good race and had a decent chance of winning.

Lazy Pat ran a gutsy race and came second in the AJC City Tattersals Club Cup (a listed race). Lazy Pat was always ridden from behind, and when he came into the home straight, his jockey would encourage him to race past the other horses, and on this occasion, he didn't quite manage to get past the horse in front of him.

On Jack's way home, he called in at the hospital. He was very, very exuberant and excited to tell me about the race. That wasn't all he had to tell me, ... as he was reversing out of his parking space at the racetrack, he said 'this silly woman' ran into his car. He later admitted it wasn't the woman's fault. He hadn't looked where he was going and backed into her car and had to pay damages. I suspect he had had a few too many beers celebrating.

Jack's inquiring mind led him to an interest in Holter Monitors which are a small wearable device that records the heart's rhythm, identifying unusual heart rhythms, intermittent atrial fibrillation, and causes for sudden collapse.

While attending the 1973 Annual Scientific Meeting of the Cardiac Society of Australia and New Zealand, Jack went to the

Exhibition Hall and visited the stand of the company selling Holter Monitors. His interest in Holter Monitors developed following a string of complex patient cases. He purchased three Holter Monitors.

After using the Holter on a few occasions, we were overwhelmed by the extra work and it was evident that we needed to bring someone into our practice to put the Holters on, remove them the following day, then print out the ECG rhythm strips to give to Jack so that he could write the report. We approached my sister, Robyn, who was thrilled to be offered a part-time position, as at the time, she had two little boys, one aged 3 and the other eight months. She started in September 1974, working three days a week.

# Chapter Twelve
# The Dawn of Echocardiography
# 1975

*# In 1975 Lazy Pat won the AJC Anniversary Handicap 2400m*

Keen to purchase another yearling, Jack attended the 1975 Easter Yearling sales. He found a yearling out of Dispose by Spacebird. (Dispose was Lazy Pat's dam). He couldn't believe his luck. He loved this broodmare line because he had had so much success with it. Anxiety tempered his excitement – he desperately wanted this colt.

We inspected the colt, and he didn't disappoint. Jack spoke to the breeder, and asked him how much he expected the colt to sell for. 'Probably $30,000.00,' he answered.

Jack had the winning bid: $30,000.00, just as the breeder had suggested. Anyway, Jack was thrilled, and asked Doug to manage the colt for him.

We made a list of 12 names for the colt and submitted them to the Australian Stud Book (ASB), but none were acceptable. Shortly after our knockback from the ASB, Jack saw his friend Andie at the races. Andie is a racehorse owner who also has a Murray Grey Stud. Jack complained to Andie about how hard it was to name a horse. Andie offered to find a name for the colt. True to his word, ten days later he phoned and put forward the name Unwanted. What a wonderful name for a colt out of the mare Dispose.

In early 1975, Jack had become aware of new technology in cardiology: scientists were interested in using ultrasound to identify heart structures. Jack had previously attended a meeting at PHH, where Dr Harvey Feigenbaum was the principal speaker giving a talk on the detection of pericardial fluid using ultrasound. Dr Feigenbaum has since been recognised as the Father of Echocardiography.

The talk sparked Jack's curiosity and he started to read up on Echocardiography (Echo, or cardiac ultrasound). He wanted to learn how to use this cutting-edge technology. Jack spoke to colleagues to gauge their opinions and all were supportive. He decided to go ahead and become trained. He began investigating hospitals offering courses in Echo and talked to course co-ordinators, who made him aware of the need for a sonographer, as the studies were time consuming and a cardiologist's time is valuable.

He considered the advice and came to me. He said it would be sensible if I trained as well and became a cardiac sonographer, as in 1975 there were only a handful of cardiac sonographers in Australia, and all were employed by large city hospitals. At this point, there were no Echo-training facilities in Australia.

This proposition stunned me. I felt my lack of formal education would be an impediment, but strangely, this didn't worry Jack. He was of the opinion that I had sufficient knowledge and intelligence to master this application, and together we would manage. He said he could teach me the physics and science in preparation for the course, and the rest would be taught at the course.

In retrospect, Echo was, at this stage, very much in its infancy. This was a time of pioneering, exploration and experimentation.

# THE DAWN OF ECHOCARDIOGRAPHY 1975

We purchased our first machine, a Smith Kline, in 1975. It was a basic M-mode machine. As soon as it arrived, we started using it. The installation technician from Smith Kline gave us basic instructions and we practised on each other until we became familiar with the controls and how to hold the transducer with the left hand, so that the right hand was free to manipulate the controls.

We purchased Dr Harvey Feigenbaum's book on Echocardiography, which taught us how to recognise the patterns on the graph. The study is performed by placing a transducer on the chest wall over the region of the heart. Before you start, a lubricant gel is applied to the chest to give a slippery surface so that the transducer glides over the chest wall without friction. The transducer sends sound waves into the heart, the sound waves are reflected back off the walls of the heart and the valves. The reflected sound waves are received back via the transducer and the machine converts the reflected sound waves and then produces a graph which is printed on heat-sensitive graph paper.

Towards the end of 1975, a colleague of Jack's told him of an Echocardiography course at the University of Washington in Seattle (UWS). Jack phoned UWS and arranged for us to enrol in their Echocardiography course. We would be there for two to three months, attending the course and doing practical work in their Echo Lab.

The next available course started at the end of July 1976. We were instructed to read and understand all that was in Dr Harvey Feigenbaum's book before the first day of the course. It was expected that when we arrived at the university, we would have sound knowledge of the physics of ultrasound as well as an encompassing knowledge of cardiac diseases and congenital abnormalities.

*Our three little girls, Jacqueline, Rebecca and Sara*

That was easy for Jack, but for me it was very challenging, balancing my work with study and the demands of nurturing and loving three beautiful little girls.

The first chapter in Dr Feigenbaum's book was on the physics of ultrasound. The reality of what I had to achieve dawned on me. It seemed like another language to me, as I'd left school at 14 and had not studied physics or science. I had an enormous task ahead of me. Jack became my teacher, and we persevered together most nights, usually after 9 pm, sometimes for an hour, and there were times when it was longer.

Outside of those late-night sessions, Jack delivered mini lessons on cardiac diseases and congenital abnormalities and taught me about therapies and how drugs work and some of their side effects. Fortunately, a lot of this was familiar to me from typing his patient reports.

Somehow, astoundingly, we accomplished our mission, a

testament to Jack's unending patience and his brilliant teaching. He managed to analyse and dissect the science and physics to a very basic level so that I could understand and then build the topic up to where I needed it.

With this difficult phase behind me, I found Echocardiography became the most exciting, interesting and stimulating part of my life, and was surprised at how easily I met the challenge and how it became second nature to me.

This proved to be a significant turning point in my life. Jack had given me precious gifts; not only was I receiving the gift of education that I had yearned for, and which had been denied me through life's stumbling blocks, but he also gave me the gifts of self-esteem and self-confidence. And, not to forget his greatest gift of all, his love.

Now came the challenge of arranging our three-month trip to America.

We asked Vince's wife, Doreen, if she would accompany us and look after our young family while we studied at the university hospital. She was delighted! She loved our girls and was like a grandmotherly Mary Poppins. Doreen had not travelled out of NSW, let alone overseas, so this was a wonderful opportunity and a grand adventure for her. We asked a travel agent to make all the arrangements, including accommodation close to the University of Washington hospital.

Meanwhile, we were having great success with our Inverness Murray Grey Stud. Vince our farm and stud manager, took our best cows and bulls to shows this year and throughout the year our stud won 9 championship ribbons at Melbourne, Moss Vale, Canberra, Goulburn and Berry Shows, the grandest of them all being the bull Michaelong Watergate winning Senior Champion Bull and Grand Champion Bull at the Melbourne 'Royal' Show.

A splendid result for our emerging Inverness Murray Grey Stud.

In 1975 Australia experienced major upheaval in its medical system. The Whitlam Government introduced Medibank (the first version of Medicare) on 1 July 1975. The introduction of the system met with ferocious opposition from many in the medical profession.

# Chapter Thirteen
# The Amazing 'Lazy Pat'
# 1976

*For Lazy Pat 1996–1997 race results refer to Horse Lists in Further Reading.*

There was so much going on in 1976. Early in the year, Jack, John and Bob were charging ahead with plans to buy a property in Caringbah to build a medical centre. John's friend Bill had agreed to come out of retirement and build the medical centre.

Bob told John and Jack that he'd noticed an old fibro house for sale in Gibbs Street Miranda, near the railway station. It turned out to be the house where the late general practitioner Dr Ken Nolan had his rooms. Before his death in 1971, he had practised there for many years, demonstrating humility, enthusiasm and dedication toward his many patients.

It seemed like this would be the most appropriate site for the medical centre.

They bought the property and plans were drawn up for a two-storey building, seven units per floor, with underground parking.

The plans were eventually passed by Council and construction began in 1976.

This was also a triumphant year for Lazy Pat, who was now six years old. Lazy Pat was racing well and had been placed in his previous races, so Doug entered Lazy Pat in the Lord Mayor's Cup in May. Jack was excited and anxious as ever, because Doug was very confident that Lazy Pat would win.

We invited one of Jack's colleagues, Don, a general physician and a friend, to accompany us to the races. We shared our hopes that Lazy Pat would win the Lord Mayor's Cup, and suggested he come with us in our car.

Jack was driving and Don poked fun at him along the way.

'How much did you pay for your shoes, Jack?' he said.

'Oh, about $20,' replied Jack.

Don laughed and told Jack he should buy decent shoes, bragging that his Italian shoes had set him back $700.

Jack declared he could never spend that much on a pair of shoes. We arrived at the Rosehill Racetrack and as Don got out of the car, lo and behold, the front soles of his shoes dropped off. Jack and I could not believe our eyes and could not stop laughing, but Don was distressed.

'Stop laughing! What am I going to do? I can't go flopping around like a penguin all day, everyone will think I am some kind of idiot!'

We pulled out the First Aid Kit out and found some Band Aids and adhesive tape to secure his floppy soles. That should teach him to go around skiting about how much he pays for his shoes.

Lazy Pat won the Lord Mayor's Cup a Listed Race at Rosehill on 9 May. His winning time equalled the race record of 2 minutes and 32.6 seconds.

Bert Lillye covered the story in the *Sydney Morning Herald*.

*Sue accepting one of the many trophies won by their horses*

Early in 1976, Judy met Peter Roadley at a church she had joined and they started going out. The young man had immigrated to Australia with his parents when he was 12. He was an only child and has a passion for music and singing.

On 23 April 1976, Judy and Peter announced their engagement at a party we held for them at home. Judy and Peter decided to wed in June, so there was much excitement in the house. With only two months to go, there were dresses to be made, and caterers, flowers and wedding cake to be organised.

Our house was filled with joy and love, it was Judy and Peter's wedding day. Judy was filled with anticipation and expectation. The day did not disappoint, dawning glorious and sunny. The previous weeks had been abuzz with planning and organisation for their happy day. Jacqui, Sara and Rebecca were Judy's flower girls, and on the day looked so sweet in their lemon-yellow velvet dresses. Judy was a radiant and beautiful bride. The ceremony was at a church in Sutherland, followed by a catered reception at home.

Making the most of the sunshine, we held the reception poolside. In the afternoon, Peter brought out his guitar and serenaded Judy with songs he'd written for her. Everyone was very happy for Judy, and for Judy, it was a realisation of her dream.

Before the wedding, we had been house hunting for Judy, looking for a suitable home for her. Most importantly, it had to be on flat ground with no stairs, and near our home. Finally, we found a house in Caringbah, which met our requirements. It was on flat ground and with only a couple of steps and was close enough to our home, that Jack could pop in frequently on his way home. The house needed a touch of paint and a few repairs, which Peter's father volunteered to attend to and the steps would be smoothed out with ramps.

The month after Judy's wedding, Jack and I, the three girls and Doreen left for Seattle. This trip was going to be a challenge. Jacqui and Sara were 5 years old and Rebecca would turn 2 while we were away. I was so grateful to have an extra pair of hands during our trip.

Surprisingly, the flight over was not as difficult as I had imagined. Our little girls were well behaved and settled in quickly under Doreen's grandmotherly influence. I think that our lives had been so busy, travelling to and from farms and going to shows, sales, and horse races, that the girls had become adaptable. On our various trips, they would each pack a little bag with books and their favourite Strawberry Shortcake dolls to play with, making up stories and adventures which entertained them for hours.

As the plane was not full, the flight attendants had time to make a fuss over the children, handing out colouring-in books and pencils when they needed distraction, and when they seemed tired, they made beds for them on the empty seats. We were so spoilt.

The PAN AM flight took us from Sydney to Auckland, where we had a short stopover of an hour or so, then to Honolulu, where we changed planes and then on to Vancouver. At Vancouver, we caught a bus to Seattle and then a taxi from the bus station to the hotel. By the time we got to Seattle we were all exhausted; our travel time door to door was two days. Fortunately, I had arranged our trip so that we arrived on a Thursday and had a weekend for our body clocks to adjust.

I felt confident that I had anticipated every scenario and that our plans were well organised. Doreen would look after the children while Jack and I attended our teaching sessions in the hospital's Echocardiography Laboratory at the University of Washington. Part of the day would be spent on blackboard lessons and the rest of the time on live demonstrations with patients in the hospital. On weekends, we planned to spend time with the children, going to a park for a picnic, taking short drives into the countryside, or swimming in the hotel pool.

But sometimes life throws a curve ball.

We were relieved that we had arrived safely at the hotel. I had booked a suite so that we could manage our family life as best we could, and we settled in. On our second day I thought we should find out where the hospital was so that we could plan our daily trips. I called the Concierge and asked for a map and the directions to the University Hospital. Well shock, horror, the University Hospital was nowhere near our hotel.

Our travel agent, who had been recommended by a friend, appeared to me to be overly confident and boasted of her travel knowledge. However, this was not our experience. This hotel was nowhere near the University or the University Hospital, as I had requested. We had been looking forward to walking to and from the hospital, but instead, the hospital was on the opposite side of Seattle. She obviously had not done her homework, all she had to do was to look at a map.

This was so disappointing. It meant that we had to hire a car and drive on the opposite side of the road, for an hour to an hour and a half depending on traffic, across Seattle to the hospital. Then, after finishing, we had to make the nerve-wracking return-trip back to the hotel. Doing this five days a week was excruciating. We were annoyed, to say the least.

Jack was brilliant. He quickly adapted to driving on the opposite side of the road, with only a couple of near misses. I thought of Robert Burns saying in his poem *To a Mouse* – 'the best laid schemes o' mice an' men often go awry.'

But when the going gets tough, the tough get going, and so we did. It was all made possible because we had Doreen, our Mary Poppins, who didn't mind the long days looking after three littlies. She exuded a beautiful motherliness, energy and tenacity. Looking after three young children is not for the faint hearted.

Calm, kind, joyful and fun, Doreen took them on an adventure every day, giving them wonderful lifelong memories. When we arrived back at the hotel each day, the children would jump up and down, screaming with delight, telling us stories of their escapade that day.

They'd travel by bus or train, or if the destination was nearby, they would walk, with Rebecca in a stroller. One of their cherished memories is the day Doreen took them to the movies to see *Pippi Longstocking*. The three little munchkins all imagined that they were Pippi Longstocking on an adventure, and they still reminisce about it to this day.

Jack and I were enrolled in a 'Training Program in M-Mode

Echocardiography,' which was followed by a 'Training Program in M-Mode and Doppler Echocardiography' to be held in the Department of Echocardiography (adult and paediatric) headed by Dr Simeon Rubinstein, at the University of Washington, Seattle.

The second program was an introductory program into the next generation of Echocardiogram machines being developed by Advanced Technology Laboratory. It was breathtaking to be shown what was in the future, to be given a taste of what is to come.

Our time at the University of Washington was stimulating and exhilarating. We were immersed in the wonderful, exciting world of cardiac ultrasound and also introduced to the upper echelon of the university hospital's cardiac department, who were recognised throughout the medical world as leaders in Echocardiography, and in particular, Doppler Echocardiography.

We were also taken to the offices and Research Laboratory at the factory of Advanced Technology Laboratory (ATL) where the ultrasound machines were being manufactured.

One of the engineers at ATL was part of the team that developed the Black Box for aviation.

ATL was a major supporter of the university hospital and all the ultrasound machines in the hospital were ATL machines. There must have been about 20 machines in the hospital and in its Research Laboratory, where they performed Echos on dogs in their aptly named 'Dog Lab.' The dogs appeared well looked after and even pampered. The only hospitals in Australia with an Echo machine at this stage were the major city hospitals, with one machine.

During our time in the Echo Lab at the university hospital and on our tour of the ATL factory, we were introduced to new advances being developed and trialled. Jack was intrigued by their new technique, Doppler. Based on the Doppler effect, the technique used sound waves to record the blood flow in the heart. The graph displayed the direction of flow, either forward flow or reverse flow, and distinguished between laminar flow and turbulent flow – laminar flow representing normal flow and turbulent flow representing turbulent flow through a stenotic valve orifice.

The machine also produced audio of the flow of blood through the valves. Researchers were looking for a way to measure the velocity of blood flow. If they could successfully measure the velocity, they could extrapolate the size of the valve orifice, presenting a major advance in the non-invasive diagnosis of valvular stenosis.

The research team at ATL also showed us a prototype two-dimensional sector scanner. Jack was enthusiastic and placed orders for the M-mode/Doppler machine and a forward order for the two-dimensional sector scanner.

We loved our stint in Seattle, where we were offered wonderful hospitality wherever we went. People were fascinated by an Australian family 'living' in their city and invited us to their homes, which were almost always built from beautiful timber, perhaps due to the abundance of trees in their forests. With its vast waterways against a backdrop of snow-capped mountains, Seattle is stunning.

After the completion of our Seattle programs, we followed up with a further one-week Training Program on M-Mode Echocardiography at the University of Oregon, Portland.

On our way home, we visited the Echo Labs of other university hospitals in California. We wanted to visit as many Echo Labs as we could so that we could collate ideas and standards from each, and look at how they set up their labs. This information would help us set up our own labs at home, one in TSH and one in Jack's consultation rooms.

Back in Sydney, Jack met with the Chief Medical Officer

(CMO) of TSH and offered to set up an Echo service in TSH. He told the CMO we would provide a machine and ancillary supplies and be responsible for the servicing of the machine. Our Echo service would be free to the hospital and offered to all patients, both private and public. All we needed was a room.

Jack told the CMO that I would perform the Echos and he would interpret the graphs and write the report. The service would be free until a Medibank number was available, and then only the private patients would be billed. The service would remain free to the hospital and public patients.

Late 1976, our offer was accepted and when our new ATL Echo/Doppler machine arrived, we moved our Smith Kline M-Mode machine to TSH. We were given a room on 2 West where we performed M-mode Echos on in-patients every morning from 7:30 am.

Although largish (H 160 cm × W 60 cm × D 70 cm), the machine was easily transportable, having four wheels on its base, and for the patients who were too ill to be moved, we took the machine to the bedside to perform the Echo. The freedom to easily move the machine around the hospital was a great asset.

We performed Echos on Jack's patients as well as patients referred by other doctors in the hospital. A provisional report was written in the patient's notes at the time of the Echo and an official report was delivered the following day with a copy to the referring doctor.

It was a very hectic life, organising three little girls, Jack's medical practice and Echo service at the hospital, and a farm with shows to go to and racehorses racing. We went to the farm on the weekends when Jack was not on call. When he was on call at TSH we stayed at home as the farm was a two-hour drive away, too far if there was an emergency.

On one of our precious weekends at home I could hear a loud knocking noise which I couldn't identify. I found Jack and he was a mystified as I was. He went to investigate and found Rebecca sitting in the boot of his precious Rolls Royce with a hammer, she was having a lovely time banging the boot of the car with the hammer, she did such a good job, the car had to be sent for repairs!

The Medical Centre was completed and opened in March 1977. Jack, John, Bob. and Gilbert all purchased suites in the new building. It didn't take long for the building to be fully occupied. It was a great success. There were male and female toilets on each floor, and a lift which serviced the garage level, ground floor and level one.

Jack and I had designed our suite, which featured two generously sized consultation rooms, a reception area, waiting room and a toilet for ourselves and our staff (which was considered a luxury). To accommodate our elderly and disabled patients, the suite was situated at the front of the building, on the ground floor.

## Chapter Fourteen
## **The Brothel**
## **1977–1978**

One Saturday afternoon, Mark L., Jack's friend in the RAAF in WWII, phoned Jack for a chat, out of the blue. He said he had been thinking of Jack and wondered how Jack had become such a popular doctor. He suggested that they should catch up and discuss a property he considered a good investment. He arranged for Jack and I to visit him at his new home in Bellevue Hill, and said he had also invited Jack's friend and colleague, Gilbert, and his wife, Judy.

Mark's new home had been the boarding house for a private school in the area. He was thrilled because it had a shower room with six showers and six toilets, which would solve the problem of the bathroom rush for his young family. The main bedroom was bigger than some people's homes.

We had a beautiful day, sitting in the sun enjoying a magnificent lunch prepared by Mark's wife, Beverley. After lunch, he told us about his proposal. He had found a property in Kings Cross and thought Jack and Gilbert might like to join him in this venture.

Jack was keen as he considered Mark to be a very astute property investor.

We arranged to inspect the property the following week. It was a building on a prominent corner in Kings Cross: three floors, with shops on the ground level. Mark pulled out the books and said, 'Here, have a look at the books and see for yourself the good returns.'

We looked and all appeared in order. He showed us the rooms: bare floorboards, an old iron bed, a small wooden wardrobe that had seen better days, and two old kitchen chairs. They didn't look very inviting. Still, with Mark's assurances, Jack and Gilbert decided to go ahead with the purchase, probably because of their confidence in Mark's property-investment skill.

Our investment with Mark and Gilbert seemed to be going along well. Every month or so, Mark would phone to say he was coming for a visit as he had a few 'cabbages' for us. When he arrived, he'd hand Jack and Gilbert a brown paper bag each. That was the way he ran the business.

A few months later, Mark phoned Jack and said he had been feeling unwell and was getting very breathless. Jack examined Mark and sent him for blood tests, which showed Mark had Leukaemia. He died six weeks later.

Gilbert and Jack decided they didn't have the time to manage the Kings Cross investment, and thought it would be best to sell it. Beverley agreed, she had enough to worry about. Out of the blue, she told us Mark had been paying the police to keep the place going.

This revelation shocked us, Gilbert and Jack are both men with a strong moral compass and always do what is right even when it is difficult or unpopular. – we didn't dare think – could it be a brothel???! Neither Jack nor Gilbert had any idea. Were we naïve?

# THE BROTHEL 1977–1978

Then we heard that police were cracking down on brothels in Kings Cross. The property went on the market immediately and, a week later, the real estate agent said there were two interested parties: a 'Madam' and a mystery buyer.

Gilbert and Jack decided to accept the Madam's offer, as who knows who the unidentified person would be? The Madam paid the deposit, and we signed the contract with a 90-day settlement. The 90 days came up and there was no settlement. We asked the solicitor, what should we do?

'If you knew who she's married to, you would do nothing.'

We took his advice and waited, and waited, and waited ... the wait was unendurable, we wanted to extricate ourselves from this unbelievable situation sooner rather than later. Then one day, months later, she turned up at the solicitor's office with a suitcase full of cash.

We asked the real estate agent about the unknown party and he said it was an agent for McDonalds! We should have sold it to 'the unknown buyer'.

We followed our short-lived foray into Sydney's hidden side of society, with a return to the USA in August 1977, for further studies in Echocardiography at the University of Oregon, Portland. Once again, we packed up the family, but this time, it would only be for two weeks. The course was a 'Training Program for M-Mode, and Two-Dimensional Echocardiography.'

As spring arrived, Unwanted was getting ready for his first race. Jack and Doug couldn't wait – they had great plans for Unwanted. He didn't disappoint, coming third in his first race.

At his next start, Unwanted won easily at Randwick. Jack and Doug felt that they may have a champion on their hands.

In March 1978, Unwanted came third in the Ranvet Stakes at Randwick, 2000m – Group 1. This was absolutely thrilling. Jack and Doug were ecstatic, and both considered Unwanted to be the best horse either of them had had.

*For 1978 Unwanted race results refer to Horse Lists in Further Reading.*

Unfortunately, this was not to be, as Unwanted developed navicular disease, now known as 'caudal heel pain syndrome,' and had to be retired. Unwanted did not race again. There was sorrow in the camp.

Lazy Pat was coming to the end of his splendid racing career. He had given us many wonderful, thrilling experiences watching him either win or almost win 46 times, and 10 of these races were stakes races.

*For Lazy Pat 1978 race results refer to Horse Lists in Further Reading.*

Overall, Lazy Pat raced 87 times for 6 wins, 16 seconds and 24 thirds. His prize winnings totalled $75,000.00. All six wins were in Stakes Races, seven of his second placings were in Stakes Races and three of his third placings were in Stakes Races. An extraordinary record for a $600 yearling. Neil Campton rode him 58 times out of the 87 races. A truly outstanding result.

In June 1978 we packed up the family and departed to America again, to attend a training program by Dr Rich Popp at the Department of Echocardiography at the University of Palo Alto, USA. This course was one-week full time, with one-on-one practical demonstration/learning sessions.

In September 1978 we made a quick second trip to the US, this time to San Francisco for a short course: two days full time, hands-on learning, organised by Dr N Schiller and Dr N Silverman of the Department of Echocardiography at the University of California, San Francisco.

## Chapter Fifteen
## Annus Horribilis × Two
## 1979–1984

At the beginning of 1979, my sister Robyn and I commenced a course at the Institute of Cardiopulmonary Technology (ICT) at Royal Prince Alfred Hospital, to become an Associate of the Institute of Cardiopulmonary Technology. The aim of the course was to learn to conduct electrocardiographs (ECGs) and to read ECGs, as well as understanding other cardiopulmonary technologies.

Meanwhile, our cattle stud and horse interests were expanding, and we were running out of room in Exeter, so Jack decided we should move to a larger property not too far from Sydney. He asked Vince to look for a suitable property. Vince phoned Jack the following week and told him he'd had a phone conversation with a friend of his, Ernie. We knew Ernie, who like us, was a member of the Murray Grey Society.

Ernie told Vince of a property out at Big Hill, just down the road from his place. Big Hill is 189 km southwest of Sydney. Named Mt Hannibal, the property was 1500 acres, with one house and a river running through some of the paddocks, situated in beautiful country amidst predominantly sheep-grazing properties. It was much larger than our 200-acre farm at Exeter.

The following weekend we drove down to look at this property, which was north-west of Goulburn, and about 29 km off the Hume Highway near Marulan. As we travelled down the road from Marulan to Mt Hannibal, after about 10 km, we came to the end of the bitumen road and landed on a dirt road for the next 20 km. This was not a good start. We eventually arrived and I have to say, first impressions are powerful. I thought YUCK!

It looked nothing like the Bowral farms we were used to, with green hills and immaculate paddocks surrounded by huge, mostly English, trees. However, here, the paddocks were rough and rocky, with lots of serrated tussock and thistles and a very occasional straggly tree, but when we found the river meandering through the property, it was easier to overlook some of the negatives.

The crystal-clear river ran over a bed of round, smooth stones and rocks, and along the banks stood a few elegant weeping willows, their graceful sweeping branches dancing in the breeze and playfully skimming across the surface of the river. We drove through the river, which was fun, and up to the small cottage, which sat on the crest of a small hill about half a kilometre from the start of the property.

The house was a small white weatherboard covered in cobwebs, with a corrugated-tin roof. To the right of the house, my eye was drawn to a magnificent apricot tree laden with fruit. At the back of the house, stood the mandatory corrugated-iron water tank and, keeping it company, the outdoor toilet, affectionately known as the 'dunny.'

This was a true bush 'dunny', an icon – a corrugated-iron cubicle with a door and a roof, sitting on a cement slab with a hole at the back of the slab, over which a toilet can sat, quite regally.

As there was no smelly 'dunny truck' to come and empty the toilet can, the toilet can had no bottom, and sat over the hole in the ground that would be around 4 to 6 feet deep (around 1 to 2 metres), deep enough to hold and hide all manner of secretions.

I shuddered at the thought of using that toilet. Inside, the cottage looked like no-one had lived in it for months, maybe years. Cobwebs and dust covered every surface. At least the kitchen looked serviceable, with a dirty old AGA stove and a few cupboards along one side of the kitchen, and a very dirty sink. The kitchen was big enough for a small table and four chairs. Next to the kitchen was a loungeroom.

Down the hallway, the bathroom was very basic, with a bathtub and a handbasin. Although, it too, was covered in dirt and cobwebs, you could see that it was acceptable, and would serve its purpose, after a good clean up.

Past the bathroom, there were two bedrooms. Importantly, there was power to the house.

After our house inspection, we hopped into the 4-wheel drive and drove over the entire property. Traversing the paddocks, we were amazed at the height and depth of the pastures. In some areas, the growth was as high as our 4-wheel drive vehicle.

We drove up the big hill behind the house to the highest point, where there was a Trigonometrical Station, otherwise known as a Trig Station, a permanent survey mark indicating the highest point in the area. This farm was situated in the Great Dividing Range, which stretches for more than 3,500 km, running the entire length of the Australian eastern coastline. From this viewpoint, we could see for kilometres in every direction and the only buildings in sight were two small homes, one on this property and one across the road, about a kilometre down. It felt like we were a hundred miles from civilisation.

Vince then took us to another area of the property where there is a prominent seam of marble. How interesting.

Then there was more, Vince told us that this property was part of Australia's early history, the property had been one of the land grants to Hannibal Macarthur, the nephew of John Macarthur, whose wife Elizabeth is recognised as the pioneer of the Australian fine wool industry.

However in Hannibal Macarthur's biography, there is some indication he also purchased land, so it is difficult to be adamant that this property was a land grant. Hannibal Macarthur (1788–1861) was a pastoralist, a politician and a businessman and travelled to Australia with John Macarthur in 1805.

Slowly, the powerful barriers of the first impression were slipping away, one by one. We came away feeling impressed and the touch of history was enticing.

We asked Vince to contact the real estate agent for a price guide. We had a lot of thinking to do on this one, many considerations to work through – the distance from the hospital, what if Vince decided not to stay with us, was the property too large for us to manage, how would we manage horses in this untamed environment, the lack of infrastructure on the property, only one small house, which meant that if we wanted to spend time on this property we would have to build, and so the list went on.

As we talked around these topics, I sensed that Jack was keen. I think he felt a sense of adventure and I am sure he was influenced by its powerful history and the fact that Ernie was our neighbour.

The following day Vince came back to us with the price guide: $175,000.00.

Jack and I agonised over the pros and cons and how we would manage financing this adventure. Our number one dilemma was, would Vince be prepared to move out there and run the place? It all seemed to hinge on his opinion of the property, and his take on how it could be managed.

We arranged a meeting to discuss these dilemmas with Vince and Doreen. Would they stay or go?

We felt miserable placing Vince and Doreen in this difficult situation, knowing their answer would no doubt decide our farming future.

After a few anxious days, Vince eventually got back to us and told us he would be prepared to manage the property but not live there. This was not what we had hoped for, but after giving our situation further consideration and bearing in mind Vince's age and health, this was the most sensible resolution to his dilemma.

This presented another problem, and after further discussions with Vince and Doreen, it seemed the solution was to employ another man, preferably, young and fit, to co-manage the property and live in the white cottage on the hill.

As a mark of appreciation to Vince and Doreen for their loyalty and hard work, Jack and I bought a small home in Bundanoon, so they'd have somewhere to call home.

We placed our Exeter property on the market and approached the bank for finance. As soon as finance was arranged, we put our offer in of $165,000.00 and it was accepted. Settlement of Big Hill, Marulan occurred on 31 January 1979. When I received news of the settlement, I phoned the insurance broker and arranged for insurance of the property to commence from settlement date.

Eight days after settlement, a huge bushfire swept through the property. Apparently, a neighbour was ploughing his field when the plough struck a rock, sending sparks into the dry grass. Pushed along by strong winds, a grass fire took off in our direction and developed into a massive bushfire.

The windstorm pushed the fire through our property and

further on. It was total destruction; all the beautiful tall pasture grasses and every fence was destroyed. Fortunately, the little white house on the small hill was saved; the fire went up the hill and swept around the house. The weather conditions had been hot and very dry for the last couple of years, and on this day, it was blazing hot with a fierce, hot wind. There was nothing anyone could do.

We were crushed by the news and in a state of shock. How could this happen? But there was one blessing: none of our stock had been moved to the property, otherwise we would have lost all our beautiful cows and bulls. Most importantly, no one was hurt.

What on earth would we do? It would be months before the pasture would regrow and be sufficient to feed our stock. We had to arrange for all the stock to be agisted on someone else's farm until we had adequate pasture growth.

When our shock receded and we were able to think a little more clearly, we phoned the insurance broker with the news. He said he would get back to us. He wanted to know how many kilometres of fencing were on the property. We told him we had only just settled, and had no idea about the length of fencing on the property. We phoned Vince and asked him to go out and see if he could somehow guess how many kilometres of fencing had been burned down.

The following weekend, we met Vince at the front gate of Mt Hannibal. We'd decided we had to bravely face the damage. As we approached, for as far as you could see in every direction, the ground was pitch black, not only our place but the neighbouring properties as well.

We stood at the gate, which was lucky to be standing, as its posts were almost burnt through. As we opened the gate, it dropped off its hinges. We looked around in bewilderment, the pitch-black ground was dotted with little white dots. What could they be, white stones?

As we walked in, to our amazement, we discovered the little white dots, of which there were thousands and thousands, were white mushrooms pushing their way through the black earth. We dug down into the soil and found that 2 to 3 cms of the earth was blackened, telling us that the fire was so fierce, it had burnt the soil.

Vince estimated there would have been 10 to 15 miles of fencing (16 to 25 km). Having taken out the insurance policy the day we settled, we figured we should be covered for the cost of re-fencing. Leaving Vince with the task of finding agistment for the stock and finding someone to rebuild the fences, we drove back to Sydney, stunned by the devastation.

We notified the insurance broker, who came back with the news that the insurance company would only pay 30 per cent of the cost of re-fencing the property, as they considered that the fence that had been burnt down would have been more than 10 years old. And they wanted two quotes for the fencing.

We could not argue the point because we had no idea how old the fencing was. We asked Vince to go ahead and get two quotes for the fencing, as requested. Vince laughed. 'I will be lucky to get someone to come and work out here, let alone finding two people willing,' he said. I hoped Vince would find them.

Unfortunately, trying to get someone to work out at Big Hill was a huge hurdle, and in the end, there were no fencers available, so Vince and a couple of mates ended up building the new fences. It was a huge task. The materials alone cost $10,000, and then there was the cost of labour.

Some weeks later, Jack woke up at 3 am with chest pain. I phoned my sister Robyn, who lived not far from us in Caringbah, and asked if she could come and take the children to her home as

I was leaving straight away to take Jack to the hospital. I thought he was having a heart attack and I wasn't sure how long I would be away.

I phoned the RMO and told him I was on my way, and he arranged for a wheelchair and nurses waiting for us as soon as we arrived. Everyone went into action. Jack was placed on a trolley bed and taken straight to the CCU, where they took an electrocardiogram which confirmed that he had had an inferior infarct.

The doctors in CCU asked me to perform an echocardiogram to assess his left ventricular function. It was a significant infarct. He deteriorated quickly, there was a sense of real urgency in his room, and I was scared. Everyone was doing their best to keep him alive. He was given morphine for the pain and unfortunately, he had an allergic reaction which made him violently ill.

The next day, I brought our girls in to see their Daddy, as the doctors were not sure if Jack would survive. Those sweet little darlings quietly walked into the coronary care unit cubicle to see their precious Daddy, who had tubes coming from every orifice of his body and wires attached to every limb, six electrodes attached to his chest, and a monitor above his bed which signalled every heartbeat.

He was barely conscious and did not respond when his little ones came into his room. Their eyes were wide open in alarm, but they were trying to be brave. Quietly, they walked up to the bed, one at a time, kissed his hand and said, 'I love you, Daddy,' with tears rolling down their sweet little faces. (Jacqui and Sara were 8 years old and Rebecca was 5). They were frightened, just as I was frightened. They didn't want to go home without their Daddy.

It was touch and go at first, but eventually we slowly inched to the end of the first week. It was a tough week, but Jack was still with us. He was so determined he was not going anywhere but home, to the house we had built together with love.

In the first few days, I had to make some fast decisions. First off, I cancelled his appointments at the surgery for the next month. I thought I would wait and see how things worked out before I cancelled further appointments. It was a challenge for our secretary, as everyone wanted to know what had happened. She had to triage the patients into two groups: urgent and non-urgent. The urgent patients were told to contact their general practitioner immediately, and the non-urgent patients were put on a list to be seen at a later date.

I phoned Vince at the farm; he was shaken by the news. I reassured him that he still had a job, and that we needed to keep everything rolling along until Jack recovered. I said this with my fingers crossed and a prayer. Vince told me Jack had arranged for him to buy 20 Murray Greys that week. 'Under the circumstances, we need to cancel the purchase immediately,' I said. 'We can re-negotiate if Jack recovers and can return to work.'

At the end of the first week, we were very cautiously optimistic.

Once Jack started to recover, he regained his spirit, and was determined to get back to work ASAP. He was ordered to sit back and do what he is told. He spent ten days in hospital and on returning home, began regaining his strength and taking daily walks with Ben, our family dog. Ben was a beautiful rough collie, a long-coated breed popularised by Lassie in the movies. The breed is intelligent, loyal, protective, gentle and friendly, used and bred for herding sheep in Scotland.

Although we called Ben our family dog, he was really Jack's dog. Ben was very loyal to Jack. If anyone came to the house, Ben would go and stand between Jack and the visitor – Jack was his master. Jack and Ben had attended dog-training classes, which turned their relationship into one of deep loyalty. Ben watched Jack's every movement, waiting and watching to see if Jack picked up his lead, the signal to go for their walk. Jack's rehabilitation started slowly with he and Ben going for a gentle, short walk to begin with, then building on this until he was walking 5 km each day, sometimes twice a day.

In those few weeks of Jack's recuperation, he and Ben must have walked at least a hundred kilometres together around the streets of Lilli Pilli.

The stress of not having an income, and bills and wages still to pay, weighed heavily on my shoulders. We had taken out income protection insurance for Jack before his health scare, and I put in a claim.

An agent from the insurance company came to our home to complete our claim. He had no time for pleasantries. We had given him a doctor's certificate stating Jack's hospitalisation, his state of health and the length of time he was unable to work. Surely that was enough evidence of his illness and inability to work?

After he left, I felt anxious for Jack, and wondered if we would see any money.

Mercifully, after a month, we started receiving payments. It was a great relief as our bank balance was well and truly in the red, and I just kept my fingers crossed that Jack would soon be well enough to go back to work, but there was no way I was going to mention this to him.

Life was on hold while Jack was off work for six weeks. He spent his days reading, catching up on the medical journals he'd stockpiled beside his bed, and indulged in a little television.

He was so glad to get back into the thrust of life. He was much slimmer, having dropped from more than 90 kg down to 70 kg. He looked trim and shiny, with a bright face and sparkling eyes.

I think doctors benefit greatly from being on the other side of the desk. They develop empathy and understanding from being a patient. Not that Jack lacked these qualities, he had them more than anyone else I knew, but his near-death experience certainly deepened these attributes.

Our lives gradually slipped back into our busy routines, with the addition of a brisk walk every morning.

As soon as we'd recovered from the ruinous bushfire and Jack's unexpected coronary occlusion, we started looking at project homes. We needed a house so that we had somewhere to sleep and eat on our weekend visits and during the school holidays.

After looking at many project homes, we finally decided on an AV Jennings project home. While we waited for a house to be built, we bought a caravan to use on our visits to Mt Hannibal. It was such a good idea and so much fun.

We chose a site beside the river to park the van. It was idyllic. We built a fireplace with the river stones and some nights, when the weather was fine, we cooked our steaks or chops on the river-stone fireplace. The caravan had three bunks and a double bed, with a table and bench seating for meals. We had a generator to provide electricity for heating and cooking, and most importantly of all, we had a toilet and a shower.

Jack was kept busy retrieving fresh drinking water from the tank at the little house on the hill, and keeping the generator running on cold nights. And so, this was our accommodation while we waited for the house to be built. During the August school holidays, we spent a week in the caravan at the farm. I remember one day was so chilly, we had to take the girls for a run up and down a hill to warm them up. There was a lot of laughter.

Vince had been managing the property since the bushfire, and as we did not have many animals on the property, he was mostly occupied with the fencing he'd been erecting with help from friends and neighbours.

At last, the moment arrived where we had adequate fencing and we had a joyous time welcoming our cows and bulls to their new home. This brought us to the next issue: Vince needed help, so we advertised for a young stockman.

Eventually, a young couple applied, Tracie and Ian, who were both in their mid-twenties and had a baby. They came for an interview and as they were the only applicants, we said, 'When can you start?'

We were so lucky, they slotted smoothly into the situation and were happy with the white weatherboard house on the hill.

Our pastures were starting to flourish, and everything started to feel normal. Since we had a large property with plenty of pasture, Vince suggested we buy a small flock of sheep, and with our neighbour Ernie's advice, we bought 200 ewes ready to drop their lambs and enough rams to service this number of ewes.

Our girls loved the sheep, because they are small animals, and they could handle them without getting hurt too much. They had so much fun.

Tracie and Ian taught our girls how to ride and how to muster sheep, although occasionally a horse would arrive home without its rider. Sometime later, the rider would return looking sore and sorry, having fallen off her horse and then endured the long walk home.

They also taught the girls about crutching sheep (removing wool from around the tail and between rear legs) which is necessary to prevent flystrike, and they watched the shearing and helped with sweeping the shearing-shed floor. This was all a great outdoor country experience for our girls and ourselves.

In November 1979, our family went to the US so that Jack

*Working on the farm at Big Hill*

and I could attend the Annual Scientific Meeting of the American College of Cardiology in Houston, Texas. During the meeting, Dr Nelson Schiller invited us to spend two days on our way home at Dr Schiller and Dr Silverman's Department of Echocardiography at the University of California, in San Francisco.

There, we were treated like royalty and the staff were very happy to share their knowledge, skills and expertise in the expanding world of echocardiography. We learnt many tricks and new methods, not only from the doctors themselves but also from the sonographers who were all recognised for their outstanding expertise.

We extended our stay and were treated to gracious Californian hospitality in their homes, where we were introduced to artists and entertainers. What we learnt from Nelson Schiller and his sonographers was invaluable and gave us the skills to be the best in echocardiography back home.

Our experience during our many visits to America, is that Americans are very generous imparting their knowledge and skills.

We ended the year on a high note: Robyn and I passed our exams and were now Associates of the Institute of Cardiopulmonary Technologies.

*For 1980 Courses and Conferences refer to Travel Lists in Further Reading.*

Our AV Jennings home was completed and we now had a comfortable place to stay on our weekends and school holidays at the property.

Meanwhile, Echocardiograhy was evolving rapidly, with the introduction of new methods and procedures, and the American university hospitals were developing new diagnostic techniques.

We now had 2D (two dimensional) sector scanners, which gave a moving image of the heart on a screen. What a thrilling advance! When we first started doing 2D Sector scans it was surreal, it reminded me of when we first experienced black and white television for the first time.

The full procedure could be performed in an ordinary room with the patient lying on a bed or an examination couch and a sonographer sitting beside the patient, holding a transducer on their chest. Immediately, the 2D sector scanner allowed us to see everything happening inside their heart. We could see if there was a damaged wall of the heart (heart attack), and determine if it was a small segment or a large segment. We could see if there was a diseased valve which required surgery, or if the patient had fluid within the double layered, saclike structure around the heart (pericardium), and so many other diagnoses could be seen simply and swiftly, without an anaesthetic.

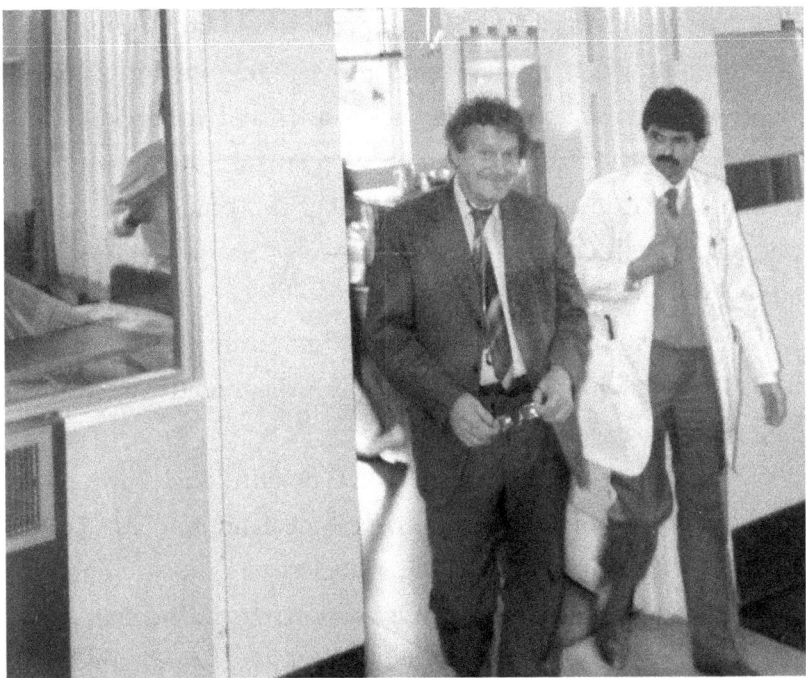

*Jack working at The Sutherland Hospital in the Coronary Care Unit*

The machines were mobile, and in the hospital, we could move the machine from patient bed to patient bed with little trouble. We could also push it from ward to ward and transport it in the hospital lifts.

What an exciting time we live in.

**Doug > Court Case Nov. 1980**
Doug, Jack's longtime friend from the horse-racing world, told us that many years before, when he'd first arrived in Sydney, he met Mr C, who owned a property – an old home with stables at the rear – in Randwick. Doug was looking for stables so that he could commence horse-training in Randwick. Mr C and Doug had come to a gentleman's agreement that Doug could use the house and stables if he maintained the property and paid the council rates,

and that when Mr C died, the property would be Doug's....

However, when Mr C passed away, Doug was instructed to vacate the premises. He came to Jack to ask his advice. Jack spoke to our solicitor who said he would be happy to take the case to court.

The court case was heard in November 1980 and Jack's solicitor phoned after the proceedings ended. 'We lost the case,' he said, adding, 'we had the wrong judge.'

It was an unhappy day for Doug. I don't think he ever got over it. Sadly, a few months later, Doug was diagnosed with bladder cancer, and passed away shortly after.

Each year we attended the Annual Scientific Meeting of the Cardiac Society of Australia and New Zealand, and the Annual Scientific Meeting of the American Society of Echocardiography,

Whenever we travelled overseas for conferences and courses, we took our girls with us and arranged for nannies at our destinations. We believed that our travels would be a great education for them as well as teaching them to be resilient and accepting of the challenges put before them. I taught them how to pack their own bags and be responsible for what they forgot. They learnt to always pack a book to read and a plastic bag for when they were car sick. They were very independent at an early age.

We arranged to attend an Echocardiography Conference at Newcastle-on-Tyne in August 1981. After the conference, we rented a Campervan and drove around England and Scotland, or rather Jack drove and I navigated, which was calamitous at times because I have a right/left dyslexia, in other words, if I said go right, I really mean left and vice versa, but we managed with a few harmless mishaps.

The Campervan was small but comfortable, except there was no toilet, which occasionally became an issue, but I remembered from my boarding school days the value of a bucket in these circumstances and so we purchased a red plastic bucket which came in handy when the situation was urgent. The girls were a bit shy about sitting on a bucket, but they soon learnt that it was better than the alternative. We had to hold Rebecca over the bucket, otherwise she would have fallen into it.

The camping sites were usually racetracks, Jack felt right at home. He would always try and park the van as close as possible to the finish line.

Rebecca had her 6th birthday on a racetrack in Scotland. We couldn't find a birthday cake so we went to the supermarket and bought a packet of six jam rollettes, popped a candle in each and sang 'Happy Birthday' to her. She was just as happy with her jam rollettes as she would have been with an elaborate birthday cake.

(Robyn and I passed our exams, and we were now Members of the Institute of Cardiopulmonary Technologies.)

We were enjoying Mt Hannibal on our free weekends and school holidays, but the good times were about to come to a close.

One night, we had a call from Doreen. Vince had collapsed at home and had been taken to hospital. Jack, who'd been monitoring Vince's heart for the last couple of years, arranged for Vince to be transferred to POW Hospital for tests.

The results indicated he needed urgent surgery for mitral valve replacement. Vince had his mitral valve replaced by a mechanical valve and, as Vince was in his late 60s, it seemed highly improbable that he could continue to do farm work and he reluctantly resigned.

Our weekends were very busy, we had many projects, and our girls were always included in the work. Jack wanted to clear one of the paddocks of all the stones on the surface of the ground, as he had plans for a horse-training track. This was rock picking at its worst. We all ended up with raw blistered fingertips, even though we wore protective gloves.

Then there were weekends when the family would go out in the paddock to chip thistles and serrated tussock. Poor Rebecca was only about 7 and would get so tired, we often found her lying on the ground with her little head on her chipper, sound asleep

Compared to other properties in the area, ours was one of the smallest, at 1500 acres. Our neighbour Ernie and his wife Betty came for a visit to give advice and to help us crutch our sheep.

Another neighbour who lived on the other side of the road, about a kilometre away, was a single man who lived on his own. He was a crop duster pilot, and had a small rough runway on his property.

The next neighbours were two brothers five or six kilometres away, who lived in a mudbrick hut – you could not call it a house, it had a dirt floor and no running water inside. When one brother married, to celebrate, they arranged to have water brought to the house, but not inside, just to the back door!

## 1982

Jacqui and Sara were making plans for their 11th birthday and wanted to bring some friends to the farm for the weekend. We suggested that they bring a friend each and their friend should come home from school with them on the Friday and return to school on the Monday.

We drove to the farm on the Saturday morning, after Jack had finished his ward rounds at the hospital. We turned off the highway at Marulan and drove along the road, and as we came to the dirt road, one of the friends started crying and saying she wanted to go back home. We cajoled her and told her we were a long way from her home, and we would take her home tomorrow.

She sobbed all the way to the farm. I was hoping that when we got there and she saw a normal-looking home and lots of lovely animals to look at, she would be distracted and settle in. All seemed under control, I was busy unpacking the car and organising the food, all the while thinking about the party we were planning for the evening.

Suddenly, my girls came running in to say their friend who had been crying in the car had run away. Oh my goodness, where did she think she was going? We were miles from anywhere and it would soon be dark. Jacqui, Sara and Rebecca ran off after her, she hadn't gone far. They managed to bring her back home. We started the birthday preparations, put on some party music and managed to distract our little friend. I hoped she wouldn't run away again.

I asked the girls if they knew why she'd become so frightened. Our only thought was that this dear girl had lived in a home unit all her life and the farm was a very foreign environment for her, with the enormous open spaces. She was probably used to being closeted and close to everything and maybe she had not been away from her mother before. I thought about how lucky our girls were to have this wonderful adventureland, where they could explore and experience a taste of farm life, and run around so free, play in the river, help with the cows and sheep and watch them have their babies, and best of all, they'd learnt to ride a horse.

The party was simple with plenty of party food, soft drinks, and music. The girls had also devised a few simple games with party prizes. There was enough to make their friend smile, and she went to bed without tears.

We woke up early the next day and cooked their favourite breakfast of pancakes, bacon and eggs, with maple syrup. After breakfast, we took them for a ride in the 4-wheel drive and pointed out the cows and calves, sheep, lambs and horses, but the girls' friend was anxious to go home, so we went back to the house and packed up the car and returned to Sydney. 'I don't think we'll do this again,' I thought.

In May 1982, we were off to the USA again, for further teaching sessions in echocardiography.

Meet the Masters in Echocardiography, Santa Ana, California, USA (one week full time)

The early 1980s was a breakthrough time for our Echocardiography practice. Jack wrote three papers which he presented at various cardiac conferences.

The first paper was accepted by the *Medical Journal of Australia* in 1981:

'Echocardiographic Observations in Myocardial Wall Motion'.

This paper was one of the first papers in the world to describe normal and abnormal wall motion of the heart. To prepare the paper, Jack and I studied the cardiac wall motion of every patient admitted to The Sutherland Hospital with chest pain. We were not told the electrocardiograph (ECG) results, this was to prove that you could determine the site and size of an infarct by Echo.

We spent six months gathering information for the paper.

The second and third papers were not as demanding, as they were specific diagnostic findings, and were a description of an unusual and rare cardiac abnormality

The second paper was accepted by the *Australian and New Zealand Journal of Medicine* in 1982:

'Pseudoaneurysm of the Left Ventricle Diagnosed By Two-Dimensional Echocardiography'.

The third paper was accepted in the *American Heart Journal* in September 1983: 'Echocardiographic Diagnosis of Right Ventricular Thromboembolism'.

It was impressive to have a paper accepted by the prestigious *American Heart Journal*.

When you submit a paper to these journals, the paper is scrutinised by a panel of doctors who are your peers and have been chosen from the top echelon of the medical fraternity and whose opinion is highly regarded.

In August 1982 Jack's sister, Thelma was admitted urgently to Prince of Wales hospital with a cerebral aneurysm. We were all devastated at the diagnosis.

Thelma came to work in Jack's practice in 1977 as a stenographer. She was an excellent stenographer, much better than I had been. She was quiet and efficient, and everyone enjoyed having her in our office. Unfortunately, this tragic diagnosis meant that she could no longer work.

We started looking for a replacement and we were very fortunate to find Adele, who had been looking for a change of jobs. Adele was the perfect choice for us; she was attractive and well groomed, with a sparkling personality and good humour. She seemed to know everyone, and with her inclusion in our little office, the place hummed along nicely. In the years to come, she became my 'right hand', and I relied on her, at times, very heavily. We're still close friends.

## 1983

In 1983 Jacqui and Sara started high school. Deciding which school to send our daughters to was one of the hardest decisions we'd have to make. Jacqui and Sara had always attended separate schools to encourage them to be independent of each other. Jack and I discussed high schools for the girls at great length. We both preferred that they attend an all-girls school.

We talked to as many people as we could about schools, in particular, we listened to our friends Frank and Margot Broderick, who also had twin girls. Frank was a general physician with a special interest in nuclear medicine and a longtime friend and colleague of Jack's who'd encouraged Jack to go into Echocardiography. His wife, Margot, was a physiotherapist who now worked as Frank's practice manager and assisted with his nuclear medicine practice.

Frank and Margot's girls were our babysitters, they loved coming to our house because we had television. Frank and Margot had banned TV from their house so the girls were not distracted from their studies. Their girls loved tennis and were always keen to babysit our girls during the Australian Open.

It was Frank and Margot who suggested to us that we should think about sending the girls to separate schools when Jacqui and Sara were about to enter primary school. We followed their advice at that time and decided to continue with separate schools into their high school years.

Frank and Margot chose Meriden and MLC at Strathfield for their girls, and after looking at the schools and attending an open day at each, we chose to follow in their footsteps. We also decided to send Rebecca to MLC, as she was starting Year 3, so it would be a good time for her to move.

We felt Meriden was an appropriate school for Jacqui, as it was a smaller school, and she would be less likely to feel overwhelmed. The larger MLC would suit Sara as she was more competitive, and would enjoy the rivalry. This meant that they could all travel together.

In the beginning, I drove them to and from school each day, and when we arrived back in the afternoon, they would sit at a desk in the waiting room and do their homework. As time went by and the girls became confident and found friends who lived in the Sutherland Shire, they started to travel by train each morning, which was a big help for me. I continued to pick them up in the afternoon, which I enjoyed, it was my special time with the girls where the outside world could not intrude.

This also gave me an opportunity to discuss any issues that the girls may have at school and also to have frank discussions on controversial matters such as drugs and interpersonal relationships.

I'm not sure how much they listened.

On 1 February 1984, the highly controversial Medicare system was brought in by the Hawke Labor government. Besides the name change from Medibank to Medicare, the health-care system remained very similar to the one introduced on 1 February 1975.

Early 1985, we were at our Big Hill farm during the school holidays. The girls had been out riding and when they returned, they put the horses in the small yards intending to give them a brush down, then feed and water them.

Without warning, the horses started fighting and biting each other and I could hear Rebecca screaming, she was in the middle of this violent mayhem. Our farm manager, Ian, jumped in and quickly moved the horses into another yard. Rebecca was laying unconscious on the ground.

Jack jumped into the yard and as he cradled Rebecca in his arms, she slowly regained consciousness, but she was having difficulty breathing. Jack shouted to me to get the car, 'We have to go to a hospital!'

The car was at the back of the house, about half a kilometre away, so I ran across the paddocks, grabbed all our bags and wallets, jumped into our station wagon and drove like a mad thing across the paddocks to the yards, wildly bumping and jerking across the uneven terrain.

Sara and Jacqui jumped into the back of the station wagon, and Jack carefully lay Rebecca down along the back seat. He sat on the seat next to her so that he could monitor her vital signs.

'I don't know how serious her injuries are, she needs X-rays,' he said, remembering there was a radiologist's strike this weekend.

'We'll have to go to The Sutherland Hospital where I know the radiologists, and I can call Tom, I'm sure he'll come and X-ray her.'

We set out for Sydney. The farm was 29 km from Marulan and 20 km of that was a dirt road littered with potholes, so I had to drive slowly and carefully along this segment, as we didn't know the extent of Rebecca's injuries, specifically, if she had spinal injuries.

Once we got on to the sealed road, I drove carefully but fiercely to Marulan. Then it was more than a two-and-half hour drive from Marulan to The Sutherland Hospital.

Along the highway, I drove like a bat out of hell, well above the speed limit, hoping that a police car would pick me up and give us an escort to TSH. Fortunately, there was not a lot of traffic on the road.

While I drove, Jack was continually checking Rebecca's vital signs. We pulled up to the hospital in less than two-and-a-half hours, a record-breaking trip and not one police car in sight. Jack organised for a stretcher and took Rebecca in to be X-rayed. The radiologist arrived 15 minutes later, and they X-rayed her back and head.

She was battered and bruised all over her torso and there was a hoof-print on her throat which explained why she was having trouble breathing. Half an hour later, the radiologist emerged with a smile and told us he could not find any broken bones, but there was a lot of soft tissue damage and swelling. He said he did find she had one less vertebra than normal, but this was congenital.

Rebecca was lucky, and we were all crying with relief. We took her home and all took turns looking after her and spoiling her. She could not walk for a few days, so we had to carry her to and from the bathroom and the bedroom. Through the daytime, we made a bed for her in the TV room next to the kitchen.

On our second day at home, Mum and Dad came to visit Rebecca. We had just carried Rebecca back from the toilet when Dad collapsed onto the kitchen floor. Jack rushed over and checked for a pulse. He looked up at me and shook his head. 'Ring for an ambulance,' Jack called out.

As Jack rolled Dad over to clear his airways and start CPR, Dad vomited and coughed.

Within minutes, the ambulance came and took Dad to TSH, where he spent a few days recovering. Fortunately, studies showed it was not a heart attack – he must have had a syncopal episode.

Rebecca was slowly recovering. As the swelling subsided, she began taking a few steps, and each day, she could manage more than the previous day. By the end of the second week, she had recovered, but still had large areas of bruising.

After Rebecca's accident, I could not bear to go to the farm. Even thinking about going gave me an intense anxiety attack, something I had never experienced before. Jack and I discussed the pitfalls of running a farm so far from Sydney. This was further exacerbated by Ian and Tracie deciding to hand in their resignation. They wanted to be nearer to family, as the long drive to Goulburn for supplies made life difficult for them. After arduously discussing this together we made the decision to put the property on the market.

Our Annus Horribilis was not finished with us yet.

KL had been our accountant for years. Back in 1960, when Jack was first looking for an accountant, George, Jack's solicitor, had referred him to KL's firm. When Jack first started with this firm, his affairs were handled by a senior accountant of the practice, and when he semi-retired, Jack's affairs were handed over to KL.

Jack was very happy with KL, so when KL announced he was going out on his own in 1981, Jack told him we'd follow, as he knew and mostly understood our complex tax affairs.

Our affairs were complex because we had two businesses: the medical practice and a mixed-farming enterprise of stud-cattle breeding, thoroughbred-horse breeding and horse racing. The taxation rules for primary production are somewhat straightforward, however, when you mix horse racing with thoroughbred breeding, the rules become more complicated and, at times, obscure.

Because our accountants did not have any experience in thoroughbred breeding/horse-racing accountancy, I decided to study and understand all the tax rules and regulations in relation to these two amalgamated entities, as it was important that we understood and agreed with their tax advice. If we did not agree with their tax advice then we sought a second opinion from an expert in the field.

Everything seemed to go along nicely until one day in 1981, KL's wife phoned us to say that KL had a brain tumour. He died shortly after.

A few months later, the Australian Tax Office (ATO) contacted us and accused us of not submitting tax returns for three years, and if we didn't submit them immediately, we would have to pay interest on all the outstanding taxes and we would be heavily fined.

We were in a state of shock and could not understand what had happened.

From our standpoint, each financial year KL had prepared a tax return which KL asked Jack to sign. He asked Jack for a cheque for the tax owing, and Jack handed a signed cheque to the Australian Tax Office to KL. We were of the understanding that the tax return and the cheque were forwarded to the ATO each financial year. As far as we were concerned, we had complied with the requirements of lodging our tax returns via KL.

This was not good. It looked like we could be in a precarious financial situation

Jack phoned George (our solicitor) and told him about KL and the ATO and asked if he could recommend another accountancy firm. George suggested we phone a friend of his, a Mr S who had an office in Miranda.

We contacted Mr S and he said he could not take us on as clients, but he had an energetic young man who had recently joined his firm who was more than capable. His name was Terry.

Terry became our accountant and was indeed all that Mr S had described. He asked us for all our tax records so that he could reconstruct our tax returns to send to the ATO. All our records were with KL, so we contacted KL's wife who said that KL had stored all his client's records in a locked garage and that we would be welcome to go there and retrieve what we needed.

We went to the garage to retrieve our records, expecting to find a box with our name on it for easy identification. But no, the garage was full of boxes which had no identifying labels. We had no alternative than to take all the boxes home to find our records.

The boxes contained a jumble of clients' records. We sifted through thousands and thousands of pieces of paper looking for our records for the last three years, and occasionally Terry would come and give us a hand. As we retrieved our records, we placed them in chronological order and then Terry prepared the tax returns based on the evidence we could find.

Terry said the ATO also wanted the details of every bank account (including the ones for the children and myself), as well as every credit card account number. They really were determined to find something, anything at all!

In the meantime, the Sheriff arrived at our home with a subpoena demanding $250,000.00 which the ATO claimed was owing. Jack immediately contacted George and asked him 'what can we do?' He said if you don't have the money you have to sell your house ASAP.

We followed his advice and put our Lilli Pilli house and our adjacent vacant block of land on the market, we told the real estate agent that we needed an immediate sale. We sold our house and the adjoining block of land, and settled on 1 March 1985.

This meant that we would have to find somewhere to live. Jack and I considered our finances and tried to work out how much we should spend on a home. I began hunting for a house in the Sutherland Shire.

After three weeks, I was becoming desperate. There was just nothing on the market that we could make do with, within our price range, so with grave reservations I started looking outside the Sutherland Shire. Eventually I came across a home in Lugarno, and took Jack to have a look.

'Is this all you could find?' he said.

I felt my chest tighten, so much so I could hardly breathe, then tears welled up in my eyes because, unfortunately, it was the only house for sale big enough for our family in our budget.

We ended up buying that house. It was a pleasant enough home; to some, it might have been a palace. It was a white stucco two-storey house with the living areas on the ground floor and the bedrooms and bathroom on the upper floor. However, as you walked in the front door you were smacked in the face by the most garish carpet I have ever seen: a bright orange, brown and black floral design, so glaringly lurid. It was everywhere – dining room, lounge room, up the staircase and in the bedrooms. It was disgusting, and we all hated it!

While everyone was complaining, I said, 'Look at least we have a home and when we have the money, we can change the carpet.' However, there was another challenging aspect which we struggled to endure and that was the almost negligible back yard. From the back door, it would have been barely five metres to a massive wall of rock, 15 metres high, the full width of the property, which blocked all the precious sunlight, delivering a gloomy sense of incarceration.

These might have been the features which made the property more affordable. We nicknamed the house our Italian grotto. We had one more complication. We needed an extra bedroom, as my 25-year-old old brother, Stephen, had come to live with us the previous year. At Lilli Pilli, he'd lived in 'the dungeon,' which he loved, but in this house, we would need to create another bedroom.

Fortunately, we found a builder who could start the alterations as soon as we settled on the property in early March 1985. He suggested that we enclose the balcony for the much-needed bedroom.

However, life is never easy. When you are on a downer, everything around you seems to spin out of control. Not long after we moved in, we found our peace and quiet continually disrupted by noisy neighbours. To make life more intolerable, Stephen's car, which he parked in the street near our house, was continually being vandalised.

Surely things must start to improve?

We continued our battle with the ATO. They called a meeting with us in our accountant Terry's office in Miranda, with Terry, the two ATO agents, Jack and myself.

Terry introduced us to the agents, who were gruff and hostile. Without preamble, they launched an attack and asked Jack if he gambled. Jack, being honest said, 'Yes,' but what he didn't say was that his bets were occasional, maybe once or twice a month, and usually never more than $10. He was not a real gambler, in the true sense of the word.

Then they asked if we took any cash out of the practice payments, and Jack replied that his office staff take all the payments, write receipts and bank the money. 'I don't see the money,' he explained.

They continued with their aggressive interrogation. They wanted to know how we'd paid for living expenses during six weeks in March-April two years ago? We hadn't drawn money from the bank during this period, they said. Please explain.

Jack, who had an excellent memory, thought for a while, then said he'd won a trifecta at the races, and we had lived off the proceeds.

'We want to know the racetrack, the day and time of the race and the names of the horses in the trifecta,' the agent replied.

Can you imagine having to dredge up information like that from two years ago?

At home, Jack found his diary from two years ago (never again would I complain about his pile of diaries). He'd recorded the date of the race, the racetrack, which race, and the horses' names in the trifecta and how much he had won.

At the follow-up meeting, Jack gave the ATO officers the trifecta information. They were stunned. They had clearly not expected Jack to produce this evidence, which was authentic and faultless.

After further questioning, they eventually admitted KL had not sent in the tax returns but he had sent in the cheques, which covered the outstanding taxation, and we did not owe the ATO any money at this time. Not one cent!

The ATO agents were less than happy, and as they left Terry's office, they couldn't help themselves. Approaching the door, they stopped and turned around and said, 'Don't forget, we will be back, we will be watching you, year after year.'

Oh my goodness!

We have always been meticulous with our tax records. We were let down by our accountant. But their retaliation made us resolve to be more scrupulous about our tax affairs and hopefully we now had a principled and conscientious accountant.

What a relief after all the months of stress and anxiety, trying to find invoices, receipts and putting all the pieces of the jigsaw together, having to sell our precious, beautiful home with a pool and an adjoining block of waterfront land. Then buying a house in our budget, which we all hated.

All for nothing! We had lost the home we built with love in our first year of marriage. Many tears were shed over this loss, we were in mourning – it was like we had lost our best friend. We were not at fault and did not owe one cent to the ATO. What a senseless sacrifice.

However, we were relieved at the outcome, knowing that the months of distress and anguish were at last over. We could not believe that our battle with the ATO was finished and in the end, we were unimpeachable, yet in the process, we'd had to sell our treasured home and adjoining land at fire-sale value.

We were having trouble reconciling the loss.

## 1985

Our second Annus Horribilis is still not through with us.

## Chapter Sixteen
## Flood Waters
## 1985–1986

It seemed an easy decision. We would sell Mt Hannibal, and buy a farm near Bowral.

Once again, every weekend, we packed the family into the car and inspected farms in the Southern Highlands. We had been searching for about a month and could find nothing suitable. We were becoming disheartened.

The real estate agent phoned again, he had another property to show us, it was a duck farm! We laughed. Horses, cattle, sheep, and now, ducks! We went along and had a look. It was in an idyllic area of the Southern Highlands. Driving into the property, we took in the breathtaking view – emerald paddocks so perfectly manicured, they seemed freshly mown.

Along the fence lines, stately pines and rugged gum trees led the way, yet as we drove over the paddocks, we could see they were muddy and water-logged. We quizzed the real estate agent about the soggy paddocks, but he was not to be thwarted.

'That is not a problem, drainage can be easily fixed,' he said to Jack. 'I will take you to a farm which has solved the issue of wet paddocks with excellent drainage in every paddock, and you will see the solution is not expensive.'

We had fallen in love with the duck farm and were keen to explore the drainage solution.

The agent made a phone call and arranged for us to see the property with the drainage solution. He said we could go straight away to look at the property, located just at the back of Bowral.

He took us back to Bowral, drove to the Burradoo railway station and followed the road past Oxley College, a private school. We continued about 100 m and crossed a river. A further 100 m and we were at the farm gates. We had driven less than a kilometre from Burradoo Station, and the beauty of the landscape floored us.

We drove through the gates and toured the paddocks, the agent pointing out the drainage channels designed to make their way to the river.

'Who owns this farm?' asked Jack.

'Mr Pockley,' answered the agent. 'He has had it on the market for a couple of years.'

Jack was astonished. 'This farm is for sale?'

'Yes,' replied the agent. Jack could barely hide his bewilderment. 'Why has no one showed me this farm? This is exactly what I want.'

While not as immaculate as the duck farm, it had many other attributes, one being that it was only 2.5 km from the Bowral CBD.

After a further half hour of questions and answers, we made an offer. By the time we got home, we had a phone call to say that our offer had been accepted and we sent a cheque for the deposit and settled on the property six weeks later, in July 1985.

We could not believe our luck. The property was 200 acres with only a hay shed and a few shelter sheds in the paddocks. Mr

Pockley had run steers on the property for years and we were told by others that the property had not been fertilised during that time. The fellow who was managing the property did not believe in fertiliser.

We recognised a couple of issues that would have put people off buying the property. The railway line ran all the way along the western boundary, and secondly, the river flooded if more than four inches of rain fell at one time. Neither issue worried us, as we felt the advantages far outweighed the negatives.

I have always loved trains, so that was a plus for me, and we decided that when the river flooded and we couldn't cross it, we could always go out the Moss Vale end of the property. The farm had two entrances, one at Burradoo (Bowral) and the other at Moss Vale.

During the settlement period, we put into motion selling the sheep and most of the cattle, only retaining 80 cows plus their calves and a dozen bulls. We sent the horses to a spelling farm while we organised horse fences on the property, as the existing fences were barbed-wire suitable for cattle, but not for horses.

We contacted a local real estate agent to sell the Big Hill property. Two weeks later, he phoned and said he had an overseas buyer wanting to buy the property, sight unseen. We asked about the buyer, and were told it was a Japanese company.

'I'm sorry, I can't sell to the Japanese, no matter how much he might offer,' replied Jack, who still had painful war memories. The agent was disappointed.

A month later, we had another offer, this time, from an acquaintance in the horse industry: Bill, a Sydney opal dealer who owned a few good racehorses. Bill was not afraid of spending money when he wanted to buy a racehorse. He was an interesting man, good-humoured and sociable, generous and kind.

Bill and his wife had two teenaged sons and owned an opal-jewellery shop in Sydney. When they wanted opals, they went out to the opal fields and purchased the opals from the miners. Bill told us his wife was the one with the nous and the eye for a good opal, as well as the knack of bargaining with the miners. We affectionately nicknamed Bill 'Billy Bunter,' in our private conversations, never to his face. If you saw him you would understand, he had a round face, a round head, and a round torso sitting on a pair of stiff legs which meant that when he walked he waddled, but when you engaged with him in conversation you became unaware of his 'Billy Bunter' features, he was so amiable and charming interspersed with sparks of wit.

We could not understand why he wanted to buy this property, as he always presented himself as someone who owned prestigious properties, such as his home in sought-after Mosman. One would assume that if he wanted to buy a farm, he would be looking around Bowral, not a rough and tumble place way out in the sticks.

Anyway, never judge. We were grateful he wanted to buy our farm. Always one who had to make a deal or have the last say, he asked if we would throw in the ride-on mower. We were happy to give it to him.

He said he wanted to ride the ride-on mower. Now, to understand how incongruous this sounded, Bill had a rotund figure and was, let's say, a little more than awkward, so it came as no surprise when he later told us that when he was mowing the lawn, it had the temerity to tip him off in the middle of the house garden. When he recovered and regained his composure, he swore he would never get on one again. From then on, he enlisted one of his sons to do the mowing.

The Burradoo property was very run down. Almost all the fences needed replacing and the paddocks were suffering from lack of fertiliser. We organised for a fencer to start ASAP, and redesigned the paddock plan. Our plan had a central laneway, running north to south, from one end of the property to the other, and all the paddocks ran off this central laneway. This made moving livestock easier, having the central laneway straight to the shed area, where we'd build yards and other infrastructure.

My parents were living in Bowral and my father, who'd been born into a farming family, offered to help out. But after a few weeks, the workload became too much for him. He suggested a friend of his, who was also an experienced farmer, might be interested in coming to manage the farm.

This was a good idea and would take the pressure off my father and Jack. Dad's friend had experience handling horses, which was a bonus. We had a chat to Dad's friend and he became our new farm manager. Slowly and surely, things started to take shape.

With no house on the property, building a house was top priority. Time was of the essence, so we chose to look at project homes to begin with, to see if

a) a house could be built within six months and

b) if we could find a layout that suited our family.

After a lot of indecision, we settled on a two-storey home with AV Jennings. We made a few changes to the house plan and they promised to build it within six months. The site would have to be on the highest point of the property, due to the flooding risk.

AV Jennings put the plans into council and they hoped to commence in October; the build would take 16 weeks. We spent a day choosing bricks, tiles, paint colours, floor tiles, carpets, kitchen appliances, kitchen cupboards and bench tops, bathroom tiles and light fittings. What a mad day that was.

As they'd predicted, Jennings began building in October, and just after the slab had been laid, the rain started. It was unrelenting.

The delivery trucks were so heavy that they were getting bogged in the muddy track and our farm manager had to use the tractor to pull them out. The rain slowed progress, and everyone started to get anxious.

Finally, the bad weather broke, and the house-build started to progress. It wasn't long after the frame was up that a council road builder came to the farm and offered our farm manager hot asphalt left over from one of his projects, at a reduced cost. This was perfect. We could use it to build the 900 m road from our front gates to the house. We had to buy extra asphalt to finish it off, but it was still economical and definitely worth it.

During construction of the fences, yards, roads and house, we travelled to Bowral most weekends and stayed overnight at a motel so that we could keep track of progress and work at the farm. Each weekend, we planted native trees along the fence lines, anticipating that one day they would grow into tall trees offering defence against the winds. Our aim each weekend was to plant 350 tubestock, which was very ambitious, but most of the time we met our target.

Meanwhile, on the home front, we were becoming disenchanted and unsettled with our abode at Lugarno. Our nights were continually disrupted by noisy neighbours and, by this time, poor Stephen's car had so many scratches, dents and scapes, it needed a re-spray.

Jack and I started to seriously think about living at the farm. We made enquiries at the private schools in the Southern Highlands. One of the high schools that appealed to us was Oxley College, which was almost on our farm boundary. It was a new school to the area, having opened in 1983.

However, Rebecca was only going in to 6th class and so the choices for her were either Bowral Public School, or Gibb Gate, a private primary school at Mittagong. These were heavy decisions to make. The girls were settled in their schools in Sydney. It had always been our choice to keep Jacqui and Sara at different schools, but if we moved to Bowral, the twins would attend the same school. Jacqui and Sara were delighted with the idea.

The key to our dilemma was that we were so disheartened with city living and believed the girls would be better off in the country, yet there were many other problems to reconcile. The crucial one for me was how would Jack manage running his practice in Miranda from Bowral?

How would he cope when the hospital called in the night and on weekends, and he had to dash to the hospital? It would be a round trip of four hours! Jack seemed unconcerned, he said he would love to live on the farm. He reminded me that he had turned 60 and would be retiring from the hospital in 1990, when he turned 65. I think he had an alluring idea of retiring to the farm, but that was still five years away.

I couldn't shake off my feelings of foreboding for him. Would moving to Bowral give him too much stress, with the daily grind of a four-hour drive as an added burden?

There were a lot of heart-wrenching discussions about schools too. The girls were doing well at their respective schools, where they'd both made lovely friends. At this key, impressionable stage of their young lives, how would they manage a move to a country school where they knew no one? And would the Bowral schools offer the same educational standards?

We agonised over it all for a week or so, and then one morning, Jack announced, 'We are moving to the farm.' Decision made, the heavy load of uncertainty lifted and we started making plans. We made arrangements for Jacqui and Sara to start at Oxley College in Year 10, and Rebecca to start at Gibb Gate in Year 6. Jacqui and

Sara could walk to school from home, and Rebecca could catch the Gibb Gate bus from Oxley College.

During the build of the house, we had had a number of Council inspections. On the last inspection, the inspector left a note for us saying it was a pleasure to inspect this build, it was the best that he had seen. We marvelled that a project home should be given such an accolade.

We looked into heating for the house and decided on a hydronic system. We favoured one that used a huge furnace which heated water pumped through pipes to convector panels in every room of the house. Each convector panel had a control knob, so that the heat in each room was independently controlled. The other plus for this style of heating was that we could heat the swimming pool (which we planned to build) utilising a heat exchanger. The furnace would be in a fully enclosed room adjacent to the pool room, which meant that all the dirt and dust from the furnace was isolated from the pool. The furnace could burn anything, usually wood, but we could burn household rubbish, and bales of hay that had become mouldy and could not be used for feed.

The house was not completed in time for the girls to start school, so we spent two weeks in a motel, the Ivy Tudor, which was comfortable. Oxley College was about a kilometre from the motel. Rebecca walked to Oxley College with Jacqui and Sara and caught the Gibb Gate School bus from there.

Jack had the hardest task. He had to drive to TSH do his ward rounds, then go to his rooms at Miranda, then drive home. I went with him at least four days a week, and we shared the driving, although Jack liked to drive. He seemed to manage these long days – the only drama was if he had a call through the night from the hospital and had to drive there and back. Fortunately, it was a rare occurrence, most things he could handle over the phone. Strange, isn't it? When we'd lived in Sydney, he would have jumped in the car and gone to the hospital.

Moving day arrived, and there was great excitement and anticipation in the family. My wonderful friend Wendy had offered to help with the move and arrived nice and early to give me a hand. She'd travelled all the way from Sylvania to Bowral to help me, what a friend.

And of course, it rained. Fortunately, we had the tar-sealed drive, which meant we didn't have to worry about mud being tramped into the house. We survived and had most things sort of in their place so that we could spend our first night in our beautiful new home. We were all so excited.

Our 'Italian Grotto' was put on the market and did not sell until 3 April 1987.

Jack loved being on the farm. He started a vegie patch and planted an orchard with apples, plums, pears, and cherry trees. He arranged for two young ladies to design and build a garden around the house; the house yard was approximately 2 acres.

A tennis court and fibreglass swimming pool were being installed. Living in Bowral, where the weather is cold for three quarters of the year, the pool would have to be enclosed and heated. We had a few quotes on a pool enclosure, but they were all so expensive, I suggested to Jack that I should get an Owner/Builder Licence and do it myself. It would cost half the price. I got my licence and started to organise the trades people.

The fibreglass pool was delivered and installed followed by preparation of the pool surround and then pouring of the concrete. After the concrete was cured, the brickies arrived to build the walls and install the windows and door frames. The company making the roof trusses phoned to say that there was a delay and they would not be delivered for two more days.

The night of that phone call, a mini cyclone swept over the farm and blew all the walls and windows into the pool. Fortunately, the pool had been filled with water, which minimised the damage to the pool, but it was a tough and messy job pulling the bricks, smashed glass and tangled window frames out from its depths.

We postponed the roof trusses and organised a rebuild and managed to complete the pool enclosure without any further dramas.

Jack loved observing the cows and was excited when the horses started coming back. After six months on the farm, Bill phoned and said he would like to come and look at our Murray Grey bulls. He arrived on a Sunday, looked at the bulls and announced he wanted to buy all 12 of them. Usually when someone comes to buy a bull, they buy one bull, not 12. Oh well, that was Bill.

While we were driving Bill around the property, he revealed that he and his wife had split and he was negotiating to buy the next-door property at Big Hill.

Our family eased into country living. Our occasional challenges were mostly to do with juggling our itineraries, until one Friday afternoon. Jack and I were at the practice, taking a rare lunch break when our secretary told us she had an urgent call from my father. He said the river had flooded and asked if we wanted him to pick up the girls from school?

This was a shock. We knew the river flooded, but did not expect it so soon. Surely it hadn't rained that much? Gratefully, we accepted dad's offer. To be on the safe side, we cancelled our appointments so we could leave as soon as possible. We started our journey home to Bowral just after 3 pm.

The rain was torrential and almost-cyclonic winds buffeted the car, making it hard for Jack to keep it in the one lane.

We took our usual route home via Appin. As we approached

the bridge, a short distance from our turn-off to Appin, the car in front of us towing a caravan was hit by a fierce gust of wind and the car and caravan slewed across the road in front of us. The caravan was breaking up in front of our eyes. Jack swerved to the side of the road trying to miss a collision and the flying debris. Fortunately, Jack was driving slowly due to the conditions and had such a split-second reaction that he was able to miss hitting the caravan.

Regrettably, the car, van and debris stretched across the road and there was no way for us to drive around the car and van. We knew we were trapped, and we knew we could not stay in the car, as visibility was so poor that the oncoming traffic probably would not see our Jeep and if they hit us, we mightn't survive. So, we left the car and looked for a safe haven somewhere. We couldn't stay on the side of the road as that was just as hazardous.

The rain and wind were fierce, the wind was so tumultuously turbulent that we were being buffeted around so badly we had trouble staying upright. Our clothes were completely saturated and our shoes filed with water. We desperately clung to each other and swam our way through the torrential downpour, it was like passing through a never-ending automatic car wash, only worse. We frantically tried to move forward, but the ferocity of the wind kept pushing us back. Inch by inch, we slowly passed the car and van, and then, we heard an almighty crash.

As expected, a truck struck our car, and in no time at all there were six vehicles involved. As we were standing there, shell-shocked, a man came up to us and reminded us that there was a restaurant just up the road. We struggled across to this safe haven and asked if they would phone the police. Luckily, no one had been injured as yet.

The wind was so strong it blew panels off the restaurant's roof.

The police arrived about 30 minutes later and started to sort out the mess. As soon as we were given the go ahead to leave, we did, both drenched to our skin, and unsure of how much damage had been done to the car – something to worry about later.

We were jubilant when the car's engine turned over and we could drive off, well, sort of, it was a very slow, jerky journey and we were not sure how far our car would take us, but we decided to push on, as the wind and rain were relentless and at least we were out of it.

We took the turn off to Appin, proceeding at snail's pace, it was tortuous. Going up the hills was excruciating, but we persevered, keeping our fingers crossed that our trusty Jeep would get us home. We crawled through Wilton, and then on to the freeway. It felt like we might make it home. Our pace meant we were a nuisance on the freeway, but there was little we could do about it, we just had to keep going.

At the turnoff to Mittagong, the car was chugging and grinding and getting slower and slower and then, on the outskirts of Mittagong, our trusty car gave up the ghost. We picked up our brief cases and other bits and pieces and tried to hail someone down, hoping someone would take pity on us. Eventually, a fellow in a ute stopped to pick us up. He said we could get in the back of the ute, out in the rain! He obligingly drove us to Bowral, and we phoned my dad to come and pick us up and drive us to the back entrance of the farm.

By now it was dark. Little did we realise the severity of the flooding. When we got to the back of the farm, we saw the whole farm was flooded except for our precious home sitting on top of the small hill, about a half a kilometre away, quarantined from the flood waters.

Dad dropped us about 50 m from the back gate and we started

# FLOOD WATERS 1985–1986

*The flood*

wading towards it. The water was not friendly, it swirled around us, trying to knock us off our feet. We clung to each other for support and in our free hand we tightly held on to our briefcases. The rain still fell, and darkness descended over the farm.

Dad shone the car headlights so that we could find the back farm gate. We warily climbed over it. As we waded through the dirty, muddy water, it became deeper and we had to try and distinguish the fences and gates in the darkness. We needed to find the gates, because the fences were made of barbed wire and not safe to climb over.

The flood was now up to my waist and, at times, my chest. We did our best to wade through the swirling water while holding up our brief cases and at times clinging to each other, shivering not only from the cold but also with fear and trepidation that the water would deepen as we slowly made our way in the dark.

At last, we found our way to the central laneway. This was a blessing because we knew once we climbed over this gate, we had about 600 metres of swirling flood waters to wade through and one more gate to climb and we would be on an asphalt roadway instead of slushy, gooey mud, which was so hard to walk through.

We waded and stumbled ever so slowly through the swirling waters. Still clinging to each other for physical and moral support, we made our way along the laneway searching for the last gate, the gateway to safety. When we finally found it, we wearily and gratefully climbed over our last obstacle. We were safe. We held each other, crying with relief and shivering uncontrollably from the emotional trauma of the last few hours. We were so cold and soaked, a muddy mess from head to toe, and our shoes were caked in inches of thick, gluggy mud.

At our front door, we stripped off all our clothes, took off our mud-laden shoes, and headed straight to the bathroom to have a wash. But that was not to be. There was a complete blackout in the area, therefore no water, as all our water was pumped by electricity from the water tank to the house, so we just had to make do with drying ourselves off with towels and wiping off as much mud as we could so that we could put warm clothes on.

We put buckets outside to catch water so that we could wash the mud off our feet, legs, hands and faces. Then, we had a hot drink and something to eat. We lit the open fire so we could heat water and cook a meal, which ended up being baked beans on toast. We huddled close to the fire for warmth.

Fortunately, our home phone still worked, and we talked to our girls and told them we were safe and that they were to stay with my Mum and Dad until it was safe for them to come home. They cried because they wanted to come home. Jack organised someone to pick up the car and spoke to the farm manager, telling him we had arrived at the house, and would try and feed the cows and horses until he could get in.

The next day was spent checking on the animals and feeding them. Jack said that one of the neighbour's cows had broken through the fence and got into the hay shed and eaten so much hay she'd laid down and died.

The following day I was so ill I had to stay in bed, and poor Jack had to do all the jobs himself. We still had no power, but we did have food and a fire. On the third day the water started to recede, and the sun managed to find its way through the clouds.

On the fourth day, we could see the devastation of the floods. We had fences down and debris everywhere. But with the power back on, at last we could have a shower and wash the dirt off our bodies and out of our hair. We phoned our girls and told them they could come home tomorrow. They were so excited that they could at last come home.

I recovered from the flu and resumed duties. Jack was much stronger than I, he soldiered on every day without complaining, but he looked exhausted. It was wonderful to have everything return to normal. The farm manager would be busy repairing the fences and getting rid of the debris.

# Chapter Seventeen
# The Evolution of 'Inverness'
# 1986–1993

With further purchases of yearlings, and some of our race fillies were being retired for mare duties, the concept of our thoroughbred stud was evolving. We decided to carry on the name of Inverness, and so Inverness Thoroughbred Horse Stud became a reality.

Australia was experiencing an economic slowdown and Jack thought this presented an opportunity to buy good broodmares as foundation mares for our stud. He bought Miami Vice, Rosalina, Audeena, Shinakima, and Threesome. Later, he purchased Tynia, A Star is Born, Maximum Effort, Melrose and I'm in Business These mares were all very well bred with plenty of BLACK TYPE. We went over to New Zealand to buy a stallion and came home with two stallions and more broodmares. The stallions were Sackford and Phizam.

Our lives settled into a hectic rhythm of work and travelling. Jack still consulted in his rooms five days a week, as well as looking after all his inpatients in TSH and in Kareena Private Hospital, which was across the road.

He drove to and from Miranda each day, about two hours each way, then on the weekends when we were home, we had farm work and farm meetings to discuss mare matings, as well as business affairs to attend to, including financial decisions and marketing strategies. We also attended frequent horse-race meetings in Sydney, regional areas and interstate; horse sales four or five times a year in Sydney, interstate and internationally, as well as medical conferences nationally and internationally four or five times each year.

This was our life for years to come.

Unfortunately, our farm-managing arrangement was coming undone. Our farm manager found the work more than he could handle and asked if his son could come and work with him. Sadly, his son was very lazy and so this arrangement did not work out and the farm manager decided he would leave us.

We advertised for a new manager and we were delighted when an amiable young man with horse experience applied for the job. He came for an interview and he started work immediately. He asked if his wife could work with him. We were happy to accommodate this, as the horse stud was growing and it was obvious we needed more employees.

Judy's Great-Aunt Muriel Gillett passed away 22 October 1987.

Muriel had been a wonderful friend and it was a pleasure to have her in our family. She was fondly called Moo Moo. Whenever she visited, she would always bring a gift, usually a small tin of beetroot, or a small tin of tuna or some other grocery item. She also never forgot the children's birthdays. She would give me a small amount of money to purchase a suitable gift for each of our daughters on their birthday.

She was so sensible, she realised that she had no idea what to buy the girls and so decided to give me the task. She loved our children and adored Judy, she phoned Judy almost every day. She left most of her estate to Judy, a blessing that enabled Judy to have a pool and make other home improvements.

Early 1988 I had a terrifying attack of chest pain with shortness of breath. Jack took me to Bowral Hospital where they performed an ECG which was normal. Thank goodness. But I was still in pain and short of breath. Jack took me to TSH, where they X-rayed me to rule out gall stones.

The X-ray showed a mass of tiny gall stones which was causing all the trouble.

Gilbert was called and he decided to perform a cholecystectomy. One week post-op, Jack took me home to Bowral to recuperate. A few days later, Jack lovingly made me a cup of coffee and unfortunately, I had a terrible reaction to it (I haven't touched coffee since). I fully recovered and returned to work three days a week.

Jacqui and Sara completed their Higher School Certificate in 1988.

Jack received an invitation from Merck Sharp and Dohme (MSD) to attend a cardiac conference in Paris in late November of 1988. MSD invited him as their guest with all expenses paid, that is, his business class airfares, accommodation and meals.

We had a family discussion about the conference, and we asked the girls if they would like to come. However, the conference dates coincided with Jacqui and Sara's Year 12 Formal, a very important social event for Year 12's.

Finally, we decided to go, leaving a little earlier so we could take the three girls with us. We told Jacqui and Sara that this trip would be their 'schoolies week,' as we were not keen for them to participate in a 'schoolies week' on the Gold Coast. We agreed that the girls would return home earlier than Jack and I, so that they could attend their Formal and we could attend the conference.

The conference venue in Paris was the Hotel Lutetia, a luxury hotel in an excellent location. The few days we had with the girls prior to the conference were amazing. There was a transport strike, so we had to walk everywhere, a blessing in disguise, because we found you see so much more on foot than if you were travelling by car or train.

We walked the streets of Paris, taking in all the usual tourist destinations – the Champs-Elysée, the Louvre, the Eiffel Tower, the Notre-Dame Cathedral. We walked to Montmartre, took a boat ride on the River Seine, and of course, there was plenty of shopping. Jack and I took the girls to the airport for their adventure-flight home without parents (I was more worried than they were). We'd arranged for someone to meet them at the airport and take them home to Bowral.

Jack asked MSD if I could attend the conference as I was an integral part of his cardiology practice. They were delighted to have me join.

The conference was officially opened at a lavish dinner in an exclusive restaurant, Le Pre Catalan situated in the Bois de Boulogne, a rambling park west of Paris, covering 2090 acres (845 hectares).

All the guests were picked up from the hotel and taken to the restaurant by bus. The bus trip was an experience! We were taken through the park, and, along the road, we were treated to 'ladies of the night' exposing themselves as the bus passed by. They were wearing fur coats and as the bus approached, they opened their coats wide to expose their scantily-clad bodies. Great entertainment for the gentlemen.

One of our cohort told us that at this restaurant we'd need two credit cards to pay the bill. As we approached, it was indeed a magnificent sight. We entered the restaurant via a massive marquee draped in white silk and festooned with oversized sparkling chandeliers.

A line of waiters greeted us, each holding a tray of champagne-filled glasses. After an appropriate interval to mingle and sip our drinks, a waiter led us into the restaurant to our table. We had been placed at a table for eight, alongside other English-speaking couples. Our conversation was a little formal to begin with, as we introduced ourselves and made small talk.

The conference co-ordinator made a welcome speech and invited us to enjoy our evening. The first course arrived, with a waiter per person. The immaculately uniformed staff paraded out, holding silver platters covered with a silver dome, and each waiter ceremoniously stood behind a guest.

Then, when the maître d' gave the command, the white-gloved waiters, with perfect timing, placed the platter on the table in

*Jack and Sue at a conference*

front of their guest and, on a second command, removed the silver dome. The precision was breathtaking! It was all so meticulously orchestrated. This performance repeated for all four courses, each accompanied by a matched wine. What a splendid night! [Le Pre Catalan was opened in 1856 and in 2007 received 3 Michelin Hats.]

The conference commenced daily with breakfast at the hotel, followed by lectures. Lunch was served in a hall adjacent to the lecture rooms. Long tables were laden with platters of the most delightful hors d'oeuvres and petit fours, served with red and white wine.

The lectures were in English, though their accents made it tricky for me to understand (Jack seemed to catch the gist of the topic). At the end of the conference, we flew home the following day into the arms of our three precious girls who were full of stories of their adventure flying home, sans parents.

## 1989

Jack had a car accident on the way home from TSH.

Fortunately, the car suffered more injuries than Jack, although he was shaken up.

Following this catastrophe, we decided we had to return to the Sutherland Shire to live, before a more serious accident happened. The plan was to rent a home while we looked around for somewhere permanent. We found a home to rent in Woolooware Road, Cronulla, near the Royal Motor Yacht Club, and settled in nicely.

Shortly after moving, I was admitted to TSH for removal of my left ovary. Unfortunately, it took me longer than expected to recover, probably because it had only been a year since the cholecystectomy.

## THE EVOLUTION OF 'INVERNESS' 1986-1993

Our change of abode coincided with Jacqui starting a course at Ryde TAFE, studying horticulture, and Sara going to the University of New England at Armidale to study economics. Sara lived on campus and Jacqui stayed with Jack and I. Later, Jacqui transferred to Wollongong TAFE and lived at the farm.

Meanwhile, Jack had become aware of the use of ultrasound to study the carotid arteries. Vascular surgeons told Jack that if we could do these studies, they would refer patients to us.

We searched for a Vascular Workshop and found that the ATL company in Seattle were hosting a workshop on ultrasound of the carotid arteries. Here was our next venture. It did not take me long to become proficient in the carotid-artery study, which I found less complicated than a cardiac study.

On 21 August 1990 Jack turned 65 yr and this was a date that he wasn't looking forward to as it meant that his life would change, as this was his retirement date from his position at Public Hospitals. In 1990 all doctors employed in Public Hospitals were required to retire when they turned 65.

Sutherland Hospital gave Jack a wonderful farewell reception. There were speeches acknowledging his tireless dedication and commitment to the hospital and his patients, and his unwavering drive and determination to open an Echo Lab in The Sutherland Hospital. He was so determined that The Sutherland Hospital should have an Echo Lab that he offered to provide the Echo machines and ancillaries plus my services and Jack's services for free until Medicare had an Item number for the Echo study. ..The Echo Lab was opened late in 1976. The Hospital appreciated the immensely significant contribution made by Dr Jack Woolridge. There were many handshakes and tears.

Of course this didn't mean that he would be fully retired, he would continue consulting in his rooms at Miranda and his patients who needed hospitalisation would be admitted to Kareena Private Hospital. The word retirement was not in his vocabulary. He still had so much more to achieve, there were ambitions and aspirations still to be fulfilled and further accomplishments and successes yet to be reached.

January 1991 – Jack's hunger for learning new things was insatiable. When the vascular surgeons asked Jack if we could do ultrasound studies of the arteries and veins in the abdomen and legs, we were on our way back to Seattle for a further workshop.

My armamentarium of ultrasound studies was growing. But wait, later that year, Jack found another workshop for us to attend – on transcranial doppler evaluation. We were now equipped to examine the flow of the arteries in the head.

During the first transcranial doppler study carried out in our rooms, we found a mobile blood clot in one of the patient's cranial arteries. A eureka moment for us, but not for the patient.

Jack was keen to buy another racehorse and so we booked a holiday on the Gold Coast to attend the Magic Millions Yearling sales in January 1992. We purchased a filly that caught Jack's eye, firstly because of her breeding and secondly, he liked the look of her. We named her Telephone Girl.

Meanwhile, Jacqui had to do work experience as part of her horticultural course. She secured a stint at Milton Park, Bowral. She enjoyed learning in their world-renowned gardens, but as the work grew heavier, it worsened her chronic back pain (she has spinal scoliosis). She decided to change career paths and enrolled in an Ella Bache Beautician course – a positive move. She thoroughly enjoyed the course and opened a salon.

At the same time, Sara was unhappy at Armidale and also chose to shift career path, to become an Echocardiographer, like her mother. Jack and I were happy for her to change and arranged for her to start working at Jack's practice.

By 1992 it was becoming obvious that we'd outgrown our Miranda rooms, so we looked at the vacant suites next door, a new office block completed in 1990. The developer was hoping to fill the ground-floor suites with medical practitioners, and most of the suites were still empty. We contacted the selling agent and chose Suite #12 on the ground floor at the front of the building. A ground-floor suite has always been our priority.

One of the great attributes of the #12 suite was that it was big enough to accommodate Jack's office needs as well as a separate beauty salon for Jacqui. We arranged for a company called Spinners to do the fit-out for both medical practice and the beauty salon.

We drew up plans and delivered them to the manager at Spinners, who assured us he had a capable young man – John – who would complete the work. The Spinners' Manager was correct; John was efficient and his workmanship could not be faulted. We moved in during 1992, all of us thrilled with our new office and Jacqui excited with her new salon.

During the build, Jacqui and John started going out together. John was a personable young man with a 4-year-old son, Brandon. Brandon would come with his dad when he worked on the weekends. John was a good father. He and his wife had divorced and Brandon lived with John and John's parents, Elaine and Don, who helped care for Brandon while John worked.

After we moved into the new building, we placed our old suite with a real estate agent and sold to Dr David Mann.

## 1993

*For Telephone Girl 1993 race results refer to Horse Lists in Further Reading.*

Rebecca completed her Higher School Certificate in 1992 and could not make up her mind what she wanted to do, eventually deciding to work on the farm. Jack and I agreed to this, though we wondered if she realised how hard farm work can be? Still, she seemed to settle smoothly into her new occupation.

Our Stud was expanding and we needed more accommodation for the people who worked for us. We planned to build a house, but due to council limitations, we were limited to building on the back 100 acres of the farm, which was disappointing as we would have preferred to have all the infrastructure in one area, close to the entry of the farm.

Once we got over this disappointment, we settled on a site approximately halfway to the back gate. Keen to build as soon as possible, we chose an Ausco home, a pre-built home built in Wagga Wagga.

On 29 October 1993, we received building approval from the council to build the manager's cottage on Lot 14 McCourt Rd Burradoo, our chosen site. The house was transported by truck and came in two sections. When it arrived, it was lifted on to the brick-foundation piers, built prior to the house sections arriving.

The house had three bedrooms, one bathroom, living room, laundry, eat-in kitchen and a front verandah. The total cost of the house was $85,610.00 and it was ready to live in a week after it arrived on the farm. The bathroom came with a toilet, shower, bath and vanity basin, and the kitchen came complete with cupboards, a sink, taps and a stove.

Ausco organised an electrician to hook up the pre-wired electricals, and a plumber to connect the water taps to the water supply and the toilet to a new septic installation, which we organised through a local plumber. We also arranged for a water tank to be delivered and then connected to the new house.

## Chapter Eighteen
## Sweet Dreams, Then a Nightmare
## 1993–1994

In winter of 1993 we moved into an apartment in Cronulla, after months of inspections, due to our indecision because the apartment appeared to us to be too small, as our previous apartment in Sylvania had been expansive with five large bedrooms and a huge living area.

We were now left with large furniture that would not fit into our new abode, and so we gave away most of it, but kept the most sentimental pieces, including artworks. Among these was an extraordinary Chinese painting of eight galloping horses. The horses are in shades of grey through to black and are painted on white silk. There are no background drawings, it is simply eight galloping horses, and, of course, 8 is a significant number in Chinese culture, it is a sign of luck. Jack received the painting from a Mr T, a Chinese gentleman who had been a longtime patient.

I remember this day, it was during the 1970s. Jack called me into his room to assist with Mr T's stress test, and as the consultation was coming to a conclusion, I witnessed the following scene: Mr T reached into his briefcase and retrieved a small plastic bag, about 20 cm × 15 cm.

The plastic bag appeared old, dirty and tattered and looked like it had been sitting in a shed somewhere for many years. Mr T solemnly presented the plastic bag to Jack, who fumbled with the bag, looking slightly embarrassed.

Mr T kindly offered to assist. Jack appeared grateful to be relieved of the responsibility of opening the tattered bag and gently handed it to Mr T, who slowly and carefully eased out what looked like a piece of white material from its confines.

He unfolded the fabric with great reverence. Jack and I were both stunned to see this magnificent piece of art unfold before our eyes. The fabric, which Mr T said was Chinese Silk, measured 1.90 m × 0.86 m, and the painting, as Mr T explained, was by a famous Chinese artist, the first to paint horses in European style.

Mr T solemnly folded the piece of silk and returned it to its tattered incarceration.

Mr T lived in Cronulla with his wife, an attractive, delightful woman, who was shy and unashamedly a Christian who volunteered her time to charities. Mr T travelled frequently to China on business. He told Jack during a consultation that he was trying to arrange finance to build freeways in China. He said that banks in Australia did not have the wherewithal for the sort of money he needed for his project, and so he was seeking finance from banks around the world. He expected to find the appropriate finance in Germany, England or the USA.

Mr T came across as a pleasant, quiet and unassuming man. We took the little tattered plastic bag and its contents home and placed it in a drawer for safe keeping.

Our little plastic bag and its treasure moved with us from house to house until it was rediscovered one day in 1987. Both Jack and I were guilty of completely forgetting about this gracious gift from Mr T.

I felt so conscience-stricken, it shook me out of my apathy and sent me with the silk treasure to an art framer in Miranda Fair. I was unaware that the gentleman who owned the framing shop was Chinese, which turned out to be the perfect scenario.

I gently exposed the silk painting on the desk in front of the shop owner, whose face erupted with delight. He could not contain himself!

'Do you know what you have here?' he said, over and over again.

I told him the story and he shook his head in disbelief. He told me that the artist's name was Xu Beihong. I asked him if he would write the name down for me. He asked me which frame we wanted, and I decided to accede to his discretion.

The result was excellent. He told me he'd had to frame the piece in a specific way so as to preserve the silk and the painting. He chose a beautiful rosewood frame with a special glass to protect the painting, and the result magnified the beauty of the art.

The painting followed us through a number of house moves and, on the last move, the removalists let it slip out of their hands and it dropped heavily on the pavement. Much to our relief the only damage was a chip off the corner of the frame, otherwise all was well. It could have been a disastrous accident, as, if the glass had shattered, it would have torn the silk and probably destroy the painting.

Over dinner one night, we were talking about 'our painting' and our young ones Googled Xu Beihong and his work. Suddenly, the room erupted; his original artwork was bringing millions of dollars! The following day, I phoned Sotheby's and told the story

*Painting of 8 galloping horses by Xu Beihong*

and asked if they could value it for me, they agreed and asked for a photo with the dimensions of the painting.

We duly followed through, everyone excited with anticipation. Three days later, I received a phone call from the auctioneers.

'I am afraid, Madam, your painting is a copy, probably by one of Xu Beihong's students. One notable characteristic is that the signature is embroidered. Therefore, it is not worth very much, but if you have pleasure from it, then keep it and enjoy it.'

The family's jubilation deflated. We all had had such wonderful dreams of wealth and had spent the money many times over. A few years later, we heard from a friend of Mr T's that the Chinese Government had cancelled the highways Mr T had been building for the last three or four years and that he'd lost all his family's wealth. He'd had to sell their large glamorous home and buy a very modest home.

So embarrassed by their loss, the family had become virtual prisoners, too ashamed to face their friends. Mr T died a short time later.

How sad life can be sometimes, but a joyful occasion was on the horizon.

## SWEET DREAMS, THEN A NIGHTMARE 1993–1994

Jacqui and John were married on 20 November 1993 at our Bowral farm. The eve of the wedding dawned a hot November day, beautiful, with blue sky and sunshine. A huge marquee was erected in the garden next to the house, and trucks pulled up with chairs, tables and the floor for the marquee.

Everything was going according to plan; Jacqui was having a wedding rehearsal with her bridesmaids and our friend Lyn. Lyn had been a singer on the TV program *Bandstand* and was our neighbour when we lived at Lilli Pilli. She offered to sing at Jacqui's wedding and had come to the farm for a practice. She was to sing as Jacqui emerged from the house to walk along the pathway to the gazebo in the rose garden, Jacqui's chosen venue for the ceremony. The practice looked and sounded delightful, and everyone seemed to know what they should be doing.

Just on dusk, a mini cyclone swept through the farm. The wind was ferocious and the rain torrential, and in the midst of the mayhem, Rebecca remembered that the sound equipment was in the marquee getting wet. The call went out to the boys to help bring all the electrical equipment into the garage out of the storm. The boys said they had to try and tie down the marquee as it looked like it would be blown to Sydney.

The cyclone lasted 30 to 45 minutes and we were so relieved when the wind and rain eventually died down. We fearfully ventured outside to check the damage. Miraculously, we still had an upright marquee. The chairs and tables had been blown about but there appeared to be little damage. We would have to wait until morning to decide what was needed by way of repairs. At least the sound equipment had been dried successfully with hair dryers.

The next day dawned wet and freezing cold, with a maximum temperature of 10 degrees. How disappointing. The grounds around the marquee were an absolute quagmire of mud, water and slush. One of the boys had an idea and called on a friend to help him. They brought in metres and metres of artificial grass. They covered the mud and slush with sand and then laid the artificial grass over the sand.

Men were laying the wooden flooring in the marquee and setting up the tables and chairs. The flowers arrived and the girls set about decorating the marquee. There were people everywhere. Someone was dispatched to pick up the wedding cake, a Croquembouche (this traditional French wedding cake is a tower of cream profiteroles, placed in a conical shape, drizzled with caramel toffee).

The rain unfortunately did not abate, and Jacqui was beside herself, she had been dreaming of exchanging vows in the rose garden.

We were all dressed, ready for the occasion, and opened a bottle of champagne to toast the day.

It was still raining. The Minister Rev Alan Wilson arrived and asked where the ceremony was taking place, and we told him of Jacqui's wishes. He said, 'I am not going out in the rain,' and Jacqui said, 'I am not going to be married in the house,' and so we had a standoff.

Guests were arriving and sheltering in the marquee.

The standoff continued. Jacqui was upstairs, and the Minister was downstairs, both adamant. I had to make a decision. It was obvious we could not ask everyone to stand in the rain while Jacqui and John were married.

I asked a few of the strong young men to move the furniture out of the dining/lounge room so that we could hold the ceremony there. I thought the large bay window would be an ideal place for John and Jacqui and the minister to stand.

I asked the boys to leave some chairs so that older people could sit, and everyone else could stand where they were comfortable. I managed to convince Jacqui that this was the only way she would be getting married today. She conceded after many tears.

We patched up her makeup and organised the bridesmaids, and the junior attendants, John's son Brandon and Judy's daughter, Elizabeth, both 8 years old and perfect for junior attendants. The plan was that the attendants would walk down the stairs and into the lounge room followed by Jacqui and Jack, accompanied by the music, with Lyn singing.

It ended up being a lovely, intimate affair, and everyone was happy. After the ceremony, we all headed to the marquee. The caterers had arrived during the ceremony and had everything ready to go as guests entered the marquee and were ushered to their tables. We celebrated well into the night.

Shortly after Jacqui's wedding, my mother was hospitalised due to ill health. She had been experiencing short-term memory loss since she was in her mid-50s. She was now 70. During her hospitalisation, she suffered hallucinations and her short-term memory loss markedly deteriorated. This was distressing to watch.

## 1994

*For Telephone Girl 1994 race results refer to Horse Lists in Further Reading.*

Early 1994 brought tragedy. Jack's friend Lou L and his second wife, Joanne, were flying back to Sydney from Port Macquarie in Lou's plane, a Beechcraft Baron. Lou had often invited Jack and I to fly with him in his plane, but because I was apprehensive about flying in a small aircraft, we declined his many invitations.

On this day, 17 February 1994, Lou was apparently flying low in overcast weather and crashed into Diamond Head, just south of Port Macquarie. Lou had two other passengers who both survived with significant, life-threatening injuries. Lou and Joanne did not survive. Jack and I felt the loss of our friend.

Rebecca came to us with another proposition. She felt she had worked out her apprenticeship at the farm and now wanted to attend Wollongong Tafe and study Japanese for Hospitality. At the same time, she managed to secure a job at the Briars, a popular restaurant in Bowral which has accommodation, and a facility for weddings and other celebrations. She was happy with her new occupation.

My mother, Ruby, was diagnosed with Alzheimers', what a tragic diagnosis.

In early 1994, we purchased 2 × 100-acre blocks, Lot 10 and Lot 11 Windella Road (off Oldbury Road) Moss Vale. Beautiful country, gentle rolling hills with plenty of feed and water, perfect for us to run extra steers and spell broodmares.

Sara met Doug early in 1994. Doug is good-looking, a Tom Cruise look alike. He is a Vet and a Queenslander and loves cricket, so he and Jack have this commonality. Sara and Doug were married on 15 October 1994 at the charming Uniting Church at Sutton Forest, followed by a beautiful reception at The Briars. Fortunately, there were no mini cyclones at Sara's wedding!

The following month, on 7 November, after a disagreement, Jack wrote a love letter to me and put it on my pillow.

### Dec 1994 Jack – Another heart attack

Jack developed significant chest pain one night in December 1994. I took him to the rooms and had a look at his heart on the Echo machine, he had a wall motion defect which suggested he was having an infarct (a heart attack).

I phoned Roger and he said to jump in the car and bring Jack straight to POW. He said he would arrange Jack's admission so that there was no hold up. When we arrived, we were met by a wardsman and wheelchair at the front door. The wardsman quickly wheeled Jack to the Intensive Care Unit (ICU) where Roger assessed Jack.

Roger told me Jack had suffered a subendocardial anterior infarction, which was what I was seeing on the Echo.

Roger arranged an angiogram, which showed a 90 per cent obstruction in the left anterior descending coronary artery, an 80 per cent obstruction in the proximal left anterior descending artery and a 30 per cent obstruction of the distal left main coronary artery. There was also a complete obstruction of the proximal right coronary artery, which caused his previous infarction.

He was in a lot of trouble. He needed urgent surgery for quadruple coronary artery grafts. Roger spoke to the cardiothoracic surgeon, who was in theatre.

Jack deteriorated quickly, and Roger arranged for an aortic balloon pump, usually only used in life-threatening situations. Roger hoped it would keep Jack going until the surgeon was available to operate. Roger informed the surgeon of Jack's deterioration. The surgeon said he would operate on Jack as soon as he had finished the case he was operating on. Jack was taken into theatre about midnight.

It was a long agonising night. Jacqui, Sara and Rebecca joined me in the waiting room, where we huddled together, trembling with trepidation. There was an air of foreboding and many tears were shed and lots of hugs were shared between us. We could not bear the thought of losing Jack. We needed each other's company and support.

The surgeon eventually came out, looking exhausted and

dishevelled but with a quiet smile on his lips. Softly, he murmured that all went well. Oh, thank you so much.

To our disbelief, following a marathon surgical procedure, Jack made a fast recovery.

He was discharged on the fourth day, post-op. Oh! What a wonderful day that was. I picked him up from POW, still in shock that I was actually taking him home.

Approaching Miranda, he said, 'Let's call in to the Rooms so we can see how things are going.'

Can you believe it? After all he'd been through, his first thought was, 'Can I go to my office?' How could I refuse? Even though he looked, and was, very unwell. Everyone was shocked as he walked in, or should I say, shuffled in, squeezing my hand tightly for support.

An expression of delight lit up his face as he walked through the door, and we could all feel the thrill and sense the triumph he felt with every step. He could not wait to get back to the coalface. Slowly, he made his way into his room, relishing every step. Slowly and guardedly, he sat in his big chair behind the desk and then breathed a great sigh of pleasure. His face glowed with gratification that he could at last come and sit in *his* chair overlooking *his* domain.

Adele, our secretary, fussed over him, and brought him his favourite cup of coffee, and they chatted about some of the patient dramas that unfolded during his absence.

'When are you coming back to work?' she asked, cheekily, to which he replied, just as cheekily, 'Tomorrow.'

Somehow, I managed to keep him at home for the next four weeks. Adele and I managed to keep the office under control, and then, on the fifth week, we gradually came back to work. The first week, we worked half time, which he found exhausting.

He was so determined to increase the workload, that by the sixth week, he was back to full time: 6.30 am to 9 pm Monday to Friday, followed by weekends at the farm.

His physical activities were severely restricted for six weeks to allow the healing of his ribs, and his leg and chest wounds. In the by-pass surgery, they'd opened his chest and cracked open the rib cage to access the heart, and following the grafting of the arteries, the rib cage is wired back together and the chest closed.

Besides the chest wounds, Jack had 15 cm wounds on both calves from surgery to harvest his veins to use for the by-passes of his coronary arteries.

When Jack returned to his consultation rooms, Sara and I performed all the physical work in his office – taking blood pressures, performing ECGs, Echos and stress tests. Other duties included assisting patients on and off the bed, and helping the elderly dress and put on their shoes, etc.

At the farm, he was restricted to a slow car ride on the asphalt road, or a gentle walk in the garden. He was so pleased when his penitentiary term was over.

## Chapter Nineteen
## A Win, Then Mutiny
## 1995–1996

It was a typically busy day at work when I received a phone call from the editor of a thoroughbred-horse magazine. Part of our marketing strategy for the stud was to place advertisements in thoroughbred-horse magazines, advertising our stallions and yearling sales.

The editor informed me that we had won a trip to Ireland. I could not remember entering any competition and he explained that everyone who placed advertisements in their magazine during the month of February received an entry into the competition. Inverness Stud was the winner.

The prize was return airfares to London for two, with accommodation and an invitation to attend the Royal Ascot meeting on Thursday, which is traditionally Ladies' Day, and the Gold Cup, a Group 1 race.

Jack and I could not believe our unexpected good fortune.

Taking advantage of our windfall, we invited our stud manager and his wife to join us as a reward for their work in establishing our stud.

It was a welcome opportunity to visit thoroughbred studs in Ireland and establish valuable contacts, while promoting our stud.

## 1995

*For Telephone Girl 1995 race results refer to Horse Lists in Further Reading.*

*For Give Us a Go 1995 race results refer to Horse Lists in Further Reading.*

In early 1995 Rebecca started a hospitality course at Macleay College, Sydney.

This was also the year Jacqui's first baby (and our first grandchild), Talissa Jean was born.

Jacqui and John decided that Jacqui should be an at-home-mum, which meant that her beauty salon was no longer needed, and we could now incorporate this area into our office.

Jack had a meeting with his friend and colleague Roger and invited him to practice from our suite of rooms in Miranda. Roger was delighted, and so were we. Roger was an interventionalist physician and his practice would harmonise with Jack's practice.

We organised a fit out, extending the waiting room and creating another consultation room for Roger. Roger started practising from our rooms in early 1996.

## 1996

*For Dream Catcher 1996 race results refer to Horse Lists in Further Reading.*

Rebecca was also starting something new. She wanted to go backpacking in England, where she'd meet up with two friends

# A WIN, THEN MUTINY 1995–1996

and backpack together. We said OK, with a proviso – that we buy her a return ticket, so that if she needed to or wanted to return to Australia, she'd have a ticket ready to fly home.

Reluctantly, we helped her buy her backpack, sleeping bag, and other backpacking essentials. When she packed her pack and put it on her back, I could not imagine her going very far with such a huge bag on her back!

We said a very teary goodbye. She wasn't sure how long she would be away, maybe a year? Each day she was away was agonising for me, I missed her so much. At first, she did not communicate with us, and then, about three months later, we had a very teary daughter on the phone.

She abruptly finished her call, and I said to Jack, 'Something is terribly wrong, Rebecca's crying and not saying anything. I am going to phone her back and tell her she doesn't have to stay away, she can come home immediately.'

She was home within a week. The day of her return was one of the best days of my life, to feel her in my arms safe and sound.

We decided to sell the two 100-acre blocks at Moss Vale that we'd purchased in 1990. The logistics of sending someone to check on the cattle and horses were weighing on us.

Jack and I went to the Magic Millions Sale at the Gold Coast in January 1996. As usual, Jack had been studying the sale catalogue over the Christmas break and had chosen a few yearlings to look at.

We arrived at the Gold Coast a couple of days before the sale, and the day before the sale, we went to the sale complex to look at the yearlings Jack had marked in the catalogue. We were looking at fillies, mainly, but a young colt caught his eye, and he liked its breeding. I didn't like it that much, but I'd learnt to go with Jack's judgement and intuition.

I thought Jack had lost interest in the colt, but as the colt came into the ring, I noticed that Jack wasn't sitting next to me, he had slipped away. As the bidding started, I had an intuitive feeling that Jack might be somewhere watching the bidding, to see where it might lead to.

Just as the bidding started to warm up, I caught a glimpse of him on the other side of the ring, and sure enough he was bidding. I shook my head and laughed. He bought the colt for $12,000.00. Jack came back with a cheeky grin, and I said, 'I saw you.' He laughed.

We arranged for a carrier we'd used previously to transport the colt to our farm. The colt arrived in Bowral two days later, which surprised us, as we had anticipated an earlier arrival. We named the colt Count Scenario.

When we arrived at the farm the following weekend, we had a major falling out with our farm manager. Jack told him we were disappointed in him and asked him to improve his performance.

He retaliated and said he quit. Jack kept calm, saying, 'I want that in writing by 12 noon.' To our surprise, he arrived with his letter just before noon, but he wasn't going quietly. He rounded up the other staff members and told them he was leaving, and if they had any sense, they would leave too.

Within days, they all left, except for one 18-year-old girl, one of the junior staff on the stud. She quietly did what she was told and was still learning how to handle horses. She was the only one prepared to stay and work until new staff were employed.

But he hadn't finished; our now ex-farm manager phoned all the clients who had broodmares on the stud and told them he was leaving immediately and there would be no one to look after their horses and they should come and take their horses to another stud as soon as possible.

Up until then, we had not had much to do with our junior

staff member. We knew this young girl by sight, she was average height, and was slightly built with dark unruly hair. She was quiet, always polite and pleasant, with a sweet, shy smile and eyes now clouded with apprehension.

All we could do was ask her to manage as best she could. She said she knew which feeds to give the mares and stallions.

This was a disaster for our stud. We were still feeling our way into the thoroughbred-breeding industry. Our racehorses were doing well and winning races. We were worried that this upheaval at our stud would severely set back our reputation in the stud industry, as news like this travels fast, and the truth gets lost and becomes distorted.

# Chapter Twenty
## Resuscitation
## 1996–2000

The day our farm manager resigned, Jack phoned Inglis', the premier stud and stock agents in Australia, and enquired about finding a new farm manager.

The next day, Inglis' phoned to recommend a man named Ross Bone. They said he was well liked, had an excellent reputation and was a hard worker. Jack phoned Ross and told him we were looking for a manager and would he be interested?

Jack explained our plight and that, under the circumstances, we needed someone to start immediately. Jack suggested we meet at our stud, have a talk and look at the property, and, if we liked one another, he could think about our offer.

The following day, Ross arrived at the farm with his wife, Narelle. We showed them around and introduced them to our loyal junior farm worker.

We had an immediate rapport with Ross and Narelle. They were obviously good people and looked like they had worked hard most of their lives. Ross was friendly and knowledgeable, having worked in the industry for years. He told us that after his father

*Ross Bone our Farm Manager*

kicked him out of home when he was 14, he went jackarooing up north, where he learnt a lot about horses in his early years.

We offered Ross the job and he said he would come if his wife could have a job too. This was perfect, as we urgently needed staff. Unfortunately, Ross said he could not start straight away, as he felt he had an obligation to his present employer to finish the foaling season. He told us that his present employers had been good to him but offered limited opportunities for promotion.

Ross recognised we were in a bind, with only one teenaged girl working on the farm, and suggested Narelle could start straight away. He told us she was a great worker and organiser. We agreed and Ross said he would start as soon as he finished the season, and would liaise with Narelle every day as he completed his stint at the other stud.

Ross' loyalty to his employers was a great sign to us that we were employing someone of high integrity and honour, rare traits to find.

While we could never have expected one young girl to manage the stud – an enormous task for anyone, let alone someone so young and inexperienced – we were grateful for her loyalty and the enormous effort she had put in to keep the stud running.

We were also thankful that she'd been so brave to stay when everyone else left. This would have taken a lot of courage and our stud would not have survived without her. Who would have thought that an 18-year-old girl could look after 45 broodmares and foals and two stallions on her own? We were amazed at how hard she worked, the long hours she put in, and her devotion to duty, which demonstrated her resilience, strength of character, determination, bravery and maturity.

Narelle arrived at the stud the following day. Jack and I were back in Sydney working, and so Narelle was on her own with our junior and together they not only fed and looked after the horses, but they also cleaned and tidied the stables and sheds which had been neglected; they were full of cobwebs, rubbish and dirt.

She found farm tools everywhere, not only in the sheds, but out in the paddocks, so she cleaned them and placed them in their rightful place. She gave all the farm vehicles a thorough clean.

The manager's cottage and staff quarters also cried out for much needed attention.

Narelle scrubbed and cleaned and after a few weeks, she had everything looking like a shiny new pin. Jack and I could not believe our eyes when Ross and Narelle showed us around. We were astounded by how much she'd achieved and felt fortunate and blessed to have her on our team.

When Ross arrived at the farm a few weeks later, things

continued to get into shape. We arrived the following weekend and spent most of the day touring the farm and making decisions. Then we came to Count Scenario in the paddock.

'Who bought this bastard?' said Ross. 'He is a horrible looking horse.'

My heart sank. I looked at Jack's face, knowing he'd be hurt by this comment. Jack had chosen the Count from the Magic Millions yearling catalogue because of his breeding; he was a Scenic colt out of the mare Rose Babu, an excellent pedigree.

Jack owned up. They had a close look at the colt and Ross said, 'His fetlock is twisted and lumpy. I don't know whether it is broken or dislocated, we had better get a Vet to have a look at him.'

Ross made a few phone calls and reported to Jack that the Count had had rotor virus as a foal, and as a rule you don't buy yearlings that have had rotor virus, as this can affect their ability to breathe adequately when they race.

What more could be wrong with Jack's treasured purchase?

Ross consulted a veterinarian, who reported to Ross, 'The fetlock is dislocated; get rid of him, he will never race.' Jack was heartbroken. Jack and Ross had a long talk and they decided to wait a while and then break him in. After he was broken in, they planned that he should have a good spell in a good paddock and then they'd reassess. I think Ross realised how much Jack liked this horse.

Weeks passed, and Ross thought the Count was improving. Ross broke him in and after riding him a few times, surprisingly he declared the Count was the best horse he had ridden – a lovely, smooth horse to ride. Ross arranged for a young girl from Tocal College to ride him every day for a few weeks and then planned to put him in a nice paddock to spell for a month or two.

After the spell, the Count was sent to horse trainer Paul Perry,

*Exercising horses at Inverness Stud*

who trained him for three months, gave the Count a run at Newcastle, and a run at Kembla, before sending him home for another spell. Paul was not enthusiastic about the horse, so we sent him to another trainer, Bede Murray, after his spell.

His racing was unremarkable until Bede put him in blinkers.

In the meantime, Ross was gathering a small team of knowledgeable, loyal workers who had previously been working on stud farms, and he managed to entice a top Broodmare Manager from another stud to join him at Inverness.

My mother's Alzheimer's deteriorated and in 1996 she was admitted to Garrawarra Hospital, Waterfall, as my father was not managing to look after her at home. She was under the care of a geriatrician.

## 1996 – Melbourne Yearling Sales

Ross prepared our yearlings for the Melbourne Yearling Sale in March.

Narelle and Ross left about a week before the sale with a truckload of yearlings. Jack and I arrived the day before the sales started. Ross took us on a tour and showed Jack the yearlings he thought had interesting pedigrees.

On our way back to the stalls where our yearlings were boxed, Ross took us to meet an Irish fellow, Dermot, the Yearling Manager for Emirates Stud, who were also selling at the sale. Their horses were stabled just down the aisle from where our yearlings were stabled.

In his inimitable, friendly way, Ross started chatting to Dermot, and then introduced us. It was the beginning of a great friendship which morphed into a successful business relationship.

At the sales, there is always great camaraderie in the stables among the stud grooms. Stud grooms are female and male and a mixed bag – some are teenagers, some old, some short, some tall, thin ones, fat ones, and they all wear the same 'uniform' of blue jeans, a shirt displaying the stud name and logo, a stud hat (also with a logo) and RM Williams™-type boots, otherwise known as a 'dealer' boot. These boots are popular because they are safe and can be slipped on and off with ease.

It was here we experienced something we'd never seen before at a horse sale: a crossdresser stud groom, a couple of aisles across. I'm sorry to say we were all at a loss for words at the vision. He was a tall man dressed as a woman, wearing flashy black tights, with a sparkly black top, and a big black studded belt around his waist. Jewellery hung off him everywhere – earrings, necklaces, bangles and rings, you name it, he had it.

If that wasn't enough, we were then traumatised by the bright

# RESUSCITATION 1996–2000

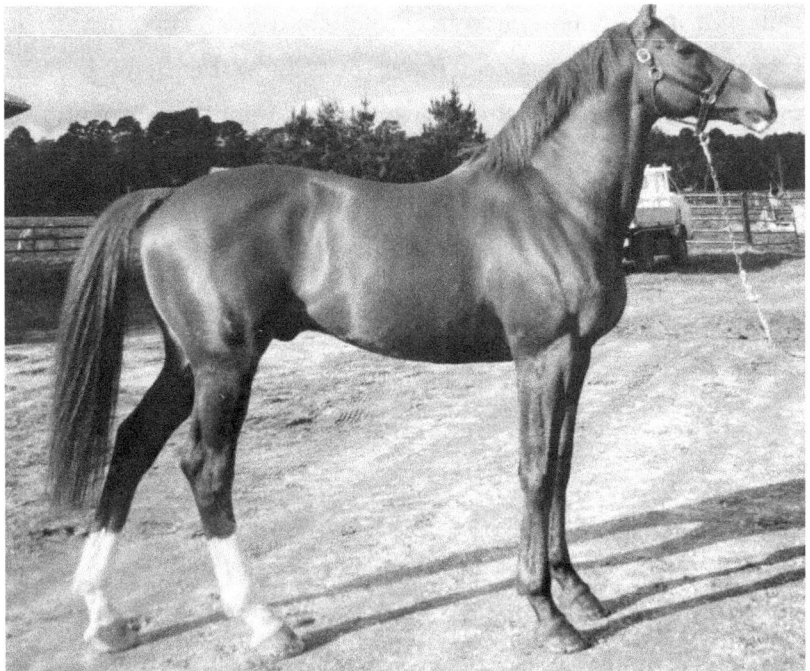

*One of our yearlings, ready for the sale ring*

red lipstick and dramatic black eye makeup. As you were taking all this in, you noticed his partially bald head and when he turned around and walked away, you saw a long, tangled, curly mess of black hair hanging down over his shoulders. Then your gaze drifted down to the black high-heeled boots.

It was almost too much for the senses, totally incongruous and bizarre. He had an older man working with him, probably in his 60s; he was short and bald and wore the traditional sales uniform of shirt, jeans, cap and boots. We were not sure if he was an offsider, or a boyfriend, but he/she was shooting fierce commands at him, in fast verbal staccato, without any pleasantries.

Mesmerising! It was hard not to miss him in all the comings and goings of the sale.

In the middle of the hustle and bustle of the sale, Ross took a call from an old friend, Stewart. Stewart and Ross had grown up in Casino and had known each other for most of their lives. Stewart owned an abattoir in Grafton and also the Turangga Thoroughbred Stud.

Stewart had heard that Ross was working at Inverness Stud for a cardiologist. He told Ross he had not been feeling well and went to see a doctor before he left for the Melbourne sales. The doctor told him he should see a cardiologist as soon as possible. Stewart asked Ross if Dr Woolridge could see him.

Ross had only been working with us a few months so he was not sure how such a request would be received. He came to us with it apologetically. Jack and I exchanged glances, we both knew our appointments were booked out for at least six months. After talking it through, we thought the best idea was for Stewart and ourselves to fly back to Sydney on Sunday and go to our rooms in Miranda, where Jack could consult and investigate him.

We successfully sold our yearlings at the sale.

On Sunday we arrived at our consultation rooms at about 2 pm. Jack consulted with Stewart, and we performed a Stress Electrocardiograph with cardiac ultrasound to evaluate his cardiac status. Jack told Stewart the results of our test were inconclusive and that he needed an urgent cardiac angiogram to look at his coronary arteries.

Jack phoned his colleague Roger to arrange Stewart's admission and angiogram at POW hospital. Stewart was shocked that Jack wanted to admit him to hospital immediately. When he gathered his thoughts, he said he hadn't come prepared to go to hospital. He had no pyjamas or toiletries, etc.

Jack assured Stewart, 'Don't worry, Sue will go and buy you some pyjamas and a toothbrush.' When I returned, I put his pyjamas and bathroom necessities in an overnight bag and gave it

*Jack at work*

to him. Stewart arrived at POW just before 5 pm. The coronary angiogram was performed the next day and he was allowed to go home the following day. Stewart was given a follow-up appointment with Jack.

At one of our weekend farm meetings, we decided to go to the Karaka Broodmare sales in May 1996. Jack wanted to buy more well-bred broodmares to breed to one of our stallions. It was important for the stud to have a successful stallion; this happens through good broodmares being bred to an appropriate stallion to hopefully produce winning racehorses.

It is a long-term undertaking, as the gestation period for horses is about 11 months. The mare's pregnancy is planned so that the foals are born between 1st August and the end of January, which is the recognised foaling season. Any foal born before 1st August (this date is recognised as the official horses' birthday) automatically becomes a yearling, that is one year old, on the 1st August, even though it may only be a few days old.

This is a huge disadvantage when they become a racehorse, because they will be racing against horses who could be a year older than they are. Foals are usually weaned about Easter, then the preparation for the yearling sales begins. Following the yearling sales, the yearlings are sent to a horse breaker to be broken in, then they have a spell, followed by a training period, and if they are precocious, they may be ready to race as a two-year-old, however, many are not ready to race until they are three years old.

The 65 per cent of thoroughbred foals that do make it to the racetrack are the result of a complex and highly choreographed breeding system designed with one goal in mind: to maximise the chances of producing a winner.

(21–23 March 1996 – attended the 11th Annual Vascular Workshop in Melbourne.)

In March 1996 a real estate agent contacted Jack and told him that 'The Stables' was for sale. This interested us because this property had a common boundary with our property, and importantly, was on the main road, Moss Vale Road, giving us a key access point.

The block had a house on it with a big block of stables which we could use for our quarantine station for our horses arriving from overseas. A quarantine station has to be isolated from the other farm animals. We said that they were asking too much, and offered $500,000.00. They came back a month later and said they would accept $555.000.00. We agreed and settled on 29 May 1996.

Jack and Ross studied the Karaka Broodmare catalogue, cover to cover, marking broodmares that were of interest, and each night,

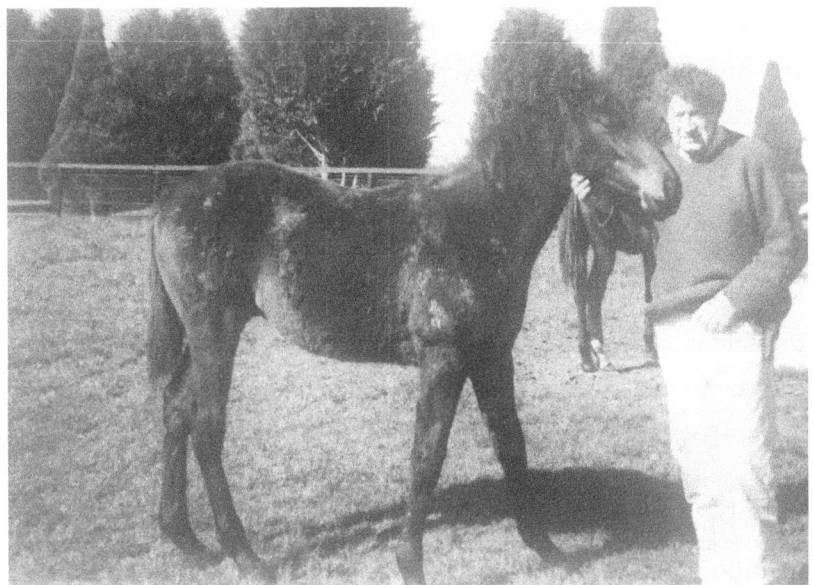

*Jack with a foal*

they'd discuss these mares, so that when we arrived at the sale venue, we were ready to inspect them.

Ross, Narelle, Jack and I, flew over to Auckland two days before the sale, thus enabling us to have enough time to inspect all the broodmares Jack and Ross had marked in their catalogues. We arrived at the sale venue very early in the morning, and started at the first mare in the catalogue, working our way through to the last mare.

Our routine was for either Narelle or I to go ahead and *ask* the groom to bring the mare out of the box and stand her while Ross examined her physically, that is, to look critically at her conformation (the horse's shape/structure), then check her mouth and teeth and look under her tail, and if she passed, he would ask the groom to take her for a walk, firstly away from us and then back towards us, to make sure that she had a well-balanced walk.

At the end of the inspection, Ross would thank the groom

and we would walk away and discuss her positive and negative attributes, and decide if we would bid on her at the auction. By the end of the day, we would have looked at more than 100 mares.

One mare stood out above all the others. Her name was Songline. We were intrigued as to why someone would sell such a beautiful mare. Ross asked the groom, who explained the owners wanted to build a house. The mare was in-foal, and she had a foal at foot, but the owners wanted to keep the foal at foot, what a shame.

Jack bid for Songline. There was a lot of interest in her, and our final winning bid was $NZ34,000.00.

By the end of the sale, we had purchased three broodmares, including Songline. We went to the office to arrange payment and organise shipping to Australia. The cost of shipping a horse to Australia was $NZ5,000.00.

(1996 – Sara had her first baby, Emily Jayne, our second grandchild.)

## 1997

*For Give Us a Go and Dream Catcher 1997 race results refer to Horse Lists in Further Reading.*

*Travel 1997 – refer to Travel Lists in Further Reading.*

In June 1997, Jack and I travelled to Orlando, Florida USA to attend the American Society of Echocardiograhy (8th Annual Scientific Meeting). Following the Meeting, we met with Ross and Narelle in Lexington, Kentucky to visit the Walmac Stud, where the renowned stallions Nureyev and Alleged stood. Next we travelled to Claiborne Stud, where the celebrated stallion, Mr Prospector stood.

Then we flew to New York. On that flight, the pilot took a detour and showed us the magnificent Niagara Falls.

In New York, we arranged for a driver to take us to Song Hill Farm in Rochester NY to inspect a stallion. We had received veterinary reports extolling the virtues of this stallion and so decided to come and inspect the stallion before purchasing him. When they showed us the stallion, we were extremely disappointed and surprised that the physical presence of the stallion was nothing like the description in the report we received. We departed without the stallion. Thank goodness we made the effort to come and look.

Our next port of call was Ireland, via London and Dublin. We travelled by car to Rathbury Stud, Coolmore Stud and Tara Stud. We returned to Dublin and attended the Leopardstown Races.

We flew to London for a few days' rest. Afterwards, we arranged for a rental car and Ross drove us to Newmarket, where we took a tour of the Newmarket Sales Complex. Next, we drove to the English National Stud, where Jeremy White accompanied us and explained all the important features of the stud.

Our journey continued on to the outstanding Floors Stud, at Roxburgh Castle. Stud employee Ted Finch took us on a delightful tour of the stud and castle.

We then travelled up to Inverness and returned to Edinburgh via Queensferry, where we had trouble finding somewhere to stay for the night. After three hours of searching, we settled on the only available room, which was at a pub right on the railway line. The next morning, we continued on to Edinburgh where Jack had a reunion with his friend and mentor, Dr Bill Price, and his wife Mary.

## 1997 The Songline Adventure

Songline's foal at foot remained in New Zealand, and was named Sunline.

Jack and Ross' judgement of Songline was vindicated in 1997 when we found out Sunline had won her first three races. Sunline had been leased by her owners to her trainer, Trevor McKee, and two others.

Trevor McKee was excited about her potential. After the third win, Ross phoned Jack and excitedly gave him the fabulous news. That weekend, we had a serious discussion about Songline's mating, as we had intended her to go to our stallion, Simonstaad. However, we all agreed that it looked like Simonstaad would not be a wise business choice. If she went to a more prestigious stallion, the financial benefit could be significant

The purchase of Songline was a turning point in our Thoroughbred Horse Stud history.

Thoroughbred-breeding theories stem from the belief that careful analysis of bloodlines can lend predictability to breeding outcomes. A well-designed mating increases the probability of the offspring's success, although many other factors also come into play. A basic understanding of these theories can give you some idea of the horse's theoretical genetic potential. However, the soundest breeding theory is the simplest one – 'breed the best to the best and hope for the best.'

The Racecourse Test (RT) is probably the most crucial selection criterion for breeding, and that is the horse's ability displayed on the racetrack. The RT measures a horse's ability to win, which requires a certain combination of speed and stamina, depending on the race in question. Racing also tests the horse's strength, soundness and will to win, all of which are inheritable to some degree.

The ultimate goal is to win elite races. Horses that fail the

RT, either because they are poor athletes or lack racing spirit, are usually poor candidates as breeding stock. When an unproven racehorse becomes a good sire or broodmare, a closer look usually shows they have an above-average pedigree.

And so, with this in mind, we set about to find what we considered the best mating for Songline. We began with an analysis of the bloodlines with a computer program produced by Frederico Tesio which reveals the bloodlines of a mare or stallion for up to 10 generations.

However, I give you a quote from Tesio himself: 'The Thoroughbred exists because its selection has depended not on experts, technicians or zoologists, but on a piece of wood, the winning post of the Epsom Derby. If you base your criteria on anything else, you will get something else, not the Thoroughbred.'

When we were deciding on our matings, we usually looked at three or four generations. Tesio's program also displayed the Dosage profile, which is a further attempt to quantify the amount of speed versus stamina in a horse's pedigree.

After studying potential matings on Tesio's program and, considering other criteria, we decided to send Songline to Octagonal.

Octagonal was bred in New Zealand at Cambridge Stud, he was in the first crop of the champion sire Zabeel and was out of the champion broodmare Eight Carat. Octagonal made his racetrack debut at Rosehill in December 1994. He won 10 Group 1 races, including the Cox Plate. He was Champion 2 Yr Old, Champion 3 Yr Old and Australian Horse of the year 1996.

The resultant foal was a splendid-looking dark-brown colt. By the time he went to the Easter Yearling Sales in 1998, Sunline had won the Flight Stakes and was starting to declare her extreme ability.

*The Inverness Stud Sale Team at one of the many sales we attended*

There was enormous interest in the Songline/Octagonal colt. Prior to the sales, we had radio and television stations requesting interviews with Ross at the stud. They arrived at the stud in the early hours of the morning with cameras and recording equipment and a host of other bits and pieces and lots of cables, a nightmare on a thoroughbred horse farm!

Ross was brilliant, he handled everyone with such ease, and when he was interviewed it was if he had been doing it all his life, no sign of stage fright. He spoke clearly and intelligently and was always obliging when asked if he would bring the colt out.

A good-looking man, with a somewhat stocky build, and slightly bow-legged, as most older horse riders are, Ross has a shock of reddish hair with the usual fair complexion and subsequently always wore an Akubra to protect his face from the sun. His Akubra was his trademark. He wore it everywhere, every minute of the day and night, except when he entered a home, office, or restaurant.

When seated, he would reverently place his hat upside down nearby or under his chair. I asked him one day why he placed his hat upside down, and he said, 'If you sit your hat on its brim, the brim will go out of shape.' He had a battered old work hat and an immaculate going-out hat. He was always neatly dressed in a pair of blue jeans and a neatly pressed shirt. His boots were always cleaned and polished.

All this attention gave us valuable media exposure worth hundreds of thousands of dollars and thrust Ross and Inverness Stud into the limelight. Ross' reputation as a stud manager was skyrocketing and he was being headhunted by some of the bigger, reputable studs, but he stayed steadfastly loyal to Jack and I.

We were at last tasting success after our years of hard work, and diligent research, acquiring well-bred broodmares with black-type in their families, and buying yearling fillies whom we felt could potentially win black-type races and then follow on as broodmares.

Black-type races are races which are either Group 1, Group 2, Group 3 or Listed races. The highest level is a Group 1 race, which is a test of class, and all the horses run with the same weight, but allowances are given for three-year-olds, fillies and mares. There are over 60 Group 1 races in Australia each year. The most prestigious Australian Group 1 races are the Melbourne Cup, Cox Plate, and Golden Slipper.

When a horse wins a Group 1 race, the horse's name is always printed in solid black print and all the letters of the name are capital letters. If the races are Group 2, Group 3 or Listed Race, the name of the horse is printed with solid black print with the first letter of the name a capital and the remainder of the letters lower case.

Ross, Narelle, Jack and I worked well together, we were compatible and understood each other's strengths and weaknesses.

When we went to the yearling and broodmare sales, Ross had connections everywhere, and with his engaging personality and industry knowledge, he talked his way into information that was vital to our decision to buy or not to buy.

Ross also had an excellent eye for horse conformation and Jack had an extraordinary innate ability to know a good horse when he saw one. Together with their thorough knowledge of blood lines, and endless hours spent reading the sale catalogues searching for our next champion, they were proving to be a winning combination.

Narelle was a valuable assistant, keeping her eye on the inspection, and timing it so that there was not a second wasted. This avoided long delays, as the grooms always brushed the horse down before bringing it out of the horsebox, and getting it to stand for Ross and Jack. This preparation always takes time. They were big days and everything had to go like clockwork because of the large number of horses we had to inspect and evaluate.

Occasionally Ross and Jack asked Narelle and I for our opinion (Jack had a great respect for Narelle's judgement).

When the sales began, we had to make sure we were at the sale ring at the right time to bid on the horse we wanted to buy.

Our stud team was further strengthened by a close friendship with the young Irishman Dermot Farrington, whom we met at the Melbourne Yearling Sale in 1996. Jack and Ross valued Dermot's advice and his International race and sales knowledge, and his contacts.

## 1998

*For Akaaber's Promise, Count Scenario, Kugelhopf, Telephone Girl, and Sunline's 1998 race results, please refer to Horse Lists in Further Reading.*

In the meantime, Jack's judgement of Count Scenario was also vindicated when the Count came 3rd in the Qld Guineas 1600m a Group 2 race at Eagle Farm \*\*. What a wonderful day for Jack.

We attended the Easter Yearling sales to buy a good filly, spent hours looking at fillies and chose a few. We were unsuccessful bidders on two fillies and then our last chosen filly came into the ring.

Jack liked this filly's breeding, she was out of one of his favourite broodmares, Donna Cara who was by Sir Tristram. The filly was by Marscay, a popular sire, so there was boldness and speed in her breeding. We decided not to bid any more than $100,000.00, and we were lucky when the hammer fell on our last bid.

On our way to the office to organise our purchase, we bumped into our good friend Bede Murray, a horse trainer who's trained a number of our horses. He said to Jack, 'You didn't buy that cow-hocked filly, did you?'

'Yes,' answered Jack, adding that he liked her. My heart went out to him.

Anyway, we pressed ahead with our business at the office. It had always been our policy to lease our expensive horse purchases and we had an arrangement in place for purchasing a filly at these sales. We completed our business arrangements and organised the transport of the filly to our farm.

We named our 'cow-hocked filly' Donna Dior, and we hoped

she would overcome her slight physical impediment. Time would tell.

(1998 – Jacqui's second baby, Ebony, was born, our third grandchild.)

## 1999
*For Akaaber's Promise, Count Scenario, Donna Dior, Give us a Go, Kugelhopf, and Sunline's 1999 race results, please refer to Horse Lists in Further Reading.*

April 1999 negotiations begin on the purchase of the stallion Lycius.

## July 1999 – First Open Day at Inverness Thoroughbred Stud, Burradoo

Our 'cow-hocked filly', Donna Dior, started her racing career, and she did not disappoint, coming 3rd in her first trial in September. She showed plenty of potential and we were more than pleased. She would now go for a good spell and return to racing early in the new year. The purchase of Donna Dior was a further demonstration of Jack's instinct to know if a horse had innate potential.

## 2000
*For Akaaber's Promise, Count Scenario, Donna Dior, Kugelhopf, and Sunline's 2000 race results, please refer to Horse Lists in Further Reading.*

20 April 2000 Rebecca and Greg married at the Uniting Church Cronulla, followed by a reception at Mariner's Cove (Rebecca worked as a wedding coordinator at Mariner's Cove, Gunnamatta Bay – it was a perfect venue for a wedding).

## Chapter Twenty-one
## Two Tragedies
## 2000–2008

On 23 July 2000 my father, Irving, had a car accident while driving to Wagga Wagga. There were no other cars involved, he apparently drifted off to sleep and ran off the road, smashing into a tree. The ambulance took him to Wagga Hospital.

The next day, a nurse helped him out of bed, and he collapsed onto the floor. An X-ray showed spinal-cord compression of C3,4,5. He was airlifted to Royal North Shore Hospital, a specialist hospital for spinal cord injuries. Surgery was performed but unfortunately dad was now a quadriplegic, to his immense distress. He would remain in hospital care for the remainder of his life. When he was stabilised, he was transferred to a private hospital in Hurstville.

Only days later, on 2 August, I was at work as usual when Adele came into my room and said, 'There is a police officer at the front desk wanting to know if you are in.'

'Are you Suzanne Woolridge?' he asked, after Adele had shown him in.

'I am,' I replied.

'You might like to sit down,' he said, and we both sat.

'Do you have a brother, Richard Mark Goodfellow?'

I said, 'Yes, I do.'

'I am sorry to say your brother has passed away in Namibia and his death is a coroner's case,' said the policeman. 'You will be notified when his case is concluded and when the body can be moved.'

This was a terrible shock because Rick had phoned me just two weeks before, to say that he was getting married and asked if I would like to come to Bangkok for the wedding.

After the police officer left, I made phone calls to my family, and we agreed to keep in touch as things progressed.

Rick passed away on 30 July 2000, his birthday. He had been working for an oil company, which had a base in Namibia. He worked with their helicopters, but I am not sure in what capacity, and worked month on/month off. He lived in Bangkok with his girlfriend, Oi.

He was on one of his routine flights from Bangkok to Namibia, and as usual, was met at the airport by an employee of the oil company who transported him to his hotel. The fellow who picked up Rick reported to his boss that he said to Rick, 'You don't look well, you should see a doctor.' Rick responded, 'It is ok, I will be ok.'

So, the chap dropped him off at the hotel. When he came back for him the next morning, Rick was not waiting in the usual designated area, so he went to the front desk and asked them to phone Rick's room. There was no answer. He waited, eventually suggesting they should go and check the room. Sadly, Rick had passed away during the night.

The police were called and his death was treated as suspicious, so it became a coroner's case.

On Sunday 13 August 2000, we received a call from an interpreter on behalf of Oi, who told us that Rick's body was in Bangkok and Oi would arrange the funeral, and could we be there.

Rick's body had been left in the Namibian morgue for two weeks while they performed the post-mortem examination. After the Coroner completed his report, Oi received notification that his body could be transported to Bangkok. The post-mortem report showed that the cause of death was pneumonia.

After we made our arrangements, we notified Oi's interpreter, and asked if someone could arrange accommodation with three bedrooms for four people.

Robyn and Stephen arrived in Bangkok on Wednesday 16 August 2000, with Jack and I following the next day.

When I packed my bag, as well as a few clothes, etc, I also packed bottles of water, packets of muesli, sultanas, nuts and biscuits, and a jar of vegemite, in case we had issues getting food.

The accommodation arranged by Oi was adequate; three bedrooms with a sitting room which had a lounge, table and chairs, plus a kitchenette.

On our first day, Oi's interpreter arrived and presented us with a large platter of fresh fruit, for which we were very grateful, it was food we could eat. She then told us that Oi has organised a massage, and after the massage, they were taking us to the Buddhist temple, and we would be expected to take food and money for the Monks every day. This was a shock, but it didn't end there.

The interpreter hurried us down to a waiting vehicle. We climbed in and buckled up our seat belts. Thank goodness we had seat belts on! The driver was swerving around people on bikes and trollies, dodging dogs and children, and managed to find all the potholes in the road. After a twenty-minute nightmare journey we were bundled out of the car.

As we stood on the side of the road, we looked around and saw a street lined with buildings which all looked much the same, except for an occasional splash of colour, mostly red and green. The buildings were mostly two floors high, some three floors, built in cement blocks.

Our interpreter hustled us in through a door of a building near where we were dropped off, and as we crossed the threshold, we were standing in a small reception area, bare of furniture and approximately 2 m by 4 m. The wall on our left had a large noticeboard with scraps of paper pinned to the board. We couldn't read any of the messages, they were in Thai.

At the end of the room was a large glass wall, and behind the glass were rows of bench seats, all at graduated heights with girls sitting on them. We looked at each other, all of us thinking, 'What are we doing here?'

Our interpreter bustled us on past the glass wall, through a narrow hallway and up some stairs. It was very gloomy, without artificial light, and there was a rank, musty smell. As we came to the top of the stairs, we walked into another hallway, but this one had a platform on one side, about 60–70 cm off the floor. This platform area was segregated into cubicles separated by curtains, and each cubicle had a thin mattress on the floor of the platform.

We were instructed to get into a cubicle, one person per cubicle, and to remove our clothes down to our undies (that was our interpretation of her broken English and hand gesticulations) and lay on the mattress. This was not my idea of fun. A group of Thai girls came in and each one popped into a cubicle, one masseur per cubicle. The girls started to massage.

I had never experienced a massage before, it is not my thing, but this experience was one of brutality – I had tears running down my face, it was so painful. After five minutes, I had to hold my hand up and say, 'Stop.' I had had enough. I quickly dressed and sat on the edge of the platform. Everyone else took my cue. We quickly departed (fortunately, the car was waiting for us at the door). We scrambled into the car, and then burst into laughter.

We waited for the interpreter. The driver took us to our next destination, the Buddhist temple. We were not emotionally prepared for this visit.

The driver pulled up at a large set of ornate, gold-coloured, wrought-iron gates, which led to a spacious quadrangle. There was hardly any grass, just dirt and pebbles with a few weeds. We crossed the quadrangle to a garish-coloured building with a platform along its front, where three monks dressed in bright-orange robes were sitting crossed legged in a prayerful pose.

We respectfully deposited the food and money in the special receptacles. Then, we were quietly ushered to the end of the platform into a room filled with the most exquisite flowers, apparently sent by Rick's employer. I have never seen so many beautiful flowers in one place before, they really took your breath away –flowers of every description, and in every colour of the rainbow.

In the middle of the room was the coffin resting on two trestles. The lid of the coffin had been removed so that we could view the body of our dear brother. We were not prepared for this. The shock was magnified by the fact that the body was now almost three weeks old and had not been properly refrigerated, and was bloated and discoloured. The interpreter encouraged me to touch him, and I shrank back into Jack's arms. We quickly exited and got into the car and asked to be taken straight back to our accommodation.

We got back to our abode feeling traumatised and shocked. We sat down with a cup of tea to settle our nerves and opened a block of chocolate to help ease our heavy hearts.

Later, we decided we should at least make an effort to eat, as it was dinner time, and the easiest solution was to have take-away from a local shop. I don't know what the food was, probably a curry? It was sort of edible and served the purpose. We went to bed to try and recover and prepare ourselves for more of the same.

Friday 18 August: We were first taken to the Buddhist's Temple for a repeat of yesterday. Being a repeat event did not make it any easier.

Afterwards, the driver took us to Rick's house. It was a two-storey house built with cement blocks, lightly rendered and painted cream, with green architraves, green front door, and a corrugated iron roof. At the front, there was a tiled patio about three metres wide, and in one corner stood a small table and chair where Oi and her mother cooked and sold noodles to passersby.

We were taken into the house via the front door, which came off the patio, and entered a room which would have been the living room as there was a large mat on the floor with colourful cushions placed in a circular fashion around the grey mat, and this was where they'd sit to eat.

Adjacent to the living room was a small kitchen, we did not go into the kitchen but we could see cupboards, a sink and a small stove. Two small bedrooms also came off the living room, with mattresses on the floor, and in one of the bedrooms, we could see a man laying on one of the mattresses

The interpreter told us that Oi's parents lived in the house as the father had had a stroke and needed to be cared for. There was also an aunt living there, as well as Oi and her two children. Oi had been the number two wife of another man who presumably was the father of her children. I guess she divorced this man and was to be married to Rick.

Stephen asked the Interpreter if he could look at Rick's

computer. We were hoping to access his files and see if there was anything we needed to attend to. Stephen found the computer in a small room where Rick had a desk and chair. Stephen tried to access the computer, but it was protected by a password and as hard as we tried, we could not work out the password. So we left without any further knowledge of Rick's financial affairs.

Saturday 19 August: Finally, the day of the funeral arrived, our interpreter arrived with the car and we were taken to the Buddhist temple. At the back of the temple was a small tower built of cement blocks, probably about 3 m tall, which was the cremation tower. There was a sloping, circuitous ramp going up the tower to the mouth of the cremation furnace. We were shuffled towards the tower; everyone was very solemn. Our interpreter came over and told us that the Monks were bringing out the coffin and we were to follow the coffin in a procession. We each received a flower to carry.

The procession took us around the tower three times, accompanied by the chanting of the Monks, and when they carried the coffin up to the mouth of the cremation furnace, we dutifully followed. The Monks sat the coffin on the ledge at the mouth of the furnace and removed the lid. We were pushed towards the coffin by the interpreter who told us to place the flowers in the coffin. The Monks then pushed the coffin into the furnace. We did not stay any longer, it was too much for us to bear, the whole event was too distressing and harrowing.

Jack and I departed that night on a midnight flight and arrived home early in the morning of Sunday 20 August. Stephen and Robyn followed the next day.

The funeral ended up costing $AUD 10,000, an extraordinary amount of money in Thailand. Stephen, Robyn and I had the unenviable task of tidying up Rick's affairs at home and we found that Rick owned a house in Moss Vale which had been rented.

We contacted his solicitor and arranged for the home to be sold and the proceeds to go to Oi. Oi phoned me every night for two weeks, wanting to know where her money was. I tried to explain to her that it takes time to sell a house, and it will probably be two months or more before we can send her the money.

Unfortunately, she kept harassing me. I was so glad when everything was finalised. Oi would be a very wealthy lady; she not only had the proceeds of his house in Moss Vale, but she would now also own the house Rick built in Bangkok. Rick did not leave a will, but we know that this is what he would have wanted. I had phone calls from Oi on and off for the next six months, always in the middle of the night, always asking for more money.

## 2001

*For Count Scenario, Kugelhopf, and Sunline's 2001 race results, please refer to Horse Lists in Further Reading.*

Tuesday 16 January 2001 – Irving died about 8.30 am. I went as soon as I could, following a phone call from the hospital, but he had passed away before I arrived. Luckily, Doug was at Cronulla, and he took me to Hurstville. I was very grateful. Doug and Stephen removed Irving's possessions, including a TV and a wheelchair. Robyn was in Canada and was on her way back, probably arriving on Friday.

Monday 22 January 2001 – Irving's funeral at Olsens'.

Sunday 28 January 2001 – Irving's memorial service at Moss Vale RSL. > 80 friends and relatives present.

6/6/2001 Sue > Kareena Hospital for surgery on throat > removal of epiglottis lymphoepithelial (retention) cyst > Dr Bob Payten

## 2002

*For Count Scenario, Great Anna, Kugelhopf, Soprana and Sunline's 2002 race results, please refer to Horse Lists in Further Reading.*

Sunline became the world's highest-earning race mare of her time. She raced on 48 occasions for 32 wins, 9 seconds and 3 thirds, earning over $11,000,000.00. She won races in New Zealand, Australia and Hong Kong.

Her major wins were the Flight Stakes (1998), W.S. Cox Plate (1999 and 2000), Doncaster Handicap (1999 and 2002, All Aged Stakes (2000 and 2002), Coolmore Classic (2000 and 2002), Waikato Spring (2001 and 2002), Hong Kong Mile (2000), Manikato Stakes (2000). She was named New Zealand Horse of the Year 1999, 2000, 2001 and 2002, Australian Horse of the Year 2000, 2001 and 2002, Australian Middle-Distance Champion 2000 and 2001, Australian Champion Filly or Mare 2000, 2001 and 2002.

Because we owned Sunline's dam Songline, our stud would now be recognised internationally, which was a great help when we were selling yearlings.

*Travel for conferences in 2002 refer to Travel Lists in Further Reading.*

(Rebecca's first baby, Ruby was born.)

We were at the farm on Sunday, when at around 4 am, we received a phone call from Doug, telling us that Sara had had an epidural bleed. We both felt extremely anxious, and started to plan our departure back to Sydney.

But then, a short while later, still in the early hours of the morning, we received a phone call from Sara's obstetrician telling us that Sara had ruptured a vein and he was taking her straight into surgery to find and tie off the vein. This is a rare, but serious, complication. During the surgery, Sara had a 'near-death experience', where she heard her obstetrician and anaesthetist talking about how they were losing her on the table. They managed to bring her back and complete the procedure. Sara said that during her recovery, the specialists confirmed to her their conversation about losing her during surgery.

Meanwhile, after a quick breakfast with Jacqui, Talissa and Ebony, we made a speedy dash to Sydney, and arrived at Kareena Hospital about 10:30 am. Sara was still in recovery and was pale and in great pain.

Jack phoned Sara's medical team to discuss her operation, her experience, and her present status.

Monday was a public holiday for the Queen's Birthday. We had a few farm problems that needed sorting out, so we went to the farm for the day. I phoned Bec and told her that we would be away for the day and she said she would come to look after Sara, as well as feed Oscar, and she planned to come again the following day.

On Thursday, Jack received a call at 6 am. Sara had severe chest pain, worse on inspiration and aggravated by lying down. We went straight to the hospital and performed an Echo which showed that she had developed pericarditis, an inflammation of the sac that surrounds the heart. She was given an Indocid suppository, which had a magic effect.

Jack and I went back to our rooms to work, returning to the hospital about 7:30 pm. By then, Sara was pretty well pain free and mobile, though still had a temperature, and was still on an antibiotic. For the first time, we thought, 'She will make it.'

This was a tough week, and yet, there was more to come.

Sara and baby were discharged from hospital and were settling in at home. Unexpectedly, eight weeks post-delivery, Sara woke with labour-like pain. Sara spoke to her obstetrician who asked her to return to the hospital. The obstetrician diagnosed retained placenta and said he would have to take her back to surgery for the procedure to remove the retained placenta, however, he told Sara he would have to do this without an anaesthetic as Sara was so unstable and not well enough to survive another anaesthetic. Sara later told me this was the most horrific experience she had ever encountered.

Doug's parents came from Brisbane to look after the family, as Sara was too ill to look after a 5-year-old and a newborn. Her recovery took about six months.

Jack and I missed Sara at work – her energy was always a good stimulus for us. But when things get tough, you just have to put your head down and work hard.

The tough times continued the following year.

On 11 February 2003, my mother, Ruby, passed away. She'd developed Alzheimer's Disease in the 1970s, though it is hard to pinpoint the onset, but in retrospect there were vague episodes of short term memory loss commencing in her mid 50's. Our first real indication was after Jacqui's wedding; when she was unwell with something unrelated and had been admitted to Bowral Hospital.

During our visits, she would often have hallucinations of huge spiders climbing the wall, and other frightening visions. After she returned home, my father told us that her memory was failing, she was forgetting where she parked the car and spent hours wandering around Moss Vale searching for it. She was also hiding things in the home and tried to ignite the microwave with a lighted match.

Dad struggled on for a while trying to look after her. He

arranged for a cleaner and when the cleaner arrived, Ruby started attacking her with a broom. This was very uncharacteristic of Ruby, who had always been a quiet, gentle, kind person.

Eventually my father asked for help. We arranged for her to see a geriatrician, who arranged for her admission to Garrawarra Hospital at Waterfall. She spent her last 20 years at Garrawarra Hospital. In the later part of her life, Boni arranged to have Ruby transferred to a hospital close to her in Queanbeyan.

My mother's funeral was held at the Methodist Church Moss Vale.

*For Great Anna and Kugelhopf's 2003 race results, please refer to Horse Lists in Further Reading.*

We arranged for another stallion, Private Call, to join our stud.
(Rebecca's second baby, Amy was born.)

*Travel for conferences and horse sales/races 2004 and 2005 – refer to Travel lists in Further Reading.*

*For Frescante and Silent Song's 2005 race results, please refer to Horse Lists in Further Reading.*

2005, Sara's third child, Charlotte Grace, was born in Bowral Hospital. Sara's obstetrician told her that because of her previous history, she would need to have a planned Caesarean section. However, six weeks before her due date she had contractions and was admitted immediately.

The next morning after the birth of little Charlotte, Sara said she felt confused, her speech was affected and she was unable to make sentences. Jack made a note in his diary that she had

Circumoral paraesthesia, as well as weakness down her left side, which progressed to global paraesthesiae.

The family was shocked to hear that Sara had had a stroke. We all rushed to her side to give her our love and the support she needed.

Charlotte, on the other hand, was a pretty baby, weighing 6lb 7 oz at birth, and was placed in a humidicrib.

Sara was treated appropriately, and we are so fortunate that she, after some time, fully recovered.

*For Silent Song 2006 race results refer to Horse Lists in Further Reading.*

*Travel for conferences 2006 – refer to Travel lists in Further Reading.*

On 8 July 2006 we flew to London to have a meeting with Dermot regarding Nuclear Freeze's return to France. On 10 July 2006 we flew to Bordeaux for a meeting with the representative from Haras des Chartrueux. On 11 July 2006 the meeting was cancelled. Dermot is upset and annoyed. We told Dermot that we do not want to send Nuclear Freeze back to France until all the outstanding moneys have been paid. On 12 July 2006 we flew back to London for a meeting with Dermot to discuss our next move.

On the 13 July 2006 we flew to Singapore, and on 15 July Jack consulted with a patient, and we departed Singapore on 16 July 2006.

Jack and I had been discussing the complex and exhausting problems of trying to run a thriving cardiology practice, together with a thoroughbred horse stud and a stable of racehorses.

We talked through the many conflicting issues of organising two very different enterprises competing for our time and finances, plus the many problems involved with employing workers for the farm, who were sometimes itinerant workers. We were becoming emotionally, physically and financially exhausted.

After many agonising deliberations, we made the decision to sell the main farm, that was Lot 13 and Lot 14 McCourt Road, Burradoo. The most unpleasant part of this was that we would have to tell Ross and Narelle.

When we talked to Ross and Narelle they were so supportive of what we planned to do, and were grateful for the years that we had together. There are some people you meet through your life, who were meant to be in your life. We will always remain friends.

Initially, we approached our next-door neighbours and friends Tony and Rowena and they agreed to buy Lot 14, which was adjacent to their property, and the sale of this block was settled on 25 May 2006.

The remaining Lot 13 was sold by auction to an owner of a Melbourne Cup winner.

We kept the remaining 100 acres on the other side of the river on Moss Vale Rd and submitted a subdivision application to the council. Our plan was to sell all except a 14 acre block which we would keep so that Jack still had a' farm' to go to, a garden to potter in and paddocks to wander through and have a horse or two and some steers. After the subdivision was completed, we built a project home by Clarendon Homes on our block.

When the house was completed, we planted a hedge of roses on the block's western boundary. We chose the rose Souvenir de la Malmaison, created in 1843 by rose breeder Jean Beluze, from Lyon, France, who named the rose after the Chateau de Malmaison.

*Farewell picnic on the lawn of Inverness Stud*

The historic manor house was the home of Josephine de Beauharnais and her husband General Napoleon Bonaparte. Josephine had created a beautiful and curious garden, featuring 250 varieties of roses gathered from around the world. It has been said Napoleon Bonaparte had his soldiers collect specimens for Josephine's garden.

Malmaison was fully restored by the famous French architect Pierre Humbert in the early 20th century and is now an important historical monument.

During the restoration, the rose Souvenir de la Malmaison was discovered and fortunately for rose lovers, it was propagated. Jack and I heard the story of Souvenir de la Malmaison and when we saw the rose, we fell in love with it.

All our horses – racehorses, broodmares, broodmares and foals, stallions, and yearlings – were sold by auction throughout 2006 and 2007.

(12/11/07 – Rebecca's third baby, Charlie was born.)

*Travel for conferences and horse sales/races 2007 – refer to Travel lists in Further Reading.*

*Travel for conferences and horse sales/races 2008 – refer to Travel lists in Further Reading.*

Jack was diagnosed with a Schwannoma of the auditory nerve.

*Jack and Sue at the races*

## Chapter Twenty-two
## Heartache
## 2008–2014

During the last four months of 2008 I had a very heartbreaking time. It was clear, not only to me, but to others that Jack was having relationship/s with other women. I was shattered and at times inconsolable, and found it difficult to work competently and to function in the manner that I was used to. After a period of brokenness I realised that if I didn't fight back I would lose the man that I had loved devotedly for 40 years, and that our children and grandchildren would lose their close relationship with Jack who they have loved and adored for all their lives. I could not sit by and let that happen. And so, I lectured myself and devised a plan to revive my relationship with Jack. During the early phase of the restoration of our relationship, we persevered with our life together, fortunately most of the time we were so busy with work and farm life that it smothered and blurred the difficult times. It was a slow, sometimes difficult process. But I endured, because I loved him so deeply and this gave me the determination and will to carry on.

I had hope, because there is one statistic clearly in favour of our relationship surviving. Apparently a divorce magazine conducted some research on infidelity and found 60–75 per cent of couples remained together after infidelity.

Throughout 2009, Jack and I worked full time, and then on the weekends we went to our Bowral property, buying Murray Grey cows and selling Murray Grey steers. Intermittently we would attend race meetings and medical conferences.

**October 2009**

Kareena Hospital called and asked me to perform an urgent Echo. Jack and I changed our appointment lists and rushed to Kareena. Unfortunately, another doctor was using the Echo machine, so I had to wait around until it was free. The doctor hurriedly returned the machine to me and I performed the Echo on the patient.

I finished the Echo and remained seated at the machine while I wrote up the findings. I stood up quickly with the Echo log

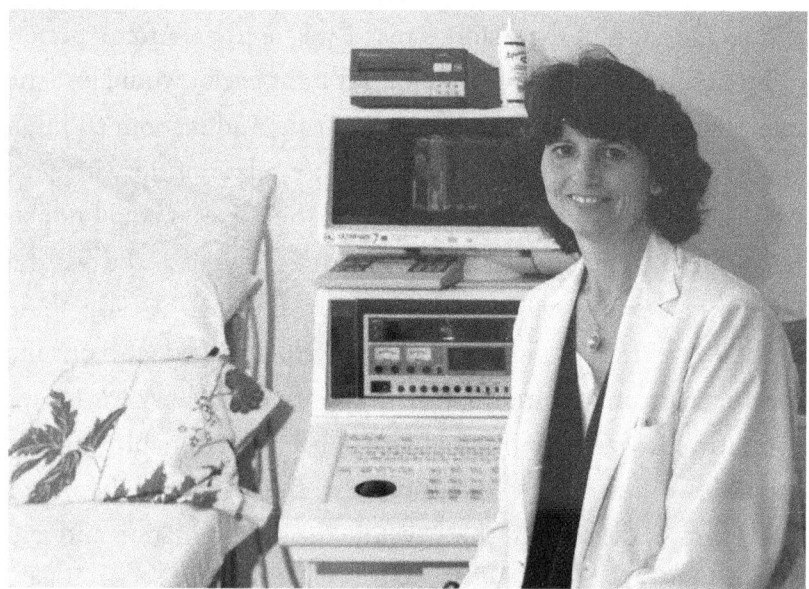

*Sue at work*

book and report form in my hands and rapidly turned around to go and find Jack. I promptly tripped on the cables and crashed to the floor, straight onto my nose, which began spurting blood. I felt dazed and stayed where I was with blood gushing from my nose.

The patient rang her bell to raise the alarm. When the nurse came in, she grabbed a pillow case and held it over my nose and told me not to move. The resident doctor arranged for me to be moved to the emergency department and plugged my bleeding broken nose. I had a follow-up consultation with an Ear, Nose and Throat surgeon, who advised me that the broken nose probably did not need surgery, but he thought I should have the bleeder cauterised.

*Travel for conferences and races 2009 and 2010 – refer to Travel lists in Further Reading.*

I felt our relationship was back on an even keel, and I was feeling more relaxed and enjoying our time together. I now felt comfortable telling him I loved him, and he would often reciprocate. At last, we had turned full circle, except for one thing: he still hadn't said that precious word, 'Sorry.'

Unfortunately, Jack had two very nasty falls at the farm, due to his poor balance from his Schwannoma, and his loss of core strength. These accidents shook his self-confidence.

We had a serious discussion about Jack's dream of retiring at Burradoo, he has always wanted to retire on a farm. Jack turned 85 in August 2010 and his mobility was waning. With his medical history, it would be sensible to be near all the medical facilities he needed.

After a lot of anguished discussions, we decided to sell our

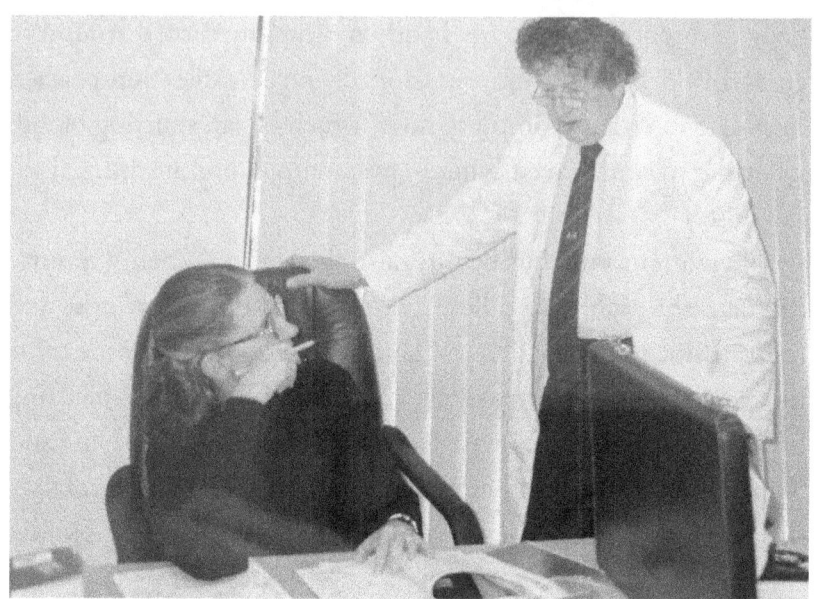

*Jack and Sue at work*

*Jack and Sue with their three girls, Jacqui, Sara and Rebecca*

house and paddocks and live permanently in Cronulla. It was a heartbreaking decision for Jack, who appeared to go into mourning for a few months but eventually recovered. I, on the other hand, would not miss the long winter months in Bowral, I was delighted to be returning to my home ground of Cronulla.

It turned out to be a most timely decision, as Jack's health was declining.

Our marital life had pretty much returned to normal, thank goodness.

*Travel for conferences and races 2011 and 2012 – refer to Travel lists in Further Reading.*

In early 2012, in his 87th year, Jack was diagnosed with an abdominal aortic aneurysm, and in May 2012 a stent was inserted to prevent an aneurysmal rupture.

Later in 2012, he had cataract surgery to both eyes, one in September and one in December.

We continued to travel and work, but at a much slower pace. We no longer had racehorses, but Jack continued to have an interest in horse racing and we occasionally went to the races and to the cricket (he had been a member of the Sydney Cricket Ground for 50 years). Horse-racing and cricket were his main leisure time passions, and close behind was his interest in rugby league.

In February 2013, Jack had a dual chamber pacemaker inserted by Roger, then, the following month, he was upgraded to a Bi-ventricular pacemaker, again by Roger.

Jack still refused to retire. When asked, he would always reply, 'Oh, sometime, maybe next year.'

As Jack's pace of life slowed, his passion and curiosity for cardiology still burned within him. He continued to read his medical journals, and enjoyed attending as many conferences as he could, always interacting with his colleagues and questioning them of their opinions on leading cardiology topics.

The 5 November 2014 was a dreadful, tragic day. John, Jacqui's husband, passed away in a surfing accident at Margaret River, WA. The whole family went into mourning.

## Chapter Twenty-three
## Going Home
## 2015–2018

In 2015, in his 90th year, Jack was using a wheelchair outside the home, and Sara and I were doing most of the physical work in the practice, e.g. blood pressures, ECGs, Stress Tests, and Echos, while Jack sat at his desk and collated and interpreted the results following an interrogation and examination of the patient.

However, we were noticing that he was becoming exhausted and fatigued easily. We often suggested to him that maybe it was time for him to retire, but he scoffed at the idea and quickly changed the subject.

I decided to make an executive decision to approach Roger and ask him if he would help me to encourage Jack to retire. Roger had a better idea, he suggested that we make an appointment for an annual check-up with, Peter a geriatrician who was also a friend, and someone whom Jack respected, and Roger would talk to Peter about our situation. Roger and I put forward a suggestion to Jack that maybe it would be a good idea if he consulted with Peter for a checkup. Surprisingly, Jack was amenable to this proposal.

The appointment was made for 10 November 2015.

And so, Jack and I went along to see Peter for Jack's 'checkup.' In the meantime, Roger had discussed my dilemma with Peter. So, Peter was clued up, and started the consultation with routine neurological tests which Jack was familiar with and he managed most of the tests. Then he started chatting to Jack about Jack's daily routines and how he was managing life, to which Jack replied he was managing well, and this was when Peter brought up the question of when did Jack think he would retire?

'Oh, sometime, maybe at the end of the year, or maybe next year,' Jack gave his usual reply.

'Why wait that long? Why not tomorrow?' countered Peter.

I nearly fell off the chair when Jack said, 'Yes, that is a good idea.' We didn't let go of that good idea: Jack retired the following day, Armistice Day 2015. He was 90 years old.

His retirement was not the way he had dreamt it. There were no cows to gaze upon, no racehorses to plan for, no paddocks to meander through, no gardens filled with rose bushes, no vegetable gardens to weed, no fruit trees to prune, and no long walks to admire the river and the trees. Instead, he was dependent on me most of the time, although Sue and Tony came to my rescue as often as they could.

We were so fortunate that with Jack in a wheelchair, we could still travel frequently with the help and assistance of Sue and Tony. And then there were times when our three girls could accompany us, and become the helpers, oh, what fun we had! The girls would take it in turns pushing Jack in his wheelchair, over cobblestone footpaths, up hills and down dales, these were fun times with lots of laughter and frivolity. Sometimes, it needed two of us to push him up the hills and across the cobblestones.

These travels helped to distract Jack from the loss of his medical world and his farm life.

*Travel for conference and leisure 2016 – refer to Travel lists in Further Reading.*

**31 October 2017 – Bravo Cruise**

Jack and I were excited – we were going on another Bravo Cruise. We excitedly anticipated the wonderful nightly concerts onboard. Our bags were packed, and we were ready to go. I arranged for a car to drive us to the Overseas Passenger Terminal at Circular Quay.

On the day of our departure we arrived just after 11 am, and went through the usual boarding procedure. I was pushing Jack in his wheelchair and we slowly made our way onto the ship. As we boarded, we passed through the doorway and the welcoming attendants, when Jack suddenly looked fearful and ill. He said he needed a bathroom urgently.

I asked for directions to the nearest bathroom and quickly pushed Jack in the wheelchair into the bathroom and closed the door behind us. I started to help Jack with his clothes when he suddenly collapsed onto the floor, violently vomiting, with diarrhoea at the same time. He was in a mess and looked distressed.

I went to the door to call for help but the door would not open and so I pressed the red emergency button. It wasn't long before there were two attendants at the door, but they also had trouble opening the door.

Eventually they found someone with a key and opened the door. They could see we were in trouble, and called for medical assistance. A doctor and nurse came along, the doctor said they would call an ambulance urgently as he observed that Jack was haemorrhaging. The doctor said, 'It looks like you won't be sailing with us this time.'

We tried our best to clean Jack up, and within a few minutes, the ambulance arrived. As we were being dispatched to the ambulance, one of the attendants told me not to worry about our bags, they would be delivered to our home, probably tomorrow.

We arrived at St Vincent's Hospital in no time at all. Jack spent three days in St Vincent's having a multitude of tests. The haemorrhage was from an ulcer, so we were lucky this happened before we sailed out to sea.

On 3 November Jack was transferred to Kareena Private Hospital, which was a lot easier for me and more comfortable for Jack, as he was among friends and colleagues, and no doubt he was spoilt. He recovered sufficiently to be discharged home on 7 November.

From then on, he was far more incapacitated. It was becoming apparent that he had vascular dementia, and I needed a lot more help looking after him. I called the Department of Veteran Affairs and arranged for assistance with showering Jack, and a nurse to give Jack his daily injections.

Jack was re-admitted to Kareena Hospital on 15 November for intractable vomiting. He quickly recovered and on the following morning he packed his things and put himself in his wheelchair and said he was ready to go home.

**Christmas 2017**
We had a family Christmas lunch at home. Sadly, Jacqui and her girls could not be with us as Jacqui was spending Christmas with her girls.

We have always had a Christmas policy that if someone has nowhere to go, they are always welcome to join us for Christmas lunch. After learning that Greg's father and brother would be on their own, we invited them to join us.

It was a big gathering! There was a lot of chatter and laughter.

Everyone seemed to have a story to tell, while we enjoyed a magnificent traditional Christmas lunch with all the trimmings, accompanied by joyful Christmas music reminding us of why we are celebrating.

By January 2018 Jack was completely bed-ridden and nurses attended him in the morning and evening.

In early March, the nurses advised me to buy a hospital bed to facilitate caring for Jack. Unfortunately, the bed did not arrive before he passed away.

**Wednesday 14th March 2018**
Jack passed away at home on Wednesday 14 March 2018 at 12.25 pm, and some of the family were here gathered around him. Fortunately two nurses were still here attending to Jack, and for that I was ever so grateful, as they were able to tell me what I needed to do. We did not know that we would lose him that day.

I was in shock. I couldn't believe it. I'd ordered a hospital bed to make him more comfortable and he passed before it arrived. We'd planned to place the bed in front of the window so that he could look out to the ocean.

Jack often told me he did not want a funeral, and asked me to promise him that I would not arrange a funeral for him. And so, I had to honour my promise, even though I knew there were many people who loved him dearly and who would want to honour him and say their good-byes.

Roger phoned and asked me what was I doing about Jack's funeral, and so I explained Jack's wishes. Roger suggested that maybe we could have a memorial afternoon tea at the RSL club, with his nearest and dearest. I talked to my girls, and we agreed to go ahead with Roger's suggestion. We phoned the RSL club, and they were very happy to assist, as Jack was a returned soldier from WWII.

It was an emotional afternoon celebrating the life of an extraordinary man. We all shed tears, and shared our emotions of sadness and loss, as well as sharing some stories of his extraordinary life, highlighting his humour, his generosity, his many sporting talents, his cardiology skills, his deep empathy for his patients, his innate ability to pick a good horse, his ability to work long, hard days. Our memories of our life with Jack are filled with firstly and most importantly love, and his extreme generosity, mixed with good humour, and a deep desire to help everyone.

Life without him will be a very different place.

**Consolation**

About six months after Jack's passing, I was on my usual early morning walk, it was a ghastly day, with torrential rain and gusting wind. There was barely a soul in sight, and I was not sure why I'd come out in such horrendous conditions.

But yes, I did know. I wanted to vent my anger. My daughter, Sara, had been diagnosed with a rare autoimmune disease, Cardio-Neuro-Behcet's, in 2010. She had been very ill for eight years, and had been urgently admitted to hospital with her eighth episode of meningitis. The doctors were not encouraging about her prognosis and during my walk in this violent storm, I cried out to God, pleading with Him to rescue Sara.

The rain was relentless and I was sobbing and pleading for divine intervention, when I was interrupted by a man's voice behind me, speaking the words, 'I am here with you,' in an authoritative voice.

I turned around to see who it was speaking to me. Who was it? Who knew about my grief and heartache? But there was no-one, the Esplanade was completely deserted, not a soul in sight.

Then I felt a warm, overwhelming feeling of peace and love come upon me.

It was Jesus reassuring me. He came to me to reassure me that HE was with me. Sara recovered from that episode of meningitis. Thank you, Jesus.

---

## Wednesday, April 18, 2018
## St George and Sutherland Shire Leader

Obituary
Legendary doctor and racehorse breeder devoted life to his patients.
*Murray Trembath*

Dr John (Jack) Woolridge made an invaluable contribution to the Sutherland Shire Community over more than 60 years and was also a highly successful race horse breeder.

A legendary figure at Sutherland Hospital due to his devotion to patients, Dr Woolridge died on March 14 after a long illness at 92.

He worked until he was 90

Dr Woolridge who lived at Cronulla, started as a GP in the shire in the mid-1950's and progressed to become a specialist general physician and cardiologist.

He was one of the first four Honorary Medical Officers at Sutherland Hospital after it opened in 1958 and he later played a major role in the opening of its coronary care unit.

Away from work, he was a passionate lover of horse racing and owned the highly successful Inverness Stud at Bowral.

His purchases included Songline, the mother of one of Australia's racing greats, dual Cox Plate winner Sunline.

Dr Woolridge bought Songline in New Zealand. The owners

wished to keep her foal, Sunline, whose success no one could have predicted.

Dr Woolridge's wife Suzanne (Sue) – his first wife Jill died after a long illness - said her husband was 'clever, charismatic and extraordinary'.

'He devoted his life to his patients with skill and saintly caring and kindness,' she said.

### *Full Life*

Jack was born in Nowra in 1925 and his family moved to Kingsford in Sydney about 1930.

Jack and his sister Thelma attended Daceyville Public School.

When he was in sixth class he sat for the Qualifying Certificate and topped the state, which saw him accepted into Sydney Boys High School (SBHS).

He passed the Leaving Certificate in 1942. When he turned 18 he joined the royal Australin Air Force (RAAF) and was posted to New Guinea and New Britain.

He started medicine at Sydney University in 1947 and graduated with honours in 1954.

He was offered a residency at St Vincent's hospital and, following that, went into a general practice with Dr Eric Miles at Sutherland.

Sutherland Hospital opened in 1958 and Jack was one of the first four Honorary Medical Officers.

Jack relinquished his general practice in the early 1960s, practicing as a General Physician in rooms at Caringbah and Macquarie Street. Jack continued working as a well respected world class cardiologist until November, 11, 2015 when he was 90 years old. *Read full obituary at www.theleader.com.au

*(printed with the permission of Murray Trembath)*

## Wednesday April 18, 2018
## St George & Sutherland Shire Leader

*Your view*
Dr Jack Woolridge was one of a kind.

Thank you Murray Trembath for your fine tribute to the late Dr John (Jack) Woolridge (*Leader* April, 18).

Having been a patient of Jack's for 38 years (from the time of my first heart bypass operation in 1978 until his retirement) I can say I have never met a more altruistic doctor.

He was devoted to his work and genuinely cared for all of his patients.

There were times when he phoned me at home after hours just to check on my progress or to learn whether a new medication was having the desired affect.

His care knew no bounds. I remember an appointment about 25 years ago when I went to see him regarding suspected angina pain. Not only did he check me out in his surgery for half an hour, he took me for a walk around the surrounding streets for 10 or 15 minutes to determine how long before the pain started.

Dr Woolridge was one of a kind. I once asked him (when he was in his mid eighties) when he planned to retire.

'I never think about retiring,' he replied.

"There's always something new to learn in this business and I'll keep going as long as I can.'

Jack did just that, travelling regularly overseas until a few years ago to attend cardiology conferences. He finally retired in 2015 at the age of 90.

*Harry Pearce*

*(printed with the permission of Harry Pearce)*

# Epilogue

In my 78th year, I was introduced to the Camino de Santiago, a spiritual walk in Spain.

My first experience was unexpected. After more than a decade of struggling with the rare autoimmune disease Neuro Cardio Behcet's, and the ensuing chemotherapy and immunotherapy, my daughter Sara was at last in remission, and starting to feel well.

She told me she and her friend Karina planned to walk the Camino from St Jean Pied de Port in France to Santiago de Compostela in Spain from May to July 2023, covering a distance of 780 km to raise money for a foundation she had set up to fund autoimmune research.

The Camino Frances, as this route is known, is one of the most popular trails for people making a pilgrimage to the Cathedral de Compostela in Santiago, which is built over the reputed burial site of St James, one of Jesus' apostles. And so, for hundreds of years, pilgrims have walked across Spain to Santiago to receive the Pilgrim's Blessing in the Cathedral.

Sara told the family of her intended pilgrimage with her friend Karina, and I and Sara's two sisters, Jacqui and Rebecca, Sara's eldest daughter Emily, my sister Robyn and her friend Sharon decided to join her and walk with her for the last 115 kms.

We had an amazing adventure!

The following year, 2024, Sara was invited to join singer/songwriter Dan Mullins on a Magical Musical Camino from Leon, Spain, to Santiago, approximately 300 kms. Sara phoned me and asked me if I would like to go with her, and I did not hesitate. Karina also joined the tour which was a great blessing as she speaks fluent Spanish.

On the Camino, there are mountains to climb, rivers to cross, villages to walk through, farms with cows and horses, dogs and cats, there was rain, and wind, and sunshine. Along the way there is the spiritual silence in the little village churches where one can go and light a candle for a loved one, and then there are the magical forests where the Presence of God descends breathtakingly upon you. And as we journeyed we were treated to Dan's evening concerts of musical delights, often in small villages but also in larger towns and in an occasional sultry city Inn. They were concerts where we could dance and sing, or just sit and listen to Dan's music and allow it to permeate our souls.

At the conclusion of this adventure, I told Karina that my life with Jack had been very much like a Camino; our lives were full of long hard days and along the way there have been many unexpected adventures and challenges. Jack would always find another mountain to climb, he wanted to be the first to reach the top of every mountain for the thrill of being the first and for the accolades, and he would always expect me to follow him and support him in every endeavour and share in the thrill and rewards. We experienced many dangerous slippery slopes where we had to hold on tight to each other to survive, but there were also many exhilarating adventures, encounters, escapades and experiences.

# EPILOGUE

And so, this was my life with Jack, full of adventures, never knowing from one day to the next what was in front of us. Our life together was special, and we were often asked, 'How do you live and work together without fighting?' The truth is we were so consumed with our businesses and family life that we did not have time for insecurities, jealousies, or worrying about who is right or who is wrong – we were busy every minute of our lives, leaving no time for arguments, just a lot of give and take, compromise, co-operation, reciprocity, adaptability, team work, and good-natured exchange of ideas. Our relationship was built on treating each other with respect and maintaining a good sense of humour.

But as you now know, in 2008, there was a brief period when everything did come crashing down, but we were eventually able to get through it and return to our life together without animosity. We learned to love each other once again.

We managed to climb our mountain separately and then realised we had to join hands to help each other on the steep downward slope, supporting each other through the slippery moments, making sure neither of us tripped and fell, breaking our renewed union.

I hope Jack's story has shown you what an extraordinary man he was: charismatic with a lust for life, visionary and ambitious, highly intelligent, with a remarkable memory. But more importantly, he exuded humility and empathy. He valued his relationships with his patients, his colleagues and the staff in the hospitals, the people he worked with in his office, and on our farms – all were treated like family.

He was loving and devoted to his children and grandchildren.

To me, in the beginning, he was my teacher and mentor, empowering me to become someone way beyond my wildest dreams. He became my husband, my lover, friend and confidante, my work-mate, play-mate and house-mate (helping with house chores when he could see I was overwhelmed). Together, we experienced life's ups and downs, learning through trial and error when to laugh and when to hurt and cry. We learnt to face each catastrophe and misfortune together and discovered the strength to go on.

In the mid 1980s, we learnt of the great health benefits of walking, and so from then on we walked for 45 minutes most mornings, quite often leaving at 5 am, sometimes earlier, and during these walks we would have our business meetings and solve our problems.

In Jack's last two years, I became his nurse and carer, entertainer and storyteller, reminding him of our many adventures. Most days, weather permitting, I'd put him in the wheelchair to take him for a stroll to the Cronulla Mall, and sit outside the Post Office, watching the world go by, enjoying the sunshine on our faces. Occasionally, an old friend, or patient, or sometimes a stranger, would stop and say, 'Hello'.

These little excursions helped to relieve the boredom but could not relieve Jack's pain and anger about being so dependent, or his fear and anxiety of further decline. He lived in fear of having to go to a nursing home. Fortunately, Jack's decline accelerated and his last few days were spent in another realm, but he was at home.

These are the lessons of true love.

May God bless your Soul, Jack Woolridge.

*The End*

*Sue walking the El Camino 2023*

# Acknowledgements

I wish to acknowledge and thank Karina Machado, my daughter Sara's friend, who offered to help me with the first editing and publishing of *Just Jack*. This book would not have been possible without Karina's encouragement brilliant editing and her devotion to the task was the catalyst for me taking the first tentative steps towards publishing.

I would also like to acknowledge and thank you too to Jared Simonis, who took time out to read the manuscript and give his advice.

A big thank you to Benny Agius (BMA Publishing Expertise) and Shaun Jury (Shaun Jury Design) for their expertise and wholehearted assistance during my publishing journey.

My most important acknowledgement is for my family, my 3 beautiful daughters, Jacqueline, Sara and Rebecca and to Judy, Jack's daughter. *Just Jack* would not have been written without their deep love for Jack and myself, their patient understanding during my days of writer's solitude, and their joyous laughter and chatter often ameliorating my days of frustration. And to Judy, a grateful thanks for all the prayers you prayed, helping me along this journey. My deepest love and grateful thanks to you all, and to all your families.

# Curriculum Vitae

**J. D. Woolridge**
M.B., B.S. (Hons) (Sydney) M.R.C.P.,F.R.C.P. (Edin.), F.R.A.C.P., D.D.U.

| | |
|---|---|
| **1931–1937** | Daceyville Public School, Nowra Public School |
| **1938–1942** | Sydney Boy's High School 1st XV, 1st XI and Athletics. |
| **1943–1945** | R.A.A.F. (Returned) '39 – '45 Star, Pacific Star. |
| **1947–1952** | Sydney University MB.BS (Hons.) |
| **1953–1954** | R.M.O St Vincent's Hospital, Sydney. |
| **1955–1956** | Clinical Assistant St Vincent's Hospital, Sydney. |
| **1956–1958** | Assistant Physician, St Vincent's Hospital, Sydney. |

| | |
|---|---|
| 1958–1959 | Department of Medicine, Dr. E.B. French, Western General Hospital, Edinburgh. Eastern General Hospital, Edinburgh. |
| 1959 | MRCP University of Edinburgh. |
| 1960–1966 | Assistant Physician, Professor R.B. Blacket Prince Henry Hospital, Sydney. Prince of Wales Hospital, Sydney. Royal Hospital for Women Paddington. |
| 1960–1966 | Associate Physician, Sutherland Hospital, Sydney. |
| 1966–1990 | Consultant Physician, Sutherland Hospital, Sydney. |
| 1976 | Seattle, U.S.A. – Training in Cardiac Ultrasound. |
| 1975–2001 | Post Graduate Training USA, UK, Europe. |
| 1960–1977 | Consultant Physician. |
| 1977 | FRACP University of Sydney. FRCP University of Edinburgh. |
| 1977– 2015 | Cardiologist |
| 1984 | Diploma of Diagnostic Ultrasound. |
| 2004 | FCSANZ |
| 11 November 2015 | Retired from private practice at the age of 90 years. |

# Publications

1. McCardle's Syndrome
   *Medical Journal of Australia* 1967.
2. Echocardiographic Observations in Myocardial Wall Motion Abnormalities
   *Medical Journal of Australia* 1981.
3. Pseudoaneurysm of the Left Ventricle Diagnosed by Two Dimensional Echocardiography
   *Australian and New Zealand Journal of Medicine*, 1982.
4. Echocardiographic Diagnosis of Right Ventricular Thromboembolism
   *American Heart Journal*, September 1983.

# Curriculum Vitae and Clinical Training

**Suzanne Ellen Woolridge, D.M.U.**
Date of birth 27 December 1945

| | |
|---|---|
| 1961–1977 | Medical Secretary |
| 1969–2015 | Personal Assistant, Office Manager, |
| (1980–2010 | Central Administrator of Inverness Murray Grey Stud and Inverness Thoroughbred Stud) |
| 1975–2015 | Cardiac Sonographer |
| 1989–2015 | Vascular Sonographer |

| | |
|---|---|
| 1976 | University of Washington, Seattle USA
Department of Echocardiography (adult and paediatric)
Dr S Rubinstein
Training Program in M-mode Echocardiography |
| 1976 | University of Washington, Seattle, USA |

|  |  |
|---|---|
|  | Department of Echocardiography, Dr S Rubinstein |
|  | Training Program M-mode, Two Dimensional and Doppler Echocardiography (one week full time) |
| 1977 | University of Oregon, Portland USA |
|  | Department of Echocardiography, Dr W Walsh |
|  | Training Program M-mode and Two Dimensional Echocardiography (one week full time) |
| 1978 | University, Palo Alto, USA |
|  | Department of Echocardiography, Dr R Popp |
|  | (one week full time) |
| Sept 1978 | University of California, San Francisco, USA |
|  | Department of Echocardiography, Drs N Schiller and N Silverman |
|  | (2 days full time) |
| 1979 | Associate Membership of The Institute of Cardiopulmonary Technology of Australia |
| Nov 1979 | University of California, San Francisco, USA |
|  | Department of Echocardiography, Drs N Schiller and N Silverman |
|  | (2 days full time) |
| Nov 1979 | Annual Scientific Meeting of American College of Cardiology, Houston, Texas USA |

# CURRICULUM VITAE & CLINICAL TRAINING

| | |
|---|---|
| April 1980 | Two-Dimensional Echocardiography Course<br>Sponsored by ATL<br>University of Washington, Seattle USA<br>(one week full time) |
| Dec 1980 | Membership of The Institute of Cardiopulmonary Technology of Aust. |
| May 1981 | Meet the Masters in Echocardiography<br>Santa Ana, California, USA<br>(one week full time) |
| Aug 1981 | Echocardiography 1981<br>Newcastle-on-Tyne, England<br>(one week full time) |
| Sept 1981 | Two-Dimensional Course<br>Technicians and Physicians Workshop<br>Phoenix, Arizona, USA<br>(one week full time) |
| May 1982 | Meet the Masters in Echocardiography<br>Santa Ana, California, USA<br>(one week full time) |
| 1982 | Department of Paediatric and Adult Echocardiography<br>Prince Henry and Prince of Wales Hospitals<br>(one day per week) |
| 1985 | Diploma of Medical Ultrasound in Cardiology |
| 1989 | Vascular Duplex Workshop<br>Professional Education, ATL, Seattle, Washington USA |

| | |
|---|---|
| 1990 | Symposium on Coronary Artery Disease<br>Department of Continuing Education<br>UCLA, San Francisco, USA |
| Jan 1991 | Echo Hawaii – American College of Cardiology |
| Jan 1991 | Diagnostic Approaches to Vascular Disease<br>Duplex and Colour Ultrasonography<br>University of Washington, Seattle, USA |
| Aug 1991 | Transcranial Doppler Evaluation<br>ATL Professional Education<br>Bothell, Washington, USA |
| Feb 1992 | Technical Seminar<br>Australasian Society for Ultrasound in Medicine |
| Aug 1992 | Annual Scientific Meeting<br>Cardiac Society of Australia and New Zealand |
| Sept 1992 | Advanced Vascular Ultrasound Techniques<br>Queensland University of Technology |
| Feb 1993 | Echo Hawaii – American College of Cardiology |
| July 1993 | Membership Australian Sonographers Association |
| 1994 | Affiliate Membership of the Cardiac Society of Australia and NZ |
| 1995 | 6th Annual Scientific Sessions – American Society of Echocardiography |
| Sept 1995 | Lower Extremity Vascular Workshop |

# CURRICULUM VITAE & CLINICAL TRAINING

| | |
|---|---|
| | Princess Alexandra Hospital, Brisbane |
| 1996 | Membership of the Australian and New Zealand |
| | Chapter of the International Union of Angiology |
| 1997 | 8th Annual Scientific Sessions |
| | American Society of Echocardiography |
| 1997 | Sonographer Membership Australasian Society for Ultrasound in Medicine |
| 1997–2010 | Registration with the Australasian Sonographer Accreditation Board |
| 1999 | Symposium '99 – Sydney |
| 2000 | State of the Art Echocardiography |
| | American College of Cardiology |
| 2001 | Chest Pain in Children and Adults, the Role of Echo |
| | Duke University USA |
| 2001 | 12th Annual Scientific Sessions |
| | American Society of Echocardiography |
| 2002 | Echo Hawaii |
| | American College of Cardiology |
| 2003 | Echo Australia 2003 |
| 2004 | 15th Annual Scientific Sessions |
| | American Society of Echocardiography |
| 2005 | Annual Scientific Meeting |
| | Cardiac Society of Aust and NZ |
| Oct 2005 | Echo Australia 2005 |
| July 2006 | Echo Alaska, American Society of Echocardiography |
| June 2007 | 18th Annual Scientific Sessions |
| | American Society of Echocardiography |

| | |
|---|---|
| **Aug 2007** | Annual Scientific Meeting Cardiac Society of Aust. and NZ |
| **Sept 2007** | Mediterranean – Cardiology Update College of Family Physicians of Canada |
| **June 2009** | 20th Annual Scientific Sessions American Society of Echocardiography |
| **June 2010** | 21st Annual Scientific Sessions American Society of Echocardiography |
| **June 2011** | 22nd Annual Scientific Sessions American Society of Echocardiography |
| **August 2011** | Cardiac Society of Australia and New Zealand Annual Scientific Meeting Perth WA |
| **August 2011** | European Society of Cardiology Congress 2011 Paris, France |
| **August 2012** | Cardiac Society of Australia and NZ Annual Scientific Meeting, Brisbane Qld |
| **August 2012** | European Society of Cardiology Congress 2012 Munich, Germany |
| **January 2013** | American Society of Echocardiography meeting > Echo Hawaii |
| **June 2013** | American Society of Echocardiography Minneapolis |
| **August 2013** | Cardiac Society Of Australia and NZ meeting |
| **August 2013** | European Cardiac Meeting. Amsterdam |
| **September 2013** | Autoimmune Conference London |

| | |
|---|---|
| January 2014 | Continuing Medical Education Conference<br>Chile |
| May 2014 | World Congress Cardiology<br>Sydney |
| June 2014 | Cardiac Society of Australia and NZ meeting<br>Dunedin NZ |
| June 2014 | Cardiostim Conference<br>Nice |
| June 2014 | American Society of Echocardiography<br>Seattle USA |
| September 2014 | Behcet's Conference<br>Paris, France |
| April 2015 | Continuing Medic |

## Suzanne E Woolridge

*Technical assistant in the preparation and presentation of the following papers*

| | |
|---|---|
| 1982 | Annual Scientific Meeting<br>Cardiac Society of Australia and New Zealand<br>'Regional Wall Motion Abnormalities' |
| 1983 | Australian Society for Ultrasound in Medicine<br>'Echocardiography in the Coronary Care Unit' |

*Technical assistant in the preparation of the following papers*
1. 'Echocardiographic Observations in Myocardial Wall Motion Abnormalities' *Medical Journal of Australia*, 1981

2. 'Pseudoaneuorysm of the Left Ventricle Diagnosed by Two-Dimensional Echocardiography' *Australian and New Zealand Journal of Medicine,* 1982
3. 'Echocardiographic Diagnosis of Right Ventricular Thrombo-Embolism' *American Heart Journal,* September 1983

**Current Memberships**
Australasian Society for Ultrasound in Medicine
Australian Sonographers Association
Cardiac Society of Australia and New Zealand
American Society of Echocardiography

# Record of Travel 1976 to 2018

From 1976 to 2018, Jack and I travelled overseas for medical conferences, horse sales and horse racing 65 times, including one trip to the USA to inspect a stallion.

**1976**

**July–August** University of Washington, Seattle, USA (1))
Dept of Echocardiography (adult and paediatric) – Dr S Rubenstein
'Training Program in M-Mode Echocardiography'
Followed by 'Training Program in M-Mode, Two Dimensional and Doppler Echocardiography'

**1977**

**August** University Of Oregon, Portland USA (2)
Dept of Echocardiography – Dr W Walsh
'Training Program M-Mode, Two-Dimensional Echocardiography'

**1978**

June — University of Palo Alto, USA (3)
Dept of Echocardiography – Dr R Popp
One week full time, one-on-one practical demonstration/learning sessions

September — University of California, San Francisco, USA (4)
Dept of Echocardiography – Drs N Schiller and N Silverman
Two days full time, hands-on learning.

**1979**

November — Annual Scientific Meeting of American College of Cardiology, Houston, Texas, USA. (5)

November — University of California, San Francisco, USA (6)
Dept of Echocardiography – Drs N Schiller and N Silverman

**1980**

April — University of Washington, Seattle, USA (7)
Two-Dimensional Echocardiography Course.
Sponsored by ATL
One week, full time

May — Meet the Masters In Echocardiography (8)
Santa Ana, California, USA, (One week full time)

**1981**

August — Echocardiography 1981 (9)
Newcastle-on-Tyne, England (One week full time)

September — Two Dimensional Course (10)
Technicians and Physicians Workshop
Phoenix, Arizona, USA (One week full time)

## 1982
**May** — Meet the Masters inEchocardiography (11)
Santa Ana, California, USA (one week full time)

## 1989
**August** — University of Washington, Seattle, USA (12)
Professional Education, ATL
Vascular Workshop

## 1990
University of California, Los Angeles USA (13)
Dept of Continuing Education UCLA, San Francisco, USA
Symposium on Coronary Artery Disease.

## 1991
**January** — American Society of Echocardiography (14)
Echo – Hawaii, USA

**January** — University of Washington, Seattle, USA (15)
Diagnostic Approaches to Vascular Disease
Duplex and Colour Ultrasonography

**August** — ATL Professional Education, Bothel, USA (16)
Transcranial Doppler Evaluation.

## 1992
**January** — Magic Millions Sales, Gold Coast Qld
Inglis Sales, Randwick NSW

**February** — Australasian Society for Ultrasound in Medicine (ASUM)
Technical Seminar

**April** — Easter Sales, Randwick NSW

| | |
|---|---|
| August | Cardiac Society of Australia and New Zealand (CSANZ) Annual Scientific Meeting. |
| September | Queensland University of Technology Advanced Vascular Ultrasound Techniques |

**1993**

| | |
|---|---|
| January | Magic Millions Sales, Gold Coast Qld Inglis Sales, Randwick, NSW |
| February | American Society of Echocardiography (17) Echo – Hawaii USA |
| April | Easter Sales, Randwick, NSW |
| June | American Society of Echocardiography (18) 6th Annual Scientific Meeting, Toronto, Canada (Held for the first time in Canada) |
| September | Princess Alexandra Hospital, Brisbane Lower Extremity Vascular Workshop |

**1996**

| | |
|---|---|
| January | Magic Millions Sales, Gold Coast, Qld Inglis Sales, Randwick, NSW |
| March | Vascular Workshop, Melbourne, Vic. |

**1997**

| | |
|---|---|
| January | Magic Millions Sales, Gold Coast, Qld. Inglis Sales, Randwick, NSW |
| April | Easter Sales, Randwick, NSW |
| June | American Society of Echocardiography 8th Annual Scientific Meeting. Orlando, Florida, USA |

## 1999

| | |
|---|---|
| **January** | Magic Millions Sales, Gold Coast Qld |
| **September** | Echo Meeting, Cairns Qld |
| **October** | Symposium 1999 – Sydney, NSW |

## 2000

| | |
|---|---|
| **January** | Magic Millions Sales and Races, Gold Coast, Qld |
| | Inglis Summer Sales, Randwick |
| **February** | On 11/2/2000 Fly Sydney to London (QF1) then to Ireland for horse sales; then fly to Paris, France and drive to Deauville, France to inspect a stallion (Nuclear Freeze). Fly from Paris to Dallas, then to Tuscon for Cardiology Conference. Fly Tuscon, Los Angeles, Sydney arrive home on 26/2/2000 (20) |
| **March** | American College of Cardiology (21) |
| | State of the Art Echocardiography, Anaheim, California, USA |
| **April** | Easter Sales, Randwick, NSW |
| **May** | 12/5/2000 Fly Sydney to Auckland, for New Zealand Horse Sales |
| **June** | 7/6/2000 Magic Millions Horse Sales, home 14/6/2000. |
| **July** | 21/7/2000 – Vascular Conference, Sydney NSW |
| | 27/7/2000 – fly to Gold Coast for Pfizer Specialist Weekend |
| **August** | 4/8/2000 Cardiac Society of Australia and New Zealand |
| | Melbourne Vic. Home on 8/8/2000 |
| | 16/8/2000 Fly to Bangkok for my Brother Rick's Funeral (22) |
| | Home 20/8/2000 |

| | |
|---|---|
| December | 24/12/2000 to Gold Coast > Magic Millions Sales and Races<br>Home 12/1/2001 |

**2001**

| | |
|---|---|
| January | Magic Millions Sales, Gold Coast, Qld.<br>22/1/2001–4/1/2001 > Inglis Classic Horse Sales, Randwick, NSW |
| February | 12/2/2001 > Melbourne Premier Horse Sales<br>19/2/2001–25/2/2001 > Adelaide Magic Millions Horse Sales |
| March | 21/3/2001–29/3/2001 > fly to Dubai for Sunline Race on 24/3/2001. (23)<br>Sunline came 3rd |

Meeting with prospective buyers for Songline yearling.
Fly back to Sydney arrive 29/3/2001

| | |
|---|---|
| April | 16–29/4/2001 – Inglis Easter Sales, Sydney |
| May | 4–5/5/2001 – Conference Sydney<br>11–13/5/2001 Fly to New Zealand > Ra Ora Dispersal Sale (24)<br>19–20/5/2001 Scone NSW Horse Sales |
| June | 16/6/2001–1/7/2001 > Fly to Singapore to consult with a patient > Fly to London then to Ireland to visit horse studs to inspect stallions who would be visiting Australia, including Coolmore Stud. Fly to London/New York/Vancouver, drive to Seattle for (25) American Society of Echocardiography (26)<br>12th Annual Scientific Sessions, Seattle, Washington, USA<br>Fly to Sydney. |

Duke University, Durham, Nth Carolina USA (27) Chest Pain in Children and Adults, the Role of Echocardiography

**2002**
| | |
|---|---|
| **January** | Magic Millions Sales, Gold Coast, Qld |
| | Inglis Sales, Randwick, NSW |
| **February** | 27/1/2002–3/2/2002 > American Society of Echocardiography (28) |
| | Echo – Hawaii, USA |
| | 11– 17/2/2002 Adelaide MM Sales |
| **May** | 10/5/2002 > Fly to Gold Coast > Races |
| | 12–14/5/2002 > Fly to New Zealand Sales (29) |
| **August** | 17/8/2002 – Fly to Melbourne for the day > Races |
| **October** | 18–20/10/2002 > Fly to Melbourne > Races |
| | 25–26/10/2002 > Fly to Melbourne > Races (Cox Plate) |
| **November** | 6–8/11/2002 > Fly to Melbourne Races (Melbourne Cup) |
| | 11–23/11/2002 > Fly to Gold Coast > Races |
| **December** | 24/12/2002–13/1/2003 Fly to Gold Coast Races and Sales |

**2003**
| | |
|---|---|
| **January** | 19–22/1/2003 Inglis Classic Sales, Sydney |
| | 30/1/2003–2/2/2003 Fly to Gold Coast – drive to sanctuary cove |
| | Astra Zeneca Cardiology Conference |
| **February** | 6–7/2/2003 > Fly to Melbourne > Races |
| | 27/2/2003–2/3/2003 > Fly to Gold Coast > Races |

| | |
|---|---|
| March | 8/3/2003 > Drive to Yarrawonga for races at Echuca then drive home |
| | 13–16/3/2003 > Fly to Gold Coast > Races |
| April | 11–12/4/2003 > Fly to Melbourne > Races |
| | 24–27/4/2003 > Fly to Gold Coast > Races |
| | 27/4/2003 > Inglis Easter Sales, Newmarket, Randwick |
| May | 1–5/5/2003 > Fly to Gold Coast > Sales and races |
| | 9–12/5/2003 > Fly to Gold Coast > Races |
| | 17–18/5/2003 > Fly to Gold Coast > Races |
| | 25/5/2003 > Open day at Inverness Stud, Bowral |
| | 30/5/2003–10/6/2003 > Fly to Gold Coast > Sales and Races |
| June | 20–22/6/2003 > Fly to Gold Coast > Races |
| | 28/6/2003 > Fly to Gold Coast > Ipswich Races |
| | 29/6/2003 > Fly to Melbourne > Inspect horses > Late plane home |
| July | 5–6/7/2003 > Fly to Brisbane > Races |
| | 24–26/7/2003 > Fly to Gold Coast FOR Pfizer Weekend Conference |
| August | 9–11/8/2003 > Fly to Adelaide > Cardiac Society of Australia and New Zealand > Annual Scientific Meeting. |
| September | 11–13/9/2003 > Mayo Clinic Echo, Sydney NSW |
| October | 18/10/2003 > Fly to Brisbane > Brisbane Races Late flight home. |
| | 19/10/2003 > Fly to Melbourne, Drive to Seymour for races |
| | Late flight to Sydney @ Kareena Hospital 10.30 pm |
| December | 23/12/2003–15/1/2004 > Fly to Gold Coast for races and sales |

## 2004

| | |
|---|---|
| January | 18–19/1/2004 > Inglis Classic Sale |
| February | 13–14/2/2004 > Fly to Brisbane > Races |
| | 24–27/2/2004 > Fly to Adelaide > Sales |
| April | 9/4/2004 > Inglis Easter Sales, Sydney NSW Fly |
| | 16/4/2004 > Fly to Melbourne and drive to Eliza Park to inspect horses |
| May | 29/5/2004 > Fly to Brisbane > Races > Late flight home |
| June | 24/6/2004–17/7/2004 > Fly to San Francisco and drive to San Diego > American Society of Echocardiography > 15th Annual Scientific Sessions. Fly to Ireland > Farms and sales > Fly to Paris > Drive to Deauville for meeting re stallion. Fly to London Then Home (30) |
| July | 22–25/7/2004 > Fly to Brisbane > Pfizer Weekend Conference |
| August | 7–10/8/2004 > Cardiac Society of Aust. and New Zealand |
| | Brisbane, QLD |
| | 13–15/8/2004 > Fly to Christchurch > Horse sales (31) |
| September | 10/9/2004 > Canberra Races |
| November | 8–14/11/2004 > Gold Coast > Races |
| | 16/11/2004 > Ryde, evening meeting on Sleep Apnoea |
| December | 25/12/2004–14/1/2005 > Gold Coast Races and sales |

## 2005

| | |
|---|---|
| January | 19–25/1/2005 > Adelaide Magic Million Sales |

| | |
|---|---|
| March | 27–30/3/2005 > Inglis Easter Sales and Races, Sydney |
| May | 14/5/2005 > Randwick Sales |
| July | 22–24/7/2005 > Fly to Brisbane > Pfizer Weekend Meeting |
| August | 4–9/8/2005 > Cardiac Society of Australia and New Zealand Annual Scientific Meeting. |
| October | 21–22/10/2005 > Echo Australia 2005 |
| December | 10/12/2005 > Rosehill Races
25/12/2005–18/1/2006 > Fly to Gold Coast > Magic Million sales and races |

**2006**

We had a gradual dispersal of our horses during 2006

| | |
|---|---|
| January | Inglis Sales, Randwick, NSW |
| March | 3–10/3/2006 > Fly to Sunshine Coast for Cardiology Conference including a Michael Crawford concert at a Coolum Beach hotel resort. |
| April | 20–25/4/2006 > Inglis Easter Sales, Sydney |
| June | 3–15/6/2006 > Brisbane sales and races
28/6/2006–17/7/2006 > Fly to San Francisco > Vancouver Board Ship for Mayo Clinic Echo Conference. 8/7/2006 > Fly to London > Meeting With Dermot Farrington re Nuclear Freeze Return to France. 10/7/2006 > Fly to Bordeaux for meeting with Alain Brandenbourger from Haras Des Chartreux. 11/7/2006 – Meeting cancelled. Dermot is upset and annoyed. We told Dermot we do not want to send Nuclear Freeze back to France until Alain Frandenbourger has |

paid all outstanding moneys. 12/7/2006 > Fly to London for meeting with Dermot to discusss our next move. 13/7/2006 > Fly to Singapore. *** 15/7/2006 Consult with patient***. 16/7/2006 > Fly to Sydney (32)

August    18–19/8/2006 > Fly to Gold Coast for Races
November  16–20/11/2006 > Fly to Brisbane Races

## 2007

January    Magic Millions Sales, Gold Coast, Qld
           Inglis Sales, Randwick, NSW
February   23–25/2/2007 > Fly to Auckland > Dunedin (33)
April      10–12/4/2007 > Inglis Easter Sales, Sydney
           27–29/4/2007 > Sydney Cardiology Meeting
May        28–31/5/2007 > ??
June       13–24/6/2007 > Fly to San Francisco > Seattle (34)

**American Society of Echocardiography**
           18th Annual Scientific Sessions
August     8–12/8/2007 > Fly to Christchurch NZ Cardiac Society of Australia and New Zealand (35) Annual Scientific Meeting
           23/8/2007–18/9/2007 > Fly To London > Edinburgh > Meeting with Dr Bill Price and Dr Ted French > Fly to Dublin for meeting with Dermot Farrington > Fly to Barcelona > Cruise on board *Norwegian Jewel* Barcelona/Rome/Naples/Pompeii/Venice/Dubrovnik/Piraeus/Izmur/Istanbul > Fly to Heathrow, London, Sydney (36)
September  College of Family Physicians of Canada Mediterranean Cardiology Update (37)

| | |
|---|---|
| October | 13–14/10/2007 > Fly to Gold Coast Races |
| Oct/Nov | 18/10/2007 > Fly to London > *Queen Mary 2* Southampton to New York Trans Atlantic Crossing > Fly new york to Sydney arrive 6/11/2017 (38) |
| Dec/Jan | 30/12/2007–3/1/2008 > Fly to Gold Coast Races |

**2008**

| | |
|---|---|
| March | 6–18/3/2008 > Fly to Los Angeles > Orlando > Miami continuing Medical Education Meeting on cruise (Dominican Republic, Charlotte, Bahamas) (39) |
| April | 25–30/4/2008 > Inglis Easter Sales, Sydney |
| June | 7/6/2008–11/6/2008 American Society of Echocardiography Toronto, Canada (40) |
| July | 16/7/2008–10/8/2008 > Fly to London, Drive to Southampton > Board *Queen Victoria* > Baltic Cruise Continuing Medical Education Meeting On Cruise > (Nth Sea/Zeebrugge, Belgium/Baltic Sea/Gdansk, Poland/Talinn, Estonia/St Petersburgh, Russia/Helsinki, Finland/Stockholm, Sweden/Copenhagen, Denmark/Oslo, Norway/Southampton) Drive to Wales, Ireland via Ferry, visit horse studs including Coolmore where we were guests > Drive to Dublin > Fly to Heathrow London then to Sydney (41) |
| September | 26–28/9/2008 > Drive to Katoomba for Medical Conference at Leura |
| December | 25/12/2008–14/1/2009 > Drive to Gold Coast for races and sales<br>Drive to Sydney |

*Lunch on the Great Wall of China*

**2009**

**April**  2/4/2009 > Fly to Shanghai for continuing medical education meeting > during the flight Jack was called to treat a woman with headache and hyperventilation > injected 25 mg promethazine. 5/4/2009 Fly to Yichang for cruise on Yangtse River and tour the 3 gorges – Xiling Gorge is the longest, the Wu Gorge is the second and the Outang Gorge is the shortest of the three gorges. The river navigates through gorges, sheer cliffs where the Meng Liang staircase from the Song Dynasty can be seen, here the river narrows to 100 metres with peaks to 1500 metres. Wanzhou, then to Chongqing a city of 32 million people, and is about the size of Austria, by 2020 the population will be 50 million. Chongqing/

|  |  |
|---|---|
|  | Shibaozhai/Wushan/Shennong/Wuhan/Beijing. The CME arranged for all conference attendees \|to have lunch and entertainment on the Great Wall of China. > Shanghai > Fly Home 21/4/2009 (42) |
| June | 4–10/6/2009 > Fly to Los Angeles then to Dallas, then to Washington CD > American Society of Echocardiography 20th Annual Scientific Sessions (43) |

**2010**

| | |
|---|---|
| June | 8–17/6/2010 > Fly to Los Angeles then to San Diego. American Society of Echocardiography 21st Annual Scientific Sessions. (44) |

**2011**

| | |
|---|---|
| June | 3/6/2011 > Fly to London, drive to Southampton > Cruise *Queen Mary 2* to New York 11/6/2011 American Society of Echocardiography 22nd Annual Scientific Sessions (45) |
| August | 10/8/2011 > Cardiac Society of Australia and New Zealand Annual Scientific Meeting, Perth WA |
| August | European Society of Cardiology Congress 2011 Paris, France (46) |
| November | 11/11/2011 > fly to Brisbane for races. |

**2012**

| | |
|---|---|
| March | 30/3/2012 > Fly to London then to Dubai > Races > Dubai World Cup > Agrame Conference at Dubai International Exhibition Centre. |

|   |   |
|---|---|
|  | 5/4/2012 > Cruise *Queen Elizabeth* > Muscat > Safaga (Luxor, Karnak and Valley of the Kings) > Aqaba (The Lost City of Petra) > Sharm El Sheikh (St Catherine's Monastery) >Port Said (Pyramids, Sphinx, and Sakkara) > Alexandria > Athens > Rome > Monte Carlo > Lisbon > Southampton. > 27–29/4/2012 > Drive to London > 22nd European meeting on Hypertension and Cardiovascular Protection @ ICC London. > 30/4/2012 Overnight Train to Inverness > P/U rental car drive to Gills Bay, catch ferry to St Margaret's Hope, drive to Ayre Hotel, tour Orkney, drive to Stromness, ferry to Scrabster, drive to Edinburgh, stay at Rocco Forte Balmoral Hotel > drive to Roslyn and head towards London 8/5/2012 fly home arrive 10/5/2012 (47) |
| August | Cardiac Society of Australia and New Zealand Annual Scientific Meeting, Brisbane, QLD |
| August | 22/8/2012–31/8/2012 European Society of Cardiology Congress 2012 > Munich, Germany (48) |
| **2013** | |
| January | 2–12/1/2013 > *Oosterdamm* cruise from Sydney > Port Villa, Mystery Island, Noumea, Ile De Pins, Sydney (49) |
|  | 18–27/1/2013 > Fly to Honolulu > American Society of Echocardiography meeting > Echo Hawaii > Fly Sydney (50) |
| June | 3–8/6/2013 > Edinburgh (51) |
|  | 27/6/2013 > Fly to Los Angeles > Dallas |

|  |  |
|---|---|
| | > Minneapolis American Society of Echocardiography |
| | 4/7/2013 > Chicago > Los Angeles > Sydney (52) |
| August | 7–11/8/2013 > Fly to Gold Coast for Cardiac Society Of Australia and NZ meeting |
| | 29/8/2013 > Fly to London then to Amsterdam for European Cardiac Meeting. |
| | Fly Amsterdam to London, drive to Southampton Cruise > *Queen Mary* 2 > New York > Newport > Boston > Boat Harbour > St Johns > Halifax > Quebec > New York > Fly To London For Autoimmune Conference |
| | 28/9/2013 Home (53) |

**2014**

|  |  |
|---|---|
| January | 18/1/2014 > Fly to Santiago > Cruise > Continuing Medical Education Conference Chile, Punta Arenas, Ushuaia Arg, Cape Horn Chile, Puerto Madryn Arg, Punta Del Este Urgu., Montevideo Urgu., Buenos Aires Arg. > 4/2/2014 Home (54) |
| February | 19/2/2014 to 14/3/2014 > Cruise *Queen Mary 2* Circumnavigation Of Australia > Brisbane > Darwin > Bali > Perth > Adelaide > Melbourne > Sydney (55) |
| May | 4–7/5/2014 > Sydney > World Congress Cardiology |
| June | 3–8/6/2014 > Auckland > Dunedin Cardiac Society of Australia and NZ meeting (56) |
| | 13/6/2014 > London > Nice > Cardiostim Conference |

|  |  |
|---|---|
|  | Fly to Seattle for American Society of Echocardiography |
|  | 27/6/2014 Home (57) |
| September | 18–20/9/2014 > Fly to Paris For Behcet's Conference (58) |
| November | 10/11/2014 > Fly to New York > Fly to Sydney (59) |
|  | 22–29/11/2014 > Bravo Cruise > Sydney/Sydney (56) |

**2015**

| | |
|---|---|
| April | 20/4/2015 > Continuing Medical Education Meeting held on *Oceania Marina* cruise > Manta, Puerto Limon, Panama Canal, Roatan, Santo Thomas, Cozemel, Miami, Port Canaveral, Charlestown, New York > |
| | 16/5/2015 *Queen Mary 2* > Trans Atlantic crossing to Southampton. > Drive to London > Fly to Sydney (57) |
| October | 24/10/2015 > Bravo Cruise > *Radiance of the Seas* > Sydney, Mare, Mystery Island, Noumea, 1/11/2015 Sydney (58) |

**2016**

| | |
|---|---|
| June | 3/6/2016 > fly to Brisbane > Cruise on the *Dawn Princess* > Brisbane, Yorkeys Knob, Alotau Ng, Darwin > The Ghan Train to Adelaide > 17/6/2016 arrive home. (59) |
| June/July | 30/6/2016 > Fly To Dubai then to Rome > *Queen Victoria* Cruise > Corfu, Kotor, Trieste, Venice, Dubrovnik, Heraklion, Kusadasi, Santorini, Athens, Dardanelles, Volos Greece, Rhodes, |

|           | Mykonos, Athens > Fly to London > Fly to Sydney arrive 27/7/2015. (60) |
|-----------|---|
| Sept/Oct  | 11/9/2016 > Fly to London then to Nice and Marsailles |
|           | Continuing Medical Education Meeting on river cruise > Arles, Auvignon, Viviers, Lyon, Chalon Sur Saone Fr > Bus to Paris > Fly to London > Fly to Sydney arrive 3/10/2016 (61) |
| October   | 6/10/2016 > Fly to Melbourne for races > Fly to Sydney 9/10/2016 |
|           | 17/10/2016 >Bravo Cruise > *Radiance of the Seas* > 24/10/2016 arrive home (62) |

**2017**

| March     | 31/3/2017 >fly to Hong Kong > *Queen Mary 2* Cruise> Bangkok, Singapore, Kuala Lumpur, Penang, Colombo, Dubai > Fly to Sydney arrive home 20/4/2017 (63) |
|-----------|---|
| **July**  | 7/7/2017 > Fly to Gold Coast for races > Home 13/7/2017 |
| **August**| 2/8/2017 > Fly to Brisbane for *Golden Princess* cruise > Brisbane, Savu Savu, Honolulu, Maui, Kona, Kauai, Papeete, Moorea, Auckland > Arrive Sydney 6/9/2017 (64) |
| **September** | 22/9/2017 >Fly to London then to Amsterdam for cruise on *Oceania Marina* > Continuing Medical Education > Amsterdam, Dover, St Marlo, Brest, La Rochelle, Bordeaux, Biaritz, Hornfleur, Bilboa, Ferrol, Oporto, Lisbon > Fly to London then to Sydney > Arrive home on 12/10/2017 (65) |

**October**  31/10/2017 > Boarded *Radiance of the Seas* for Bravo Cruise.
Jack collapsed when boarding and was transferred to St. Vincent's Hospital.

# Inverness Stud – List of Horses

(** indicates horses bred by Inverness Stud)

**List of stallions serving at Inverness Stud during the lifetime of the stud**
1. **Sackford USA** 1980 – Stop the Music USA × Bon Fille by Ben Lomond GB
2. **Phizam NZ** 1979 – Zamazaan FR × Phias NZ by Oncidium
3. **Simonstad NZ** 1989 – Kaapstad NZ × Sovereign Field SAF by Northfields USA
4. **Lycius USA** 1988 – Mr Prospector USA × Lypatia USA by Lyphard
5. **Medaaly GB** 1994 – Highest Honor FR × Dance of Leaves by Sadler's Wells
6. **Nuclear Freeze USA** 1996 – Danzig USA × Razyana USA by His Majesty USA
7. **Private Call USA** 1995 – Private Account × Euphoric by the Minstrel CAN

8. **Universal Prince 1997** – Scenic IRE × Biscay Bird by Bluebird USA

Phizam and Sackford were owned by Inverness. Nuclear Freeze was purchased by Inverness and Dermot Farrington, and then shares were sod.

Lycius, Medaaly, Private Call and Universal Prince were leased. We had 1 share in **Canny Lad** 1987 – Bletchingly × Jesmond Lass by Lunchtime)

**List of broodmares owned by Jack and Sue during the lifetime of Inverness**

1. **Abhaa** 1991 (Marscay × Rebecca Gay by Lord of the Dance)
   *Progeny bred by Inverness Stud* :
   Abhaa Fly 1999 (Hamas IRE) (7-0-1-0)
   Miss Patsy 2000 (Lycius USA) (9-0-0-0)
   Abby's Ice 2001 (Nuclear Freeze USA)
   Big Freeze 2003 (Nuclear Freeze USA) (4-0-0-0)
2. **Abby's Ice** \*\*2001 (Nuclear Freeze USA × Abhaa).
3. **Afilar** 1986 (Lord Seymour-Hi Lissa).
   *Progeny bred by Inverness Stud:*
   Manihi Freeze 2004 (Nuclear Freeze USA) (13-0-0-0)
   Dismal 2003 (Fantastic Light USA)
   Nefertum 2004 (Nuclear Freeze USA)
   Anuket 2005 (Nuclear Freeze USA)
4. **A Star is Born** 1989 (Ahanoora GB × Stage Hit by Century).
   *Progeny bred by Inverness Stud:*
   Eviotis 1998 (Octagonal NZ) (**8-1-0-1**)
   I'm a Showoff 1999 (Thunder Gulch USA) (2-0-0-0)
   Spinning Knight 2000 (Spinning World USA) (11-0-0-0)
   Angel's Star \*\*2001 (King of Kings IRE) (**9-0-1-0**).

Mighty Canny 2003 (Canny Lady) (46-3-4-2)
Tomlar Shack 2004 (Nuclear Freeze USA)

5. **Audeena** 1981 (Taipan USA × Deciana NZ)
Progeny **NOT** bred by Inverness Stud:
**Baldeen 1988** (Balmerino) **Winner 1994 STC Birthday Quality H'cap a Listed Race**
*Progeny bred by Inverness Stud:*
Respected 1992 (High Regard) **(49-6-4-0)**
Balmoral Road 1993 (Phizam NZ) **Exported to Singapore**

6. **Ballystorm** 1989 (Storm Bird CAN × Raise Rain USA by Raise a Native).
*Progeny bred by Inverness Stud:*
Frosty Bally 2001 (Medaaly GB) **(4-0-0-1).**
**Exported to Philippines 9/5/2005**
Ballyev 2002 (Fasliyev USA) **(7-0-0-1)**
Parley 2003 (Nuclear Freeze USA) **(41-2-8-6)**
Cold Ethyl 2004 (Nuclear Freeze USA)

7. **Bebhinn** 1989 (Sackford USA × Laura's Cottage IRE by Habitat).
*Progeny bred by Inverness Stud:*
**Kugelhopf 1995 (Akaaber USA)** ,578 **(66-9-5-10)**
    1st 2003 TWBA Toowoomba Cup a Listed Race
Doodling Bill 1996 (Salieri USA) **(3-0-0-0)**
Cape Hoper 1997 (Simonstad NZ) **(13-1-0-1)**
Chatswood Chase 1998 (Simonstad NZ) **(19-1-3-2-)**
Grand Beaver 1999 (Grand Lodge USA) **(20-2-0-0)**
Nibbler 2000 (Snippets) **(17-2-3-4) Exp to NZ 19/12/04**
Gautier 2001 (Peintre Celebre USA)
Bibidas 2002 (Xaar GB) (5-0-0-0)
Mournful 2003 (Nuclear Freeze USA) (17-0-0-0)
Princess Universe 2004 (Nuclear Freeze USA) (4-0-0-0)

8. **Beckie Boo**** 1995 (Last Tycoon × Olympia Fields by Tate Gallery)
   *Progeny bred by Inverness Stud:*
   Be Keen 2000 (Simonstad NZ) (22-1-0-2)
   Nuclear Speed 2001 (Nuclear Freeze USA) (14-0-2-1)
   Cristi La Boo 2003 (Lacryma Cristi IRE) (9-3-0-0)
   Pale Moon Rising 2004 (Galileo IRE) (37-1-3-3)
9. **Bedspread USA 1989 (Seattle Dancer USA × Affair USA BY Bold Lad)**
   Progeny bed by Inverness Stud:
   Blanket 2002 (Nuclear Freeze USA)
10. **BLAME 1986 (Famous Star GB × Lady Hi Bing by Royal Avenue)**
    ,200 (59-12-4-9) and stakes placed in
    1991 3rd MV WH Stocks 1600 m Listed Race
    1992 4th Rosehill Queen of the Turf 1500m Group 3
    *Progeny bred by Inverness Stud:*
    Royal Dragon 1998 (Charnwood Forest IRE) (1-0-1-0)
    Staratan 1999 (Spartacus) (37-11-6-6)
    Dammen 2001 (Canny Lad) (29-5-7-2)
    Nucleic 2002 (Nuclear Freeze USA) (11-0-0-2)
    Nuclear Reactor 2003 (Nuclear Freeze USA) **Exported to Singapore 4/7/2007**
11. **Buster's Girl 1983** (Blockbuster × Ryeborough)
    *Progeny not bred by Inverness Stud:*
    **Boisterous Lady 1992 (Rivotious USA)**
    **1998 GCTC Silk Stocking Listed Race**
    *Progeny bred by Inverness Stud:*
    Zambuster 1993 (Phizam NZ)
12. **Champagne Rouge** 1987 (Salmon Leap USA × Clystalla USA by Pia Star)).

# INVERNESS STUD – LIST OF HORSES

*Progeny bred by Inverness Stud:*
Perignon 1996 (Scenic IRE) **(46-6-9-6)**
Mr Egotist 1999 (Hennessy USA) **(16-2-4-1)**

13. **Chitter Chatter 1999** (Scenic × Media Miss) In foal to Nuclear Freeze USA.
    *Progeny bred by Inverness Stud:*
    Three Mile Island 2004 (Nuclear Freeze USA) **(34-1-1-5)**

14. **Classy Tricks 1984** (Dash o' Pleasure USA × Princess Talaria by Dignitas)
    *Progeny not bred by Inverness Stud:*
    **Valuate 1996 (Bluebird USA) (30-4-3-1)**
        1st 2000 Randwick Carbine 1600m a Listed race
        3rd 2000 Randwick Ritchie 1400m Group 3
    *Progeny bred by Inverness Stud:*
    I'm Classy 1999 (Torrential USA) **Exported to Malaysia 3/6/2005**
    Our Mate Moee 2001 (Rubiton)

15. **Coolmore GB 1985** (Ardross IRE × Laura's Cottage IRE by Habitat)
    *Progeny not bred by Inverness Stud:*
    **Paco Rabanne NZ 1992 (Kreisler IRE) (25-7-3-2)**
        1st 1995 NCRC Canterbury Stakes a Listed Race
    *Progeny bred by Inverness Stud:*
    Cool Addiction 2000 (Groom Dancer USA) **(12-1-2—0)**

16. **Corsicana 1985** (Half Iced × Smokey Princess by Sovereign Edition)
    **Race Win 1988 CJC Canterbury Belle Stakes 1200m Listed Race**
    *Progeny bred by Inverness Stud:*
    Metro Electric 1996 (Centro NZ)
    In Good Stad 1997 (Simonstad NZ)

Jolly Frog 1999 (Simonstad NZ) **(9-0-0-0)**

17. **Cri Cri (Gallant Knight × Torna). Cri Cri was Jack's first racehorse purchase.**
The following are her foals
Big Flash 1970 (Royal Sovereign) he won at least 4 races
Exeter Miss 1971 (Just Great GB)
Cuddle Daddy 1973 (Recalled GB)
Bionic Belle 1974 (Royal Sovereign)
All Tears 1975 (Imagele)

18. **Danehillcait** 1995 (Danehill × Laura's Cottage IRE by Habitat) in foal to Universal Prince.
*Progeny bred by Inverness Stud:*
Robbo's Danehill 2000 (Lycius USA) **(15-2-1-2)**
Poop Deck Pappy 2001 (Hennessy USA) **(35-2-3-5)**
Canny Cait 2002 (Canny Lad) **(2-0-0-0)**
Universal Colours 2004 (Universal Prince) **(25-1-3-3)**
   **Exported to NZ 16/6/2010**

19. **Donna Dior** 1997 (Marscay × Donna Cara by Sir Tristram). Donna Dior was purchased by Jack at the 1998 Easter Sales.
,835 **(15-2-2-1)**
**1ST 2000 MV Salinger Trophy 1600 m Listed Race**
*Progeny bred by Inverness Stud:*
Donating 2002 (Octagonal NZ)
**Galileo's Daughter 2004 (Galileo IRE) ,750 (18-1-1-3)**
   **2nd 2008 Rosehill Arrowfield Group 1**
   **3rd 2008 AJC OAKS Group 1**

20. **Dream Catcher**\*\* (Sky Chase × Showingly by Bletchingly) **(18-3-3-4)**
*Progeny bred by Inverness Stud:*
Dream Win 1998 (Simonstad NZ) **(12-1-0—1)**
Final Edict 1999 (Rubiton) **(44-10-3-6)**

Dream Runner 2000 (Lycius) **(20-2-0-0)**
21. **Eisteddfod**\*\* 2003 (Carnegie IRE × Singeing Lamp)
    *Progeny bred by Inverness Stud:*
    Suzanne 2008 (Choisir) **(37-2-6-2)**
    Default 2009 (Rock of Gibraltar IRE) **(27-3-3-2)**
22. **Fireace NZ 1989** (Straight Strike USA × Fire Mountain by Rocky Mountain)
    *Progeny bred by Inverness Stud:*
    Firestick 1994 (Sackford USA ) **(29-3-3-5)**
    Call Adair 1996 (Simonstad NZ) **(24-1-2-6)**
    Hannah's Hope 1997 (Simonstad NZ) $0 **(1-0-0-0)**
    Dance Ritual 1998 (Danehill Dancer IRE) **(5-0-1-1)**
    Regal Rendezvous 1999 (Eagle Eyed USA) $0 **(1-0-0-0)**
    Solidified 2000 (Simonstad NZ) **(73-4-8-5)**
    Hang Fire 2001 (Nuclear Freeze USA) **(37-2-2-3)**
23. **Frescante**\*\* 2001 (Peintre Celebre USA × Amwag USA) **(15-4-1-3)**
    *Progeny bred by Inverness Stud:*
    **Weekend Special 2007 (Snitzel) ,028 (23-4-7-2)**
      **3rd 2012 Flemington – Kensington 1000m Listed Race**
    Conifercone 2008 (Choisir) $0 (6-0-0-0)
    Fresnel 2009 (50 per cent Coolmore) (Fastnet Rock) **(20-3-3-2)**
24. **Glittazone**\*\* 2000 (Lycius × Regal Vacation) **(13-0-3-4)**.
25. **Great Anna** 1999 (Anabaa × Great Vintage) ) **(20-5-1-3)**
    **2003 3rd Morp. Aust Oaks 2025 m Group 1**
    **2004 1st STC EPONA STAKES 1900 m Listed Race**
    Sold in foal to Reset
26. **Grenache Girl** 1993 (Our Poetic Prince × Temperance Lady)
    *Progeny bred by Inverness Stud:*

Nuclear Wine 2001 (Nuclear Freeze USA) $0 (4-0-0-0)
27. **Grumblebum** 1999 (Charnwood Forest × Sourpuss) (12-1-1-2)
Sold
28. **Holliska 1984** (Wolver Hollow IRE × Mariska FR)
*Progeny bred by Inverness Stud:*
Arthur's Charm 1994 (Bluebird) (4-0-0-0)
Likastad 1996(Simonstad NZ) (10-0-0-0)
Derrawee Ruby 1999 (Simonstad NZ) $0 (2-0-0-0)
29. **I'm a Thunder**\*\* 1999 (Thunder Gulch × I'm in Business) (18-2-2-1)
*Progeny bred by Inverness Stud:*
Velvetere 2004 (Nuclear Freeze USA )
Spared 2005 (Nuclear Freeze USA)
Sold in foal to Nuclear Freeze $22,000
30. **\*\*I'm a Wag IRE** 2000 (Lahib USA × Amwag USA) 99-0-1-0)
31. **I'm Classy**\*\* 1999 (Torrential × Classy Tricks)
*Progeny bred by Inverness Stud:*
Nuclear Ice 2003 (Nuclear Freeze USA) **Exported to Malasia 3/6/2005**
Sold in foal to Nuclear Freeze $3,000
32. **I'm In Business 1981** (Jevington × Rain Check)
*Progeny bred by Inverness Stud:*
Private Business 1993 (Virginia Privateer USA)
**Mr Prudent 1994** (Phizam NZ)
   1st 1999 NSW Tatt's Plate 2400 m – Listed Race
   1st 2001 AJC Sydney Cup 3200 m Group 1
   3rd 2001 Caul Easter Cup 2000 m Group 3
   2nd 2002 AJC Sydney Cup 3200 m Group 1
   3rd 2002 MV Cup 2500 m Group 2

## INVERNESS STUD – LIST OF HORSES

    2nd 2002 Flem Melbourne Cup 3200 m Group 1
    2nd 2002 AJC Sydney Cup 3200 m Group 1
    3rd 2003 Bendigo Cup 2400 m Listed Race
Bel Fior 1996 (Simonstad NZ) (5-0-0-0)
I'm a Thunder 1998 (Thunder Gulch USA) (**18-2-2-1**)

33. **Imperial Elder** 1992 (Sir Tristram IRE × Dowager Empress CAN by Vice Regent)
*Progeny bred by Inverness Stud:*
Miss Goldie 1998 (Geiger Counter USA) (**3—0-1-1**)
Polish Empress 2000 (Polish Navy USA) (**7-1-2-0**)
Ping Pong Ball 2002 (Favorite Trick USA)
Basileus 2004 (Universal Prince)

34. **Just an Angel** 1983 (Yeats USA × Just Thought USA by Jacinto)

35. **Love's Ave** 1992 (Scenic IRE × Kicks for Free by Kaoru Star) purchased and raced by Jack and Sue, (**40-3-7-7**)
*Progeny bred by Inverness Stud:*
Rose of Simon 1998 (Simonstad NZ) (**4-0-0-1**)
Roman Free 2000 (Spartacus) (**30-5-2-5**)
Mr Scaramunga 2001 (Medaaly GB) (**25-0-2-3**)
Love on the Rocks 2002 (Nuclear Freeze USA) (**25-0-2-3**)
Kazmac 2003 (Nuclear Freeze USA)
Explosive Mac 2003 (Nuclear Freeze USA) (**12-1-0-3**)

36. **Madas** 1995 (Varick × La Bijou by Matrice) in foal to Universal Prince, sold $4,000
*Progeny bred by Inverness Stud:*
Lymadicus 2000 (Lycius USA) (**15-2-1-1**)
Cool World 2001 (Nuclear Freeze USA) (**23-3-5-2**)
World Wind 2002 (Nuclear Freeze USA) **Exported to Malaysia**
Sintaepung 2003 (Nuclear Freeze USA) **Exported to Korea**

Explode 2004 (Nuclear Freeze USA) **(15-1-1-2)**
Universal Jewel 2005 (Universal Prince) **(30-2-2-7)**

37. **Maximum Effort NZ** 1987 (Shy Rambler USA × Maxi NZ by Bourbon Prince USA)
    **Stakes Winner – 1991 CJC Warstep Stakes 2000 m – Listed Race**
    *Progeny bred by Inverness Stud:*
    Eyenar 1995 (Jetball) **(4-0-0-0)**
    Cut Through 1997 (Royal Academy USA) **(58-3-9-14)**
    Look of Thunder 1998 (Thunder Gulch USA)
    Sweet Spot 1999 (Royal Academy USA) **(18-1-5-3)**
    Find an Oasis 2000 (Desert King IRE) **(9-0-1-0)**
    Great Effort 2001 (Medaaly GB) **(20-3-0-1)**

38. **Melrose** 1990 (Sun and Shine X Vedo Bay by Orange Bay)
    *Progeny bred by Inverness Stud:*
    Gotti 1999 (Pentire GB) **(71-3-6**
    Desert Mel 2000 (Desert Prince IRE) **Exported to NZ**
    Strawberry Rose 2001 (Snippets) **(7-1-1-0)**
    Beauty Nuke 2003 (Nuclear Freeze USA) **(9-0-0-0)**
    Melrose Prince 2004 (Universal Prince) **(40-3-5-2)**

39. **Miami Vice 1984** (Century × Oh Calcutta by Streetfighter)
    *Progeny bred by Inverness Stud:*
    Wild Warrior 1993 (Bite the Bullet USA) **Exported to Singapore 2/4/1996**
    Sonny Crocket 1994 (Sackford USA) **(28-1-0-0)**
    Arrestad 1996 (Simonstad NZ) **(4-0-0-0)**
    Miami Pirate 1997 (Marauding NZ) **(22-1-0-0)**
    Miami Belle 1998 (Night Shift USA) **(12-1-1-2)**
    Secret Vic 1999 (Grand Lodge USA) **(1-0-0-0)**
    Tis Hopeful 2000 (Lycius USA) **(13-1-1-2)**
    Miami Ice 2001 (Nuclear Freeze USA) **(32-5-4-1)**

# INVERNESS STUD – LIST OF HORSES

Vice 'n Ice 2002 (Nuclear Freeze USA) **(8-1-0-0)**

39. **Miss Goldie**\*\* 1998 (Geiger Counter USA × Imperial Elder) **(3-0-1-1)**
*Progeny bred by Inverness Stud:*
Prima Gold 2002 (Snippets) **(22-3-6-0)**

40. **Miss Mahal**\*\* 2004 (Canny Lad × Tis Mahal)
*Progeny bred by Inverness Stud*
Iccy Sue 2008 (Nuclear Freeze USA)
Mr Armstrong 2009 (Nuclear Freeze USA) **Exported to NZ**
Devi Jam 2010 (50/50 with Coolmore Stud) (Duke of Marmalade IRE) **(7-0-0-0)**

41. **Miss Pine Lodge 1997** (Charmande USA × Dispose NZ)
*Progeny bred by Inverness Stud:*
Sack the Maid 1994 (Sackford USA) **(22-1-2-0)**
Twilight Glow 1995 (Forest Glow)
Miss Simes 1996 (Simonstad NZ) **5 (20-1-5-2)**
Simmysue 1997 (Simonstad NZ) **(27-3-4-6)**

42. **Mon Ami 1986** (Monakea × Mere by Small Time)
*Progeny bred by Inverness Stud:*
Power Park 1999 (Frenchpark GB)
Monacius 2000 (Lycius USA) **(7-0-0-0)**
Montonami 2001 (Rubiton) **(1-0-0-0)**

43. **Monet's Odyssey**\*\* 2002 (Peintre Celebre USA × Regal Odyssey) **(5-0-0-0)**

44. **Mossy Top 1981** (Twig Moss × Silent River)
*Progeny bred by Inverness Stud:*
Top County 1993 (County) **(27-5-2-1)**

45. **Musical Haze 1983** (New Regent CAN × Musique de Nuit FR)
*Progeny bred by Inverness Stud:*
She Says 1997 (Simonstad NZ) **(15-1-0-2)**

Easyline 1999 (Snippets) **(30-4-1-2)**
Buster Haze 2000 (Lycius USA) **(54-1-7-6)**

46. **Nandewar 1997** (Mukaddamah USA × Mountain Greenery USA by Prospect)
    *Progeny bred by Inverness Stud:*
    Atom Splitter 2001 (Nuclear Freeze USA) **(24-1-0-1)**

47. **Northwood Storm** 1993 (Bluebird USA × Storm Kitty USA by Storm Bird)
    *Progeny bred by Inverness Stud:*
    Halcyon Blue 1997 (Simonstad NZ) **(6-1-0-0)**
    Lodaga Sheikh 1998 (Canny Lad)
    Oh Kitty 2001 (Orpen USA) **(26-4-5-2)**
    Nuclear Storm 2002 (Nuclear Freeze USA)
    Cool Saab 2004 (Nuclear Freeze) **(25-2-5-3)**

48. **Our Lass 1995** (Geiger Counter USA X September Lass USA by Diamond Prospect)
    *Progeny bred by Inverness Stud:*
    Hudson Jack 2000 (Desert Style IRE) **(22-6-4-1)**
    Permafreeze 2001 (Nuclear Freeze USA)

49. **Pitti Palace 1985** (Arch Sculptor GB × Arouse NZ)
    **Stakeswinner 1988 AJC Reginald Allen Handicap 1400 m Listed Race**
    *Progeny bred by Inverness Stud:*
    Our Dane 1997 (Danehill USA) **(12-1-3-3)**
    Palace Night 1998 (Night Shift USA) **$3,000 (14-0-1-0)**

50. **Planned 1984 (Imperial Prince IRE × Great Future)**
    *Progeny bred by Inverness Stud:*
    Skyblaze 1993 (Aurealis) **(33-2-1-2)**
    Decree 1994 (Sackford USA) **(4-1-0-0)**

51. **Princess Aly USA 1987** (Alydar × Paddy's Princess by St Paddy)

## INVERNESS STUD – LIST OF HORSES

*Progeny bred by Inverness Stud:*
Another Native 2000 (Lycius USA) (4-0-0-1)

52. **Princes Jessie 1988** (Cheraw IRE × Handful of Gold)
*Progeny bred by Inverness Stud:*
Beat the Posse 1993 (Phizam NZ) **(8-1-0-0-)**
House on Aces 1994 (Sackford USA)

53. **Pure Ecstasy** 1997 (Thunder Gulch × Kalzao by Alzao)
*Progeny bred by Inverness Stud:*
Isotope 2001 (Nuclear Freeze USA) (6-0-0-0)
Pure Ice 2005 (Nuclear Freeze USA) (3-0-0-0)
**Sold in foal to Nuclear Freeze, with Nuclear Freeze colt at foot $6,000**

54. **Ranein 1990** (Bluebird USA × Fashion Scene by Without Fear)
*Progeny bred by Inverness Stud:*
Sir Simon 1996 (Simonstad NZ) (8-1-0-1)
Alfie's Halo 1997 (Don't Say Halo USA) (5-0-0-0)
**Dress Code 2000 (El Moxie USA) ,550 (35-3-4-2)**
   **2002 3rd Caul. Debutant 900 m Listed Race**
   **2002 4th MV Platinum 1000m Listed Race**
   **2003 5th GCST Magic Millions 1100m**
Freeze Dancer 2001 (Nuclear Freeze USA) (6-1-1-0)

55. **Real Joy 1993** (Fairy King × Viva Regina by Archregent)
*Progeny bred by Inverness Stud*
The People's Champ 1998 (Simonstad NZ) **(21-6-2-2)**
Speed at Easy 1999 (Hamas)

56. **Regal Odyssey NZ 1985** (Vice Regal × Lavender Hill by Sovereign Edition)
*Progeny not bred by Inverness Stud:*
**Regent Street 1998 (Carnegie IRE) ,600 (35-7-4-1)**
**2002 1st QTC QLD Guineas 1600m Group 1**

2002 4th GCST Hollingdale 1800m Group 2
2004 1st VRC Straight Six Listed Race
2004 3rd FLEM Yallambee 1400m Group 3
*Progeny bred by Inverness Stud:*
**Soprana 1999 (Carnegie IRE) (12-1-3-0)**
    2002 5th EF – TJ Smith 1600 m Group 1
    2002 4th Rand Furious 1400 m Group 3
    2002 4th RHL – Tea Rose 1500 m Group 2
    2002 2nd Rand Champion 2000m Group 1
Daaly Power 2001 (Medaaly GB) (14-2-3-0)
Monet's Odyssey 2002 (Peintre Celebre USA) (5-0-0-0)

57. **Regal Vacation 1984** (Imperial Prince × Outing by Boucher)
*Progeny bred by Inverness Stud*
Sleepytime 1999 (Simonstad NZ) (7-0-0-0)
Glittazone 2000 (Lycius USA) (**13-0-3-4**)

58. **Rosalina DEN 1984** (Souble Jump IRE × La Circasia IRE)
*Progeny bred by Inverness Stud*
it's my sin 1993 (Success Express) ,679 (27-5-2-4)
    1996 3rd Avon Ra Ora 1200 m Listed Race
    1997 1st OtlMRC Maori WFA Group 1
    1997 1ST BOPRC Trust Bank Classic Listed Race
    1997 1st OTAK Regency 1400 m Group 1
    1997 4th EF Byrne Hart 1400 m Group 2
    1998 3RD MORP Goodwood 1200 m Group 1
Rose of Rhyana 1994 (Sackford USA) (13-1-3-1)

59. **Rose Babu 1981** (Tattenham by Aubyn Babu by My Own)
*Progeny not bred by Inverness Stud:*
**Count Scenario 1994 (Scenic IRE) ,875 (63-12-8-9)**
    Purchased at the 1995 Magic Millions Yearling Sale

# INVERNESS STUD – LIST OF HORSES

    1998 3rd EFM Qld Guineas 1600 m Group 2
    1999 3RD WAGG Wagga Cup 2000 m Listed Race
    1999 2nd GCST Prime Ministers Cup 2400 m Group 2
    1999 2ND EFM EFM Stakes 2400 m Listed Race
    1999 1ST CRJC Grafton Cup Group 3
  Dashing Scene 1995 (Scenic IRE ) ,230 (57-8-7-3)
    2000 1st STC Kingston Town Stakes Group 3
  *Progeny bred by Inverness Stud:*
  Ceddie 1999 (Simonstad NZ) (**17-3-2-0**)

60. **Rose of Luskin 1986** (Luskin Star × Rosebrook by Vain)
  *Progeny bred by Inverness Stud:*
  Rose of Lycius 2000 (Lycius USA) (**7-2-1-1**)
  Frank's Connection 2001 (Nuclear Freeze USA) (**7-1-0-0**)

61. **Rose of Simon\*\* 1998** (Simonstad NZ × Love's Ave) (**4-0-0-1**)
  *Progeny bred by Inverness Stud:*
  Go Bossy 2002 (Nuclear Freeze USA) (**6-0-0-0**)

62. **Sarajac\*\* 1995** (Kapstaad × Shinakima by Shining Finish)
  *Progeny bred by Inverness Stud:*
  Mr Simon 1999 (Simonstad NZ) (**4-0-0-0**)
  Sarakima 2001 (Nuclear Freeze USA) (**32-0-1-4**)
  Uncle Nick 2002 (Nuclear Freeze USA) (**2-0-0-0**)
  In the Realm 2003 (Nuclear Freeze USA ) (**5-0-0-0**)

63. **Satin Poppy GB 1992** (50 per cent share) (Satin Wood IRE × Primatie FR by Vaguely Noble)
  Gaitero 2003 (Encosta De Lago)

64. **Shinakima 1982** (Shining Finish × Edging Up USA by Snow Sporting)
  **1985 1st STC Tea Rose Stakes 1500 m Group 2**

1986 1st AJC Light Fingers Stakes 1200 m Group 2
1987 1st STC Queen of the Turf Stakes 1500 m Group 3
*Progeny bred by Inverness Stud:*
Sarajac 1995 (Kaapstad NZ)
Over the Counter 1997 (Geiger Counter USA) (4-1-0-1)
Breezeway 1998 (Brief Truce USA)

65. **Showingly** 1983 (Bletchingly × Allez Show by Comeram)
*Progeny not bred by Inverness Stud:*
Z'oro NZ 1989 (Gold and Ivory USA × Showingly)
   1993 2nd RICC Stewards 1200m Group 3
   1993 2ND TER ZHFM Sprint 1400m Listed Race
   1994 1st WRC Thorndon Mile Group 1
   1994 3rd AWAP MWTU Chall 1400 m Listed Race
*Progeny bred by Inverness Stud*
Dream Catcher 1992 (Sky Chase NZ) **(18-3-3-4)**
Gold 1993 (Phizam NZ) **(13-1-1-2)**
Puissance 1997 (Simonstad NZ) **Exported to Singapore 24/9/1999**
Boliglava 1999 (Geiger Counter USA) (45-6-2-5)
Canny Go 2000 (Canny Lad) (1-0-0-0)

66. **Singeing Lamp** 1983 (Blazing Saddles × Donna Nook GB by Relko) not in foal, sold $5,000
*Progeny bred by Inverness Stud:*
Curls 1994 (Sackford USA)
Fresh Start 1995 (Sackford USA) (7-1-0-1)
Miss Fitting 1996 (Simonstad NZ) **(10-0-1-0)**
Illuminant 1997 (Dehere USA) **(38-4-2-6)**
Half Hennessy 1999 (Hennessy USA) **(25-6-3-2)**
Winner of 2003 QTC QLD Derby 2400 m Group 1
2003 QTC Grand Prix Stakes 2140 m Group 2
2002 ITC Illawarra Classic 1200 m Group 3

2002 Tatt's Ming Dynasty Q H 1400 m Group 3
Eisteddfod 2003 (Carnegie IRE)
67. **Silent Song 2001** (Stravinsky USA × Incommunicado IRE), **(31-4-6-2)**
*Progeny bred by Inverness Stud*
Fei Su 2008 (Fastnet Rock)
Love Me 2009 (50 per cent Coolmore Stud) (Rock of Gibraltar IRE) **(4-0-0-0)**
The Headmistress 2010 (50 per cent Coolmore Stud) (Dylan Thomas IRE) **(18-1-0-0-)**
68. **Skylark** 1992 (Marscay × Phantom's Lady by Sir Tristram)
*Progeny bred by Inverness Stud:*
Simple Simon 1996 (Simonstad NZ) (8-0-0-0)
Thumbalite 1998 (Simonstad NZ) (38-2-3-30
Miss Strangelove 1999 (Geiger Counter USA) (10-0-0-0)
**Clevedon 2001 (Keltrice) (21-5-0-5)**
**2005 3rd RHL Epona Stakes 1900 m Listed Race**
**2005 3rd RAND Adrian Knox 2000 m Group 3**
Vanstraalen 2002 (Nuclear Freeze USA) (46-5-6-6)
Alpha Gunn 2003 (Nuclear Freeze USA) (10-3-1-1)
Unistudent 2003 (Universal Prince) (2-0-0-0)
69. **Sleepy Seattle** 1992 (Seattle Song USA × Valderna FR)
*Progeny bred by Inverness Stud*
War Party 2004 (Catbird) **(15-1-1-2)**
70. **Smashing Belle** 1997 (Housebuster × Tri Belle)
Progency bred by Inverness Stud
Bath 2002 (Faltaat USA) **(11-1-1-1)**
Sorrowful 2003 (Thunder Gulch USA ) **(46-6-9-14)**
Smashing Princes 2004 (Universal Prince) **(8-0-0-1)**
71. **Songline** 1987 (Western Symphony × McAngus by Alvaro )
in foal to Reset, sold $210,000.00

**Sunline 1995 (Desert Sun GB) Not bred by Inverness Stud, (48-32-9-3)**

**Winner of 13 Group 1; 12 Group 2; 2 Group 3 and 1 Listed**

Songline Progeny bred by Inverness Stud:

Jessie Perfect 1996 (Strausbrook)
  (7-0-0-0)

Sunny Song 1997 (Simonstad NZ)

Octasong 1999 (Octagonal NZ)

Song of Songs 2000 (Danehill USA)

Flaring Sun 2002 (Desert Sun GB) **(13-1-0-2)**

Songstar 2003 (Galileo IRE) **(14-0-0-2)**

72. **Song of Songs**\*\* 2000 (Danehill USA × **Songline** NZ)
73. My Melody 2004 (Universal Prince × Songline NZ) (1-0-1-0)
74. **Songstar**\*\* 2003 (Galileo IRE × Songline NZ)
    *Progeny bred by Inverness Stud*
    Nowheretosomewhere 2010 (Danehill Dancer IRE)
      (7-0-0-1)
75. **Soprana**\*\* 1999 (Carnegie IRE × Regal Odyssey) ,050 (12-1-3-0)
    **2002 4th in Furious Stakes 1400 m Group 3**
    **2002 2nd in Champion Stakes 2000 m Group 1**
76. **Stars Galore** 1982 (Shining Finish GB × Zahedi NZ)
    *Progeny bred by Inverness Stud*
    In Orbit 1994 (Sackford USA) **(24-3-1-1)**
    Simons Galaxy 1996 (Simonstad NZ) **(42-2-2-7)**
77. **Sundust Rose**\*\* 1998 (Raami GB × Rose of Luskin)
78. **Sunstate** 1986 (Luskin Star × Mission by Vain)
    *Progeny bred by Inverness Stud*
    Sunny Sim 2000 (Simonstad NZ) **(3-0-0-2)**

# INVERNESS STUD – LIST OF HORSES

Samurai 2001 (Nuclear Freeze USA) **(5-2-1-1)**
Suntanned 2002 (Nuclear Freeze USA) **(65-20-4-3)**
Ansto 2003 (Nuclear Freeze USA)
Uniprincess 2004 (Universal Prince) (3-0-0-0)

79. **Telephone Girl 1990 (Been There × Miss Pine Lodge)**
    **Race Winner**
    *Progeny bred by Inverness Stud:*
    Airline 1996 (Simonstad NZ) **(51-6-9-7)**
    Damascus Calling 1997 (Salieri USA) ,795 987-12-12-13)

80. **The Fairy\*\* 1997** (Fairy King × Threesome by Zamazaan) (3-0-0-0)
    *Progeny bred by Inverness Stud*
    Ice Baby 2002 (Nuclear Freeze USA) **(8-0-0-1)**
    Ice Frost 2003 (Nuclear Freeze USA) **(4-0-0-2)**

81. **Threesome 1981** (Zamazaan FR × Hasty Way NZ)
    *Progeny bred by Inverness Stud:*
    Black Halo 1994 (Don't Say Halo USA) (35-3-4-40
    Triform 1995 (Sackford USA) (4-0-0-0)
    The Fairy 1997 (Fairy King USA) (8-0-0-1)
    Moksha 1998 (Snippets) (43-5-5-2)

82. **Tis Hopeful\*\* 1999** (Lycius USA × Miami Vice) (13-1-1-20
    *Progeny bred by Inverness Stud:*
    Tis Hot 2005 (Nuclear Freeze USA) (6-0-0-0)

83. **Tis Mahal\*\* 1999** (Scenic IRE × Must be Mahal) (3-0-0-0)
    *Progeny bred by Inverness Stud:*
    Miss Mahal 2004 (Canny Lad) (4-0-0-0)

84. **Triassic 1990** (Tights USA × Astral Row NZ)
    **Stakes Winnings**
    **1st 1993 ARC Soliloquy Stakes 1600 m Listed Race**
    **1994 WaikRC Sir Tristram Fillies Classic Group 2**
    *Progeny bred by Inverness Stud:*

Trigonometry 2003 (Galileo IRE ) (17-2-1-2)
Pride 'n Prejudice 2004 (Universal Prince) (19-4-0-2)
So You Think 2006 (High Chaparral IRE × Triassic)
Winner of 10 × Group 1:
2009 MVRC Cox Plate
2010 VRC MACKINNON STAKES
2010 MVRC Cox Plate
2010 MRC Yalumba Stakes
2010 MRC Underwood Stakes
2011 IRE Irish Champion Stakes
2011 IRE Tattersalls Gold Cup
2011 GB The Eclipse Stakes
2012 GB Prince of Wales Stakes
2012 IRE Tattersalls Gold Cup
Winner of 1 × Group 2
2010 MRC Memsie Stakes
Winner of 2 × Group 3
2009 STC Gloaming Stakes
2011 IRE Curagh Mooresbridge Stakes
So You Think was rated 133 by Timeform and is the highest rated Australian colt of the Modern Age. He stands at stud at the famous Coolmore Stud in the Hunter Valley
Triassic was exported to NZ on 13 December 2011

85. Tynia 1977 (Hotfoot GB × Royal Flare GB)
Stakes Winnings
1980 VRC Edward Manifold Stakes 1600 m Group 2
1981 VATC Tranquil Star Stakes 1400 m Group 3
*Progeny bred by Inverness Stud*
Adventurous 1993 (Fairy King USA) ,605 (10-3-2-1)
1996 1st AJC Craven Plate 2000 m Group 3
1996 1st GosRC GOSFOR CLASSIC 1600 m Listed Race

# INVERNESS STUD – LIST OF HORSES

1996 NCLE Spring Stakes 1600 m Listed Race
1996 Rand Dulcify 2000 m Listed Race
Hot Socks 1994 (Sackford USA) (6-0-1-0)
Itch 1996 (Simonstad NZ) (24-0-4-1)

86. **Una Donna NZ** 1987 (Sir Tristram IRE × Dancelot by Vain)
*Progeny bred by Inverness Stud:*
**Stormy Joe 1999** (Hurricane Sky) ,300 (24-5-6-3)
Tea Biscuit 2001 (Nuclear Freeze USA) (24-2-3-3)

87. **Welka** 1994 (Sadlers Wells × Athyka) **sold in foal to Choisir (could not find progeny records)**

88. **Western Music** 1986 (Western Symphony USA × Getting There by Jungle Boy GB)
**Stakes Race Win**
**1988 1st VRC Maribyrnong Stakes 900 m Group 2**
*Progeny bred by Inverness Stud:*
Trailer Trash 2000 (Grosvenor NZ) (11-1-0-1)
Music Medal 2001 (Medaaly GB) (11-1-0-1)
Stand by Your Man 2003 ( Nuclear Freeze USA) (7-1-0-1)
Danzmusic 2004 (Nuclear Freeze USA) (21-2-2-1)

89. **Zapolska** 1993 (Polish Patriot USA × Le Crystal USA)
*Progeny bred by Inverness Stud:*
Jericho Miss 2004 (Nuclear Freeze USA) 917-0-0-2)

90. **Zabelle** 1995 (Zedative × Amunani) not in foal

**List of racehorse stakes winners and performers owned and raced by Jack and Sue**

1. Count Scenario 1994 (Scenic IRE) ,875 (63-12-8-9)
   Purchased at the 1995 Magic Millions Yearling Sale
   1998 3rd EFM Qld Guineas 1600 m Group 2
   1999 3RD WAGG Wagga Cup 2000 m Listed Race

1999 2nd GCST Prime Ministers Cup 2400 m Group 2
1999 1ST CRJC Grafton Cup Group 3
2. Donna Dior 1997 (Marscay × Donna Cara by Sir Tristram) (15-2-2-1)
2000 1st MV Salinger Trophy 1600 m Listed Race
3. Great Anna 1999 (Anabaa USA × Great Vintage NZ) (20-5-1-3)
2003 3rd Morp. Aust Oaks 2025 m Group 1
2004 1st STC EPONA STAKES 1900 m Listed Race
4. Just Jack 1967 (Just Great GB × Lavina). Just Jack was one of the first racehorses owned by Jack and Sue, he won his first four RACES
5. **Kugelhopf 1995 (Akaabar USA × Bebhinn) ,578 (66-9-5-10)
2003 A TC Toowoomba Cup 2050 m Listed Race
6. Lazy Pat 1969 (Just Great GB × Dispose) (87-6 – 16 -24 ?)
Jack bought Lazy Pat for $600 at the Inglis Easter sales in 1970
1st 1973 Cant Alexandra Graduation Stakes 3200 m
1st 1976 Lord Mayor's Cup 2400m. Listed Race
Lazy Pat equalled the Race Record in this race
1st 197? Rand Anniversary Handicap 2400 m
1st 1977 Rand January Cup 2000 m Listed Race
1st 1977 Rand Tattersalls Club Cup 2400 m
1st 1977 WFM Australia Day Cup 2400 m Listed Race
2nd 1974 Rand City Tattersalls Club Cup 2400 m Listed Race
2nd 1976 Rand Summer Cup 2000m Group 3
2nd 1976 RHL N E Manion Cup 2400 m Group 3
2nd 1976 Rand Christmas Cup 2400 M Listed Race
2nd 1977 Rand City Tattersalls Club Cup 2400 m Listed Race

2nd 1978 Rand January Cup 2000 M Listed Race
2nd 1978 RHL H E Tancred Stakes 2400 m Group 1
Hyperno beat Lazy Pat by half a head
3rd 1976 WFM Australia Day Cup 2400 m Listed Race
3rd 1977 Rand Christmas Cup 2400 m Listed Race
3rd 1978 RHL Parramatta Cup 1900 m Listed Race

These were the only race results found in newspaper clippings kept over all these years which I could confirm. as you can see he raced 87 times for 6 wins, 16 seconds and probably 24 thirds. Neil Campton rode him 58 times out of the 87 races. A truly amazing result

7. **Miss Goldie** (Geiger Counter USA × Imperial Elder NZ) (3-0-1-1)
   3rd 2001 KGR 2 YR Classic Group 3

8. Silent Song NZ 2001 (Stravinsky USA × Incommunicado IRE) ,400 (31-4-6-2)

9. **Soprana** 1999 (Carnegie IRE × Regal Odyssey) ,050 (12-1-3-0)
   2002 4th in Furious Stakes 1400 m – Group 3
   2002 5th in T J Smith – Group 1
   2002 2nd Spring Champion Stakes 2000 m – Group 1

10. Unwanted 1974 (Space Bird USA × Dispose)
    3rd 1978 Ranvet Stakes 2000 m Group 1
    Jack purchased Unwanted at the 1975 Inglis Easter sales for $9,000. He won 2 races easily with Neil Campton as his jockey and trained by Doug Lonsdale. Both Doug and Jack considered him to be the best horse either of them had had. Unfortunately Unwanted developed navicular disease which is now known as 'caudal heel pain syndrome' and had to be retired. Jack was devastated.

**List of other racehorses owned and raced by Jack and Sue during the lifetime of Inverness Stud**

1. **Abby's Ice 2001 (Nuclear Freeze USA × Abhaa)
2. Akaabers Promise 1995 (Akaaber USA × Risque Promise) ,240 (50-9-7-5)
3. **Angels Star 2001 (King of Kings IRE × A Star is Born) (9-0-0-1)
4. Altissimo 2005 (Show a Heart × Gentle Wind) (28-2-3-2)
5. Baby Rock 2005 (Rock of Gibraltar IRE × Uberfrau GB) (31-1-4-5)
6. **Ballyev 2002 (Faslyev-Ballystorm) broken and trained, not raced – sold $1,500
7. **Beat the Posse 1993 (Phizam NZ × Princess Jessie) (8-1-0-0)
8. **Black Halo 1994 (Don't Say Halo USA × Threesome NZ) (34-3-4-4)
9. **Blanket 2002 (Nuclear Freeze USA × Bedspread by Settle Dancer)
10. **Canny Cait 2002 (Canny Lad-Danehillcait) unbroken, sold $3,500
11. **Ceddie 1999 (Simonstad NZ × Rose Babu) (17-3-2-0)
12. **Chitter Chatter 1999 (Scenic × Media Miss by Mr McGinty)
13. **Default 2009 (Rock of Gibraltar × Eisteddfod)
14. **Donating 2002 (Octagonal × Donna Dior)
15. **Dream Catcher 1992 (Sky Chase NZ × Showingly) (18-3-3-4)
16. **Frescante 2001 (Peintre Celebre USA × Amwag USA) (15-4-1-3)
17. **Fresh Start 1995 (Sackford USA × Singeing Lamp) (7-1-0-1)

## INVERNESS STUD – LIST OF HORSES

18. **Frosty Bally 2001 (Medaaly-Ballystorm) sold $1,500
19. **Gautier 2001 (Peintre Celebre USA × Bebhinn)
20. Give Us a Go 1991 (Tights USA × Lazy Dream) **(56-6-6-6)**
21. Grumblebum 1999 (Charnwood Forest × Sourpuss) **(12-1-1-2)**
22. **Half Hennessy (Hennessy USA × Singeing Lamp) trained by Bede Murray **(25-6-3-2)**
23. **Illuminant 1997 (Dehere USA × Singeing Lamp) trained by Gai Waterhouse **(38-4-2-6)**
24. **I'm a Thunder 1998 (Thunder Gulch USA × I'm in Business) **(18-2-2-1)**
25. **I'm a Wag 2000 (Lahib × Amwag) **(9-0-1-0)**
26. **Miami Ice (Nuclear Freeze × Miami Vice) **(32-5-4-1)**
27. LENT**Monet's Odyssey 2002 (Peintre Celebre USA × Regal Odyssey)
28. **Music Medal 2001 (Medaaly GB × Western Music) **(11-1-0-1)**
29. **Oh Kitty 2001 (Orpen-Northwood Storm) **(26-4-5-2)** >>sold for $6,000
30. **Perignon 1996 (Scenic IRE × Champagne Rouge) **(46-6-9-6)**
31. **Poop Deck Pappy 2001 (Hennessy USA × Danehillcait) **(35-2-3-5)**
32. **Pride 'n Prejudice 2004 (Universal Prince × Triassic) **(19-4-0-2)**
33. **Robbo's Danehill 2000 (Lycius USA × Danehillcait) **(15-2-1-2)**
34. **Roman Free 2000 (50 per cent share) (Love's Ave × Spartacus) **(30-5-2-5)**
35. **Rose of Lycius 2000 (Lycius USA × Rose of Luskin)
36. **Song of Songs 2000 (Danehill × Songline) **(1-0-0-0)**

37. **Songstar 2003 (Galileo IRE × Songline NZ) (14-0-0-2)
38. St Vincent 1976 (Scarletville IRE × Damestar) – all I could find was a 2nd at Randwick
39. **Suntanned 2002 (Nuclear Freeze USA × Sunstate) (65–20-4-13)
40. **Suzanne 2008 (Choisir × Eisteddfod) (37-2-6-2)
41. **Tea Biscuit 2001 (Nuclear Freeze USA × Una Donna NZ) (24-2-3-3)
42. Telephone Girl 1990 (Been There × Miss Pine Lodge) **Race winner**
43. **Tis Hopeful 2000 (Lycius USA × Miami Vice) (13-1-1-2)
44. Tis Mahal 1999 (Scenic IRE × Must be Mahal) (3-0-0-0)
45. **Vice 'N Ice 2002 (Nuclear Freeze × Miami Vice) (8-1-0-0) – sold $8,000
46. Yummy NZ 2005 (Yamanin Vital NZ × Capital Flight NZ) (41-5-3-7)

**List of stakes performed racehorses bred but not raced by Inverness Stud**

1. Adventurous 1993 (Fairy King USA × Tynia) (10-3-2-1)
   1996 1st AJC Craven Plate 2000 m Group 3
   1996 1st GosRC Gosfor Classic 1600 m Listed Race
   1996 NCLE Spring Stakes 1600 m Listed Race
   1996 Rand Dulcify 2000 m Listed Race
2. Clevedon 2001 (Keltrice × Skylark) (21-5-0-5)
   2005 3rd RHL Epona Stakes 1900 m Listed Race
   2005 3rd RAND Adrian Knox 2000 m Group 3
3. Dress Code 2000 (El Moxie USA × Ranein) (35-3-4-2)
   2002 3rd Caul. Debutant 900 m Listed Race
   2002 4th MV Platinum 1000m Listed Race
   2003 5th GCST Magic Millions 1100m

# INVERNESS STUD – LIST OF HORSES

4. Galileo's Daughter 2004 (Galileo IRE × Donna Dior) (18-1-1-3)
   2nd 2008 Rosehill Arrowfield Group 1
   3rd 2008 AJC OAKS Group 1
5. Half Hennessy 1999 (Hennessy USA × Singeing Lamp) (25-6-3-2)
   Winner of 2003 QTC QLD Derby 2400 m Group 1
   2003 QTC Grand Prix Stakes 2140 m Group 2
   2002 ITC Illawarra Classic 1200 m Group 3
   2002 Tatt's Ming Dynasty Q H 1400 m Group3
6. It's My Sin 1993 (Success Express × Rosalina (Den) (27-5-2-4)
   1996 3rd Avon Ra Ora 1200 m Listed Race
   1997 1st OtlMRC Maori WFA Group 1
   1997 1ST BOPRC Trust Bank Classic Listed Race
   1997 1st OTAK Regency 1400 m Group 1
   1997 4th EF Byrne Hart 1400 m Group 2
   1998 3RD MORP Goodwood 1200 m Group 1
7. Mr Prudent 1994 (Phizam NZ × I'm in Business)
   1st 1999 NSW Tatt's Plate 2400 m – Listed Race
   1st 2001 AJC Sydney Cup 3200 m Group 1
   3rd 2001 Caul Easter Cup 2000 m Group 3
   2nd 2002 AJC Sydney Cup 3200 m Group 1
   3rd 2002 MV Cup 2500 m Group 2
   2nd 2002 Flem Melbourne Cup 3200 m Group 1
   2nd 2002 AJC Sydney Cup 3200 m Group 1
   3rd 2003 Bendigo Cup 2400 m Listed Race
8. Stormy Joe 1999 (Hurricane Sky × Una Donna NZ) (24-5-6-3)
   2nd EFM Brisbane HCP 1600 m Listed Race
9. Weekend Special 2007 (Snitzel × Frescante) (23-4-7-2)
   3rd 2012 Flemington – Kensington 1000m Listed Race

www.ingramcontent.com/pod-product-compliance
Lightning Source LLC
Chambersburg PA
CBHW071952290426
44109CB00018B/1997